Freud and Tragedy

Studies in Austrian Literature, Culture and Thought

General Editors:

Jorun B. Johns
Richard H. Lawson

Heinz Politzer

Freud and Tragedy

Edited and with an Introductory Essay
by Wilhelm W. Hemecker

Translated by Michael Mitchell

ARIADNE PRESS
Riverside, California

Ariadne Press would like to express its appreciation to the
Bundesministerium für Bildung, Wissenschaft und Kultur, Vienna
for assistance in publishing this book.

Library of Congress Cataloging-in-Publication Data

Politzer, Heinz, 1910-1978.
    [Freud und das Tragische. English]
    Freud and tragedy / Heinz Politzer ; edited and with an
introductory essay by Wilhelm W. Hemecker ; translated by
Michael Mitchell.
        p.   cm. -- (Studies in Austrian literature, culture and
thought.)
Includes bibliographical references.
ISBN 1-57241-146-5 (pbk)
        1. Freud, Sigmund, 1856-1939. 2. Tragic, The. I. Hemecker,
Wilhelm. II. Title. III. Series.
BF109.F74P6513 2003
150.19'52'092–dc22   2005023436

Cover Design:
Art Director, Designer: George McGinnis

Heinz Politzer

Contents

Acknowledgment

The editor would like to express his gratitude to Mrs. Jane Politzer for the patient interest she has taken in the lengthy preparation of this edition of her husband's last important work; also to Kay Seiler for her recollections of her brother; and to Siegfried Unseld, of Suhrkamp Verlag, for allowing me access to his correspondence with Politzer and for releasing the book, which was originally to have been published by Suhrkamp.

"... as a kind of last will and testament"
Heinz Politzer's Freud project

Wilhelm W. Hemecker

> In this city where
> no bells ring
> death *is*

Heinz Politzer, who with these lines wrote his poetic testament,[1] died on July 30, 1978, in Berkeley, California, far away—
even farther than mere distance suggests—from the city where he
was born on New Year's Eve 1910, still in the "world of
yesterday," the city which, more than anything else, had formed
him: Vienna.

It was there that Politzer began his studies—German and
English—before transferring to the German University of Prague
in 1932; soon after, he was approached by Max Brod to assist in
the edition of Kafka's complete works.[2] Later *Franz Kafka: Parable
and Paradox*[3] was to become, along with *Franz Grillparzer oder das
abgründige Biedermeier* (Franz Grillparzer or The Hidden Depths of
the Biedermeier),[4] Politzer's major publication, part of an Austrian
trilogy which remained uncompleted when the great literary
scholar, writer and poet died shortly before he could finish his
study of Sigmund Freud.

With a recommendation from Thomas Mann and a grant from
the American Guild for German Cultural Freedom, Politzer
succeeded in reaching Jerusalem in 1938, where he made the
acquaintance of Martin Buber. From there he emigrated, two years
after the end of the War, to America, where he managed to
establish himself in the university system, the crowning point in his
career coming with a call to a chair at the University of California,
Berkeley.[5]

On December 31, 1968, Politzer wrote to Hans Paeschke,
editor of the monthly magazine *Merkur*, "I have spent the last three
months preparing a course of lectures on depth psychology as a
method of literary criticism and, since I must do it in English, have

written them out …. I would not be surprised if this course should turn into a book, and it is certainly the case that I could translate a chapter into German for you and *Merkur* …. What I have in mind for *Merkur* is something like an essay on 'The interpretation of Freud's interpretation of dreams.' You see, I've subjected Freud's interpretations of his own dreams to the Freudian method and the results are, to put it mildly, amazing. That doesn't mean, however, that I've forgotten the piece on Austria or the one on the generation gap."

The lectures developed into psychoanalytical interpretations of literature that were to be published in the collection of essays, *Hatte Ödipus einen Ödipus-Komplex?* (Did Oedipus Have an Oedipus Complex?)[6] The essay he had mentioned was soon ready to appear in *Merkur* under the title "Sigmund Freud als Deuter seiner Träume" (Sigmund Freud as Interpreter of His Dreams).[7] With the "generation gap," however, Politzer had touched on a topic that was to occupy him more and more until eventually he incorporated it in his project of a monograph on Freud.

This project can be traced back to the summer of 1967. "What is happening about the topics we were discussing?" Paeschke asked Politzer, who at the time was John Simon Guggenheim Fellow at the University of Freiburg. "I mean the question of the generation gap, which the students' activities this summer have rendered doubly topical for us. I keep coming back to what you said about masochism."[8] After his return to Berkeley, Politzer sketched out his observations in a longer letter, using the categories of active/passive: "How did I find America when I got back? Not in a happy state at all. What concerns me among other things is the state of the younger generation. While young Germans are active—whatever their motives and whatever their goals—here the hippies and the flower-power movement have set off an escapist trend which makes me fear the worst."[9] Paeschke's reaction was a request for a "psychological and (let's say) ethnological analysis of the younger generation here and over there."[10]

But for the moment nothing came of it. Signs, initially vague, of a connection with his Freud project first appeared in the fall of 1969 when Politzer, referring to a piece entitled "Did Oedipus Have an Oedipus Complex?" that he had written for Hessen Radio, told Paeschke that "one could use this subject as an approach to the problem of the younger generation,"[11] or, as he later wrote, "some ideas from that piece could be applied to the problem of the generation gap."[12]

More years passed. Then, in a letter from Paeschke of January 25, 1972, the expression "the post-oedipal generation" occurs. Six months later he tried again: "Nb: something on the post-oedipal generation is at the top of *Merkur*'s wish list and no one else can write it."[13] The following spring he was urging, even threatening Politzer: "I will keep pestering you about this topic as long as we remain friends."[14] And over a year later, in July 1973, he described Politzer's essay as "a project that is gradually coming painfully close to my heart."[15]

Long before this, in 1971, Politzer had alluded with a laconic remark to another project, at this point still separate from the question of the generation gap, that was to become his last. In the postscript to a letter to Paeschke, he said, "By the way, I'm writing a book on Sigmund Freud for Molden."[16] Politzer's book of essays on *Franz Grillparzer oder das abgründige Biedermeier* was just coming out and the psychoanalytical interpretations of literature, which had developed out of his lectures, appeared one after the other in specialist journals until the mid-1970s, when they were collected in the volume *Hatte Ödipus einen Ödipus-Komplex?*

Now, however, he had a bigger subject in his sights; he was going back to the source, to the father of psychoanalysis himself. He was soon talking of "notes" for a book on Freud, although in a macabre context: together with other books, Politzer said, he had entrusted them to the US Postal Service, and they had "fallen victim to a hurricane and now were bobbing along on the waves of Lake Cayuga—incredible but true." Sarcastically, he added, "Just like at home," quoting Karl Kraus's pun on the word *aufgeben*, which can mean to post a letter or to abandon it as lost.[17] Politzer gave a more precise and dramatic description of the loss in his application for a further fellowship from the John Simon Guggenheim Memorial Foundation in New York: "Finally, I wish to explain that my notes on the subject, which I began to collect in 1969, were destroyed in June 1972. This loss was caused by floods in the wake of Hurricane Agnes when I sent my working library from Cornell, where I was a Senior Fellow in the Society for the Humanities, to my home university in Berkeley. Since I did not have any copies of my notes, the result of three years' labor was lost, and it was necessary for me to begin at the beginning. At present I am reconstructing the notes."

In the same application there is a "Statement of plans" which describes the subject of his project: "My project grew out of lecture courses and seminars I have given at Berkeley and Cornell University on the applicability—and the limitations—of Sigmund Freud's teachings within the realm of literary criticism.... As my research developed it became obvious to me that Freud himself was a literary figure in his own right, possessed (if not obsessed by) an acute sense of the tragic. Both his life and his writings seemed to unfold according to the laws of tragedy. His naming the Oedipus complex after one of the most tragic heroes in Greek mythology testifies to this preoccupation ... I intend to write a critical biography of Sigmund Freud, using the techniques of psychobiography, while describing his life and works in terms of hubris, and self-transcendence very much on the pattern of tragic Oedipus, especially Sophocles' *Oedipus at Colonos*.... I further intend to demonstrate that the death-wish which Freud formulated as late as 1917, much to the dismay of his disciples, is already noticeable in his *Interpretation of Dreams* (1899), and that his paper on "Terminable and Interminable Analysis" of 1937... represents the very climax of his personal and intellectual tragedy.... I hope to be able to show a man who was neither a Victorian nor a prophet of carnality, but a profoundly innovative spirit, who eventually succeeded in conquering the death-drive that threatened to destroy him, accepting his fate—exile and death—in true tragic fashion."[18]

Alexander Mitscherlich, asked by the Foundation for an appraisal, gave the project his full support: "I don't know anyone in the world of scholarship who is better equipped than Mr. Politzer to develop this position of Freud in its relevance for our time."[19]

In the spring of 1973, Politzer came back to the question of the younger generation: "Are you there? I would love to be able to turn up at your place in Ainmiller Straße with a bottle of champagne and expound my plan for an essay on the post-oedipal generation to you; more and more things occur to me about it every day."[20] A few weeks later, he reports an exchange of views on the subject "with Alexander and Margarete Mitscherlich, who were spending a year in the USA"; Margarete Mitscherlich's book *Must We Hate?* seemed to him "an ideal starting point."[21] The "key idea," however, came to him in the summer of 1974 during "long walks" while convalescing in Großgmain in Salzburg after an operation (Politzer was suffering from progressive arteriosclerosis). "The post-oedipal generation is a mutation beyond tragedy. Their joy is for its own sake, not for eternity,"[22] he wrote, thus linking up not only with Nietzsche's *Zarathustra* ("But all joys want eternity—,/—Want deep, profound eternity!)"[23] but above all with *Freud and Tragedy*.

Back in Berkeley, Politzer's health deteriorated rapidly. "I am concentrating on … the most urgent work, that is my Freud book. That's all I have the strength for,"[24] he wrote in the middle of November. Not long afterwards, Politzer went into more detail and the connection between the topic of the post-oedipal generation and his Freud project was conclusively established: "What little strength I have left is employed on my Freud book, for the last chapter of which I have the oedipal and post-oedipal generation in mind. I'm in the middle of the second of five or six chapters."[25] But Paeschke wanted his share for *Merkur* and, with a reference to "the two Frenchmen, Deleuze and Guattari, with their best seller in France," the *Anti-Oedipus*,[26] as well as to competition from the German-speaking world, was insistent—and successful: Politzer promised him "the post-oedipal generation, just to get a bit of peace and quiet,"[27] and sent off the manuscript on March 7, 1975: "Here it is, the little monster." He had, he said, "spent the last six weeks wrestling with that and nothing else," rarely had a piece cost him such an effort. "Compared with it, my book on Kafka was a piece of cake."[28]

In a long and detailed letter, Paeschke subjected the manuscript to ruthless criticism,[29] and a meeting on April 21—once more Politzer was staying in Großgmain for his health—was devoted entirely to a discussion of the essay. Even when writing the essay, Politzer had felt unsure about it, as he told Paeschke: "Naturally I ask myself what is the reason for the immense difficulties I was confronted with. Presumably the main difficulty lies in the fact that, however much I tried, I have not sufficiently distanced myself from the material. I had hoped to overcome this difficulty by writing this essay as the last chapter of my book on Freud; in that case I presume the threads would have come together in a more coherent fashion."[30]

Finally, he recognized "that the whole thing has to be done again … with Deleuze and Guattari, naturally." At the same time, Politzer was working intensively on his Freud project: "I'm just starting on a chapter about Freud's death which will take me more or less to the end, or close to the end, of the book.... As well as that I'm enclosing an extract from my Freud-Jung chapter, somewhat irreverent, that Gert Kalow is going to broadcast on Hessen Radio for Jung's hundredth birthday."[31]

During the long days of early summer, Politzer completed the chapter he was working on. It is dated "July 8, 1975." As the manuscript reveals, he noted as possible titles "Dying and Death," "Freud and Death," "A Tragic Death," before finally deciding on "The Death Principle." "As you will already have guessed from the relaxed tone of this letter, I've managed to bump Dr. Freud off and finish the relevant chapter," Politzer joked in a letter to Friedrich Torberg a few weeks later. "With that the book is as good as finished. Except that I'll have to rewrite it both as a whole and bit by bit."[32]

Not long after, he gave a more detailed account to Alexander Mitscherlich. "It is now the middle of summer and I can give you a brief report on the progress of my Freud book. The first chapter, 'S. F. and the Tragedy of Interpretation' will appear separately in advance, in a volume about Austria.... —Good old Gert Kalow broadcast excerpts from the second chapter—on Freud and Jung, Oedipus in practice, so to speak—as a birthday offering for Jung on July 22. The chapter itself is three times the length of the text of Kalow's broadcast.—The first draft of the third chapter, 'The Death Principle' (the death principle as well as Freud's own death), is finished.—I wrote the fourth chapter, on the post-oedipal, a-tragic generation, before the third, then discarded it; I'll have another go at it during the rest of the summer."[33]

The revised version of that chapter, which was intended to appear as an essay in *Merkur* with the title "Freud, Oedipus—and then?" or "Romeo and Juliet No Longer Have to Die: Comments on the Post-Oedipal Generation" and was discarded after Paeschke's detailed criticism, was a complete reworking of the original. Politzer wanted to take a radically personal approach, using his own son as an example and "going in for biography," as he wrote to the man who was both his editor and friend. "What I would like to do, to put it briefly, is to try and paint a portrait of Stephen, bringing out the features that seem to me to be typical of his generation. With great precision, very little theory."[34] After he had completed it, Politzer wrote of a "Copernican revolution," not only in his treatment of the subject, but above all in his personal relationship with his son, Stephen Benjamin: "The fact is that for a long time I have been horrified at my own rigidity, and the essay should be read above all as an act of liberation. It is not without a touch of irony, which you found lacking in the first version, but I believe it was written as a sign of love, of a reconciliation."[35]

The essay, now entitled "Mein Sohn S. Benjamin" and with a very personal tone, finally appeared in *Merkur* in the spring of 1976.[36] While reading the proofs Politzer, usually excessively self-critical, could not help remarking "how good the essay actually is" and gave due recognition to his editor: "If I should be right, then it is thanks to you and you alone. You prompted the essay and were generous with your suggestions for improvements and got the best out of me and then cut all the superfluous material. No one else in the German-speaking countries could do that."[37]

Paeschke reported triumphantly on the reaction to the article, "Yesterday evening Jürgen Habermas spent an hour talking about your 'Son Benjamin' and nothing else; it has been very well received by all the important people over here. So you see that's the main kind of thing occupying people's minds nowadays."[38]

All of Politzer's further plans and activities were subordinate to his medical treatment. On October 22, 1976, he told Paeschke, "So that's the X-ray over with. Diagnosis: blocked arteries in both legs, operation next Monday." Politzer was hoping for "just one more year ... just one more summer" to give him time to finish his "tragic Freud."

"I'm still working on my book," he assured Siegfried Unseld, the director of Suhrkamp, where the book was to appear, "but I have been ill a lot in recent years and I beg you not to think I've been dilatory. One day it'll be done."[39] But the publishers were not happy to leave it at that. Only a few days later, Alexander Mitscherlich, the editor in charge of the series "Literatur der Psychoanalyse" for which the book was destined, was already pestering him: "May I ... most respectfully approach you with the question as to what is happening about our Freud book. You cannot deny that during the past two to three years I have made considerable concessions to you as regards patience, but now the time has come when we must think of 'Literatur der Psycho-analyse.' What is to be included in the volume, what is the situation with the table of contents? You know how delighted I would be to receive a manuscript that gathered together all the ideas we have discussed in one such volume."[40]

In his reply Politzer once more summarized the situation, adding that he had the *chutzpah* to regard the book as a signal success and naming "three main chapters:" "I. 'Sigmund Freud and the Tragedy of Interpretation,' II. 'Freud's Fainting Fits' and III. 'The Death Principle'."[41]

The first two chapters were already completed, Politzer said; the third was "finished in manuscript but not yet typed out. What still remains to be done," he went on, "is an introductory chapter comparing the Aristotelian idea of tragedy with the one Freud himself had developed in *Totem and Taboo*, plus a conclusion discussing the self-analysts and the structural analysts. And somehow I have to provide proof that anyone who does not regard Freud as a tragic figure in the Old Testament sense misunderstands him." But he also had to ask Mitscherlich to continue to exercise patience, pointing out that "You are enough of a psychologist to recognize that to bring off such an ambitious project requires good health as well as time and inspiration" and concluding that he hoped to achieve emeritus status not only from his chair in Berkeley "but also from Freud" in June 1977.[42]

In fact, though, in the early summer of 1977, a further, final chapter was written with the title that was intended for the book as a whole: "Freud and Tragedy." On July 23, 1977, he wrote to Friedrich Torberg, "I have completed—well, almost—my book on Freud,"[43] and two days later there followed a similar report: "My Freud book is finished... by and large the manuscript is there."[44]

"At the end of July," he told Hans Paeschke, "I had an operation lasting nine hours in the course of which my aorta was replaced with plastic from the ribcage to the arteries in my thighs." With reference to the Freud book Politzer said, "I practically completed it before the operation because I wanted everything wrapped up in advance. And rightly so, as things turned out." In his last letter to Alexander Mitscherlich as well, Politzer confirmed that he had managed to complete the "fourth and last chapter.... God knows how I had to struggle with fate to get it done."[45]

"The most annoying thing about the whole affair," he joked, looking for sympathy from his friend Friedrich Torberg, "is that I am a typical illustration of 'the operation was successful, the patient died' syndrome. I am very slowly starting to think about work: the

Freud book should be finished by the end of January."[46] In the middle of October 1977, he was talking, in another letter to Paeschke, about his "intention to revise and write out a fair copy of the final chapter of the Freud book,"[47] and again two weeks later, "I have the intention, as I wrote to you before, of gradually getting down to the last chapter of my Freud book again (I wrote it in the last weeks before my operation, as a kind of last will and testament); it needs a very thorough revision." How far the topic of the post-oedipal generation had by then become integrated into the Freud project can be seen from his statement: "I no longer need to link the post-oedipal generation to it, it's part of it."[48]

Politzer's last letter preserved in the *Merkur* archives reveals how incomplete the project was, in spite of everything: "I have managed to extract a short essay from the last chapter which I intend to contribute to the Mitscherlich Festschrift. The title is 'Warum Freud Shakespeares Shylock tabuisierte' (Why Freud Made a Taboo of Shakespeare's Shylock).... While I was engaged on that I realized *how much* work there is still to be done on that chapter and on the book as a whole."[49]

Politzer wanted to send the manuscript of *Freud and Tragedy*, with which he had wrestled "like Jacob with the angels,"[50] to press before the end of 1978. It was not to be. His contribution to the Festschrift on Alexander Mitscherlich's seventieth birthday was to be Politzer's last publication, appearing posthumously. An editor's note states: "The author died on 7. 30. 1978."

Notes

[1] The poem—Politzer calls it a haiku—is in an unpublished letter from Politzer to Friedrich Torberg of September 4, 1972, Friedrich Torberg's papers, Vienna City and State Library, Manuscript Collection, Vienna.

[2] Franz Kafka, *Gesammelte Schriften*, ed. Max Brod; vols. 1-4, Berlin: Schocken,1935; vols. 5-6, Prague: Mercy, 1935-37. The collection that Heinz Politzer had put together—Franz Kafka, *Vor dem Gesetz*, Berlin: Schocken—appeared in 1934.

[3] Heinz Politzer, *Franz Kafka: Parable and Paradox*, Ithaca: Cornell University Press, 1962.

[4] Heinz Politzer, *Franz Grillparzer oder das abgründige Biedermeier*, Vienna: Molden, 1972.

[5] For Politzer's biography see: "Heinz Politzer" in *Lexikon der österreichischen Exilliteratur*, ed. Siglinde Bolbecher and others, Vienna/Munich: Deuticke, 2000; also "Heinz Politzer" in volume 20 of *Neue deutsche Biographie*, ed. the History Commission of the Bavarian Academy of Sciences, Berlin: Duncker and Humblot, 2001; "Heinz Politzer" in *Internationales Germanistenlexikon*, ed. Christoph König, Berlin: deGruyter, 2003.

[6] Heinz Politzer, *Hatte Ödipus einen Ödipus-Komplex? Versuche zum Thema Psychoanalyse und Literatur*, Munich: Piper, 1974.

[7] Heinz Politzer, "Sigmund Freud als Deuter seiner Träume," in *Merkur* 24, (1970), pp. 34-48.

[8] Hans Paeschke, letter to Heinz Politzer, August 8, 1967. The unpublished correspondence between Politzer and Paeschke is in the *Merkur* archives or among Politzer's papers, both kept in the Deutsches Literaturarchiv (DLA, German Literary Archive) in Marbach, Germany. All the letters quoted below are to be found there. All translated by M.M.

[9] Heinz Politzer, letter to Hans Paeschke, October 3, 1967.

[10] Hans Paeschke, letter to Heinz Politzer, February 15, 1968.

[11] Heinz Politzer, letter to Hans Paeschke, September 4, 1969.

[12] Heinz Politzer, letter to Hans Paeschke, September 19, 1969.

[13] Hans Paeschke, letter to Heinz Politzer, July 27, 1972; postscript.

[14] Hans Paeschke, letter to Heinz Politzer, April 4, 1973.

[15] Hans Paeschke, letter to Heinz Politzer, July 8, 1974.

[16] Heinz Politzer, letter to Hans Paeschke, October 3, 1971.

[17] Heinz Politzer, letter to Hans Paeschke, August 4, 1972.

[18] Heinz Politzer, Application for a John Simon Guggenheim Memorial Foundation Fellowship. Supplementary Statement C: Statement of plans. Frankfurt City and University Library, Manuscript Department: Alexander Mitscherlich Archive. Original in English.

[19] Alexander Mitscherlich, Report for the National Endowment for the Humanities, Washington, July 16, 1973 (copy), that served as the basis for

the appraisal requested by the Guggenheim Foundation. Frankfurt City and University Library, Manuscript Department: Alexander Mitscherlich Archive. Original in English.

20 Heinz Politzer, letter to Hans Paeschke, April 30, 1973.

21 Heinz Politzer, letter to Hans Paeschke, June 11, 1973.

22 Heinz Politzer, letter to Hans Paeschke, July 24, 1974.

23 Friedrich Nietzsche, *Thus Spake Zarathustra*, tr. Thomas Common, Edinburgh: T. N. Foulis, 1909, p. 398; (*Complete Works*, vol. 11).

24 Heinz Politzer, letter to Hans Paeschke, November 14, 1974.

25 Heinz Politzer, letter to Hans Paeschke, November 29, 1974.

26 Gilles Deleuze, Felix Guattari, *Anti-Oedipus: Capitalism and Schizophrenia*, tr. Robert Hurley and others, pref. Michel Foucault, London: Continuum, 2000.

27 Heinz Politzer, letter to Hans Paeschke, January 6, 1975.

28 Heinz Politzer, letter to Hans Paeschke, March 7, 1975.

29 Hans Paeschke, letter to Heinz Politzer, March 26, 1975.

30 Heinz Politzer, letter to Hans Paeschke, February 21, 1975.

31 Heinz Politzer, letter to Hans Paeschke, June 2, 1975.

32 Heinz Politzer, letter to Friedrich Torberg, July 21, 1975, Vienna City and State Library, Manuscript Department: Friedrich Torberg's papers. These contain all the letters from Politzer to Torberg quoted below.

33 Heinz Politzer, letter to Alexander Mitscherlich, Frankfurt City and University Library, Manuscript Department: Alexander Mitscherlich Archive. This contains all of Politzer's letters to Mitscherlich quoted below. The first chapter initially appeared under the title of "Sigmund Freud und die Tragik der Interpretation" in *Dauer im Wandel. Aspekte österreichischer Kulturentwicklung*, ed. Walter Strolz, assisted by Oscar Schatz, Vienna/Freiburg/Basel: Herder, 1975, pp. 85-145. A footnote on p. 85 says his book *Freud und das Tragische* "will probably appear in 1976."

34 Heinz Politzer, letter to Hans Paeschke, July 29, 1975.

35 Heinz Politzer, letter to Hans Paeschke, September 19, 1975. Politzer goes on to indicate a possible pun on the German word for reconciliation: *Versöhnung*, which contains the syllable *söhn*, which could suggest *Sohn* = son.

36 Heinz Politzer, "Mein Sohn S. Benjamin," *Merkur* 30 (1976), pp. 236-249.

37 Heinz Politzer, letter to Hans Paeschke, March 5, 1975.

38 Hans Paeschke, letter to Heinz Politzer, July 21, 1976.

39 Heinz Politzer, letter to Siegfried Unseld, January 27, 1977. Suhrkamp Verlag archives, Frankfurt am Main.

40 Alexander Mitscherlich, letter to Heinz Politzer, January 24, 1977. DLA, Politzer's papers.

41 Heinz Politzer, letter to Alexander Mitscherlich, February 1, 1977.

42 Ibid.

43 Heinz Politzer, letter to Friedrich Torberg, July 23, 1977.

44 Heinz Politzer, letter (carbon) to Robert (Breuer?), July 25, 1977. DLA, Politzer's papers.

45 Heinz Politzer, letter (carbon) to Alexander Mitscherlich, December 16, 1977. DLA, Politzer's papers.

46 Heinz Politzer, letter to Friedrich Torberg, August 31, 1977.

47 Heinz Politzer, letter to Hans Paeschke, October 18, 1977.

48 Heinz Politzer, letter to Hans Paeschke, November 3, 1977.

49 Politzer's contribution, "Warum Freud Shakespeares Shylock tabuisierte. Zum Problem der Tragik bei Freud" appeared in *Provokation und Toleranz. Festschrift für Alexander Mitscherlich zum siebzigsten Geburtstag*, ed. Sybille Drews and others for the Sigmund Freud Institute, Frankfurt am Main: Suhrkamp, 1978, pp. 482-497.

50 Heinz Politzer, letter (carbon) to Ilse Grubrich-Simitis, February 28, 1976. DLA, Politzer's papers.

Freud and Tragedy

Sigmund Freud and the Tragedy of Interpretation

I

On October 31, 1934, Ernst Kris gave a lecture on *The Psychology of Older Biography* to the Vienna Psychoanalytical Society. In it Kris, who was qualified in both depth psychology and art history, discussed, among other things, "certain typical expressions, set phrases"[1] of biography, by which he understood motifs and situations, often of fictional origin, which were repeated in the lives of various artists separated by time and place. This observation led Kris to ask "whether a clear dividing line can be drawn between the stock of set phrases used by biography and the artist's life as he lived it?"[2] He formulated the answer in a catchphrase which was to prove exceedingly fruitful: a *"pre-lived biography."*[3] By this he referred to the fact that the biographies of later artists often seemed to be shaped decisively by those of their predecessors. He identified, as it were, stock themes of biography, such as Ernst Robert Curtius developed fourteen years later for the whole of European literature.[4] But Kris went further. For him the "extreme case" of such a "pre-lived biography" was Thomas Mann's Biblical novel *Joseph and His Brothers*, "a book which keeps suggesting the idea that the chronological succession of generations is blurred and things near and far-off in time are brought closer together by the technique of identification."[5]

Thomas Mann exacted his revenge in the speech he made on May 8, 1936, at the celebration for Freud's eightieth birthday. Without actually naming Kris, he took up the concept of the "pre-lived biography," emphasizing how eminently applicable it was to the Biblical books he was working on and pointing out that their underlying theme was the idea of seeing "life as succession, as following in others' footsteps, the identification"[6] of later generations with exemplary figures from the past. (Of course, the principle of "imitation" is not unknown either in the history of religion, or in the humanities in general.) Then, however, Mann himself went further, beyond the limit set by Kris, saying, "Alexander followed in the footsteps of Militiades, and Caesar's Roman biographers were convinced, whether rightly or wrongly, that he wanted to imitate Alexander. This 'imitation,' however, is much more than is contained in the word today; it is mythic identification, a concept particularly familiar to the ancient world, but whose influence stretches well into the modern era and is psychologically possible at any time. The antique stamp of the figure of Napoleon," Mann went on, "has often been commented on. He expressed his regret that the modern outlook did not permit him to claim to be the son of Jupiter-Ammon, as Alexander had. But there can be no doubt that he at least confused himself mythically with Alexander during his oriental adventure. And later, after he decided to pursue his fortune in the West, he declared, 'I *am* Charlemagne.' Not, be it noted, 'I remind people of him,' not, 'My situation is similar to his,' not even, 'I am like him,' but simply, 'I *am* him.'" (Three years later Mann could have continued the series of historical figures with Hitler, who invaded Poland on the same day as Napoleon had invaded Russia.) This—that is, the identification of a person with his predecessor—Thomas Mann concluded succinctly, "is the formula for myth."[7]

Translated into the language of psychology, we can presumably talk of daydreams which the great and the not-quite-so-great of history indulged in and which they personified in such striking fashion that the society of the time had no alternative but to identify them with the mythical figures on which they had modeled themselves. They—the great—are akin to writers in that their achievements (be it a play or a conquest) are to be seen as "communal daydreams."[8] The audience, in the gallery or in history, enjoys being carried away. And in this process it is impossible to ignore the decisive role played by the feeling of "following-in-someone's-footsteps," of "having-been-here-before," in brief, the sense of "mythic identification."

A daydream of a similar origin could well be behind an episode in Freud's life, recounted by Ernest Jones, which has given rise to all sorts of speculation.[9] According to this anecdote, Freud's disciples gave him a surprise present on his fiftieth birthday: a commemorative medallion with, on the obverse, Freud's profile and on the reverse a Greek design. It shows the scene in which Oedipus solves the riddle of the sphinx, but around it was the second line of the final stasimon from Sophocles' *King Oedipus*: "Who resolved the dark enigma, noblest champion and most wise."[10] "At the presentation of the medallion," Jones continues, "there was a curious incident. When Freud read the inscription he became pale and agitated and in a strangled voice demanded to know who had thought of it. He behaved as if he had encountered a revenant, and so he had. After Federn told him it was he who had chosen the inscription, Freud disclosed that as a young student at the University of Vienna he used to stroll around the great Court inspecting the busts of former famous professors of the institution. He then had the fantasy, not merely of seeing his own bust there in the future ... but of it actually being inscribed with the *identical words* he now saw on the medallion."[11]

Ernest Jones interpreted this episode as the daydream of an ambitious student who was determined to equal his masters and persuade posterity to set up a memorial to him too in the Arcade Quadrangle of Vienna University. And he points to the inscription as the key to the notable incident. When Freud reread the inscription, he blanched and his voice went hoarse because it brought the unconscious fantasy of a "mythic identification" into consciousness. And this inscription may well throw some light on an even deeper level of Freud's unconscious. Had he not, on his way to getting his bust in the Arcade Quadrangle in Vienna, solved mysteries compared with which the riddle the sphinx set Oedipus was child's play? Was there not a picture of that very sphinx on the wall of his consulting room?[12] Had he not every reason to think himself a "noble champion and most wise," even if only in the sense that he had stripped bare and stirred up the fundamental unconscious forces of the human psyche? He had headed his *Interpretation of Dreams* with the defiant, rebellious words from Virgil, "*Flectere si nequeo superos, Acheronta movebo,*"[13] (If I cannot bend the powers above to my will, I will stir up Hades). He repeated the phrase in *The Interpretation of Dreams* itself, adding in italics, "*The interpretation of dreams is the royal road to a knowledge of the unconscious activities of the mind.*"[14]

A royal road indeed! He was an enlightened Jew in the age of Franz Josef and knew perfectly well that it was not through his own deserts that he had been awarded the title of professor but through the "subversive activity" of one of his female patients in the ministry concerned so that he found it impossible to convince himself that he had succeeded in bending the powers above to his will when he stirred up the Acheron of the human psyche to such an extent that it has still not calmed down. He prefaced his book with the quotation from Virgil in order to throw down a challenge to those above and waited for the powers-that-be to take their revenge. When they did no such thing, when, on the contrary, the news of his impending appointment as professor—for the wrong reasons and with misconceived intentions—spread round Vienna, he was even able to stand back and make light of this tragic incongruity. On March 11, 1902, he wrote to Wilhelm Fließ, "The public enthusiasm is immense. Congratulations and bouquets are already pouring in as though the role of sexuality had been officially recognized by His Majesty, the importance of dreams confirmed by the Council of Ministers, and the necessity of treating hysteria by psychoanalytic theory passed by Parliament with a two-thirds majority!"[15] It was the satyr play while the tragedy was still proceeding.

His book on the interpretation of dreams was not only the royal road for Freud, it was also the crossroads in his life. It was from the interpretation of dreams that he gained the insights into the human psyche—"that most marvelous and most mysterious of all instruments"[16]—which led him from the investigation of hysteria to the theory of neurosis, to psychoanalysis, and finally to the realization that there were interminable as well as terminable treatments, incurable as well as curable neuroses.

In the middle of this crossroads, however, he encountered the shadow he was to meet again on his fiftieth birthday on Paul Federn's medallion: Oedipus. In the fifth book of the *Interpretation of Dreams*, Freud lays out before the reader the "material and sources" of dreams, in the course of which he discusses "what is known as a tragedy of destiny," Sophocles' *Oedipus Rex*, remarking that, "If *Oedipus Rex* moves a modern audience no less than it did the contemporary Greek one, the explanation can only be that its effect does not lie in the contrast between destiny and human will, but is to be looked for in the nature of the material on which that contrast is exemplified. There must be something which makes a voice within us ready to recognize the compelling force of destiny in *Oedipus* .... And a factor of this kind is in fact involved in the story of King Oedipus. His destiny moves us only because it might have been ours .... It is the fate of all of us, perhaps, to direct our first sexual impulse towards our mother and our first hatred and our first murderous wish against our father. Our dreams convince us that that is so. King Oedipus, who slew his father Laïus and married his mother Jocasta, merely shows us the fulfillment of our childhood wishes."[17]

There was a time when the phrase "our dreams convince us that that is so" did not claim to be a universally valid insight, based on the description of dreams from countless patients but was a highly personal confession. After Freud had started to interpret his own dreams, performing the *operatio spiritualis* of analysis on his own psyche, he wrote on October 3, 1897, to Wilhelm Fließ, "For the last four days my self-analysis, which I consider indispensable for the clarification of the whole problem, has continued in dreams and has presented me with the most valuable elucidations and clues .... To put it in writing is more difficult than anything else for me; it would also take me too far afield. I can only indicate that the old man plays no active part in my case, but that no doubt I drew an inference by analogy from myself onto him; ... that later (between two and two and a half years) my libido toward *matrem* was awakened, namely, on the occasion of a journey with her from Leipzig to Vienna, during which we must have spent the night together and there must have been an opportunity of seeing her *nudam*"[18]

As an interpreter of dreams, the inhibitions Freud felt with regard to his own dreams must have been considerable. Ernest Jones was one of the first to be struck by the fact that the central motif, his memory of his mother's naked body, is related in a dead language, the Latin of medicine. Jones also corrects the date of Freud's experience: it was in 1860 that the Freud family traveled from Leipzig to Vienna, by which time Freud was at least three and a half years old, his father, Jakob, forty-four and his mother, Amalia, twenty-four.[19] Even in the days before the First World War, when life expectancy was shorter, a man was not old at forty-four. If, then, Freud called his father the "old man," it was presumably in relation to his own age and, above all, to that of his mother. Also his suggestion that the "old man" played "no active part" for him is at the very least dubious. It is contradicted by a memory—undated, it is true—from Freud's "early" childhood, "in which the child, probably driven by sexual curiosity, had forced his way into his parents' bedroom and been turned out of it by his father's orders."[20] The puzzling passage in the letter to Wilhelm Fließ quoted above in which Freud talks of an "inference by analogy," which he directed from himself at the "old man," presumably means that while Freud the child was jealous of the adult, he assumed his father felt no jealousy. The "old man" could not, must not be so "active." There is a further indication of repressed aggression in the formulation used in the German: that as a child he "directed" (*gerichtet habe*) an "inference by analogy" at his father, whereas the usual form of this expression (as in the English translation) would have been that he "drew" an inference from himself onto the adult. The "old man" presumably played a much less passive role than the child was prepared to admit. Nor is the fact that this child desired his mother quite as straightforward as at first appears. His libido (another example of the Latin veil) is aroused "toward *matrem*," not "at her" or "for her" or "ad matrem" (the most natural way of expressing this would have been to use the Latin preposition.) His desire "toward" his beloved mother, whose declared favorite he was, cannot have been free of ambivalence. That probably explains the repression which even as an adult Freud does not seem completely to have overcome.

"The deepest and eternal nature of man, upon whose evocation in his hearers the poet is accustomed to rely, lies in those impulses of the mind which have their roots in a childhood that has since become prehistoric,"[21] Freud wrote in *The Interpretation of Dreams.* It is the mythical, tragic age, the age of dreams, which Freud here designates as "prehistoric." It presumably begins with a person's birth. But when does it end? The year that lies between Freud's memory of the awakening of his libido and the actual journey from Leipzig to Vienna, that is the time between the ages of two and a half and three and a half, can probably be taken as its limit. But setting this limit back by a whole year can also be seen as a "Freudian" slip arising from Freud's wish to push this incident, which appalled even him, as far back into the past as possible.

Of Sophocles' Jocasta, Freud notes, "Here is one in whom these primeval wishes of our childhood have been fulfilled, and we shrink back from her with the whole force of the repression by which these wishes have since that time been held down within us. While the poet, as he unravels the past, brings to light the guilt of Oedipus, he is at the same time compelling us to recognize our own inner minds, in which those same impulses, though suppressed, are still to be found."[22] But he sought to uncover those "primeval wishes of childhood" and bring them into consciousness. However, an analysis of the language in which his self-interpretation is couched shows that he himself was not fully conscious of his own confused emotions and that, tragically, he did not entirely understand himself.

But he continued to interpret the "prehistoric" dreams to which mankind, when it dreams them, has given the name of myth. It was a piece of our mythic heritage he brought to light, and he gave what came to the surface a tragic name: the Oedipus complex. What does it matter that most of his early patients came from the Viennese upper-middle classes? The dream of the lost paradise of childhood is universal and that is what he cleared away, patiently, layer by layer, an archaeologist of the mind, until he reached the bottom, where he found the images of a father murdered and a mother desired. In his interpretation, these images were given a meaning that was as primitive as it was intimately personal: the meaning of the nursery and the fairy tale, from which it is only a short step to myth. It was images that he uncovered, primal images if one is to believe him. It is no small part of Freud's own tragedy that he believed these images to be the result of scientific research. As such, he incorporated them in a system he erected on the basis of medicine, which he then proceeded to open up to the analysis of religion, culture, and society. No one should be surprised if this exposed faults in the system itself.

What he felt was required of him as a doctor was to heal his sick patients. From the "chimney sweeping," which his friend and teacher Josef Breuer owed to his patient Anna O, ... to the free association Freud himself got his patients to develop on the couch, the cooperation of patients in overcoming their disorder was the *sine qua non* of the therapeutic process of psychoanalysis. His aim was to bring into consciousness things that had so far been unconscious, to alleviate the fears engendered by the guilt, the primal guilt of the nursery, and to break the compulsions afflicting his patients, above all the ultimate compulsion, the compulsion to repeat. By that he understood the urge his patients felt to perform actions and bring about situations which their conscious minds recognized, albeit too late, as being harmful. He wanted to mobilize the will against irrational drives, to call up the light of day against the darkness and the confusion of dream, the labyrinths and trapdoors of which he had recognized and systematically interpreted. Later on, he himself coined the concise formula for this healing process: "Where id was, there ego shall be."[23]

By the "id" he understood the underworld elements of night and its dreams, and by the "ego" the self-aware individual obedient to the dictates of reason, whom he also saw as under pressure from the "super-ego," a force of conscience shaped according to the commandments, criticisms, and taboos of a father or some other authority figure. He himself repeatedly warned against taking this model too literally and seeing it in almost topographical terms as an "ego" struggling for its place in the sun of the "super-ego," while at the same time having to defend itself against the underworld of the "id," the unconscious. But he was the very person who encouraged this topography of the "ego." Above and below appear in the programmatic epigraph with which he prefaced his book on the interpretation of dreams, and even today the unconscious often appears as the subconscious. But as early as *The Interpretation of Dreams,* Freud had declared, "We must avoid, too, the distinction between 'supraconscious' and 'subconscious,' which has become so popular in the more recent literature of the psychoneuroses, for such a distinction seems precisely calculated to stress the equivalence of what is psychical to what is conscious."[24] But the phrase, "Where id was, there ego shall be," was something Freud was proud of; he would not hear a word against it, even though, as we will later show, it was a provocation and could even be described as the hubris of his tragedy.

II

For Freud, the process by which the hero of Sophocles' *Oedipus* gathers the evidence which eventually reveals his own guilt was a classic representation of the process by which the "id" becomes the "ego." "The action of the play," Freud says in *The Interpretation of Dreams*, "consists in nothing other than the process of revealing, with cunning delays and ever-mounting excitement—*a process that can be likened to the work of a psychoanalysis*—that Oedipus himself is the son of the murdered man and of Jocasta."[25] Oedipus, who in the first line of the tragedy refers to himself as the father of his people, resists the message from the oracle of Delphi and its interpretation by the seer Tiresias in a way that Freud could not but see as a prefiguration of the resistance he had had to overcome in his self-analysis and which he then came across again when he treated his patients. But once on his own trail, the Greek hero does not let up until he has come face to face with the truth about himself and his parentage. Then he goes and puts out those eyes which have seen too many horrors. Facing him is his wife and mother, a haven of calm for the impetuous, ruthless man. It is she who, close to the climax of the tragedy, is given the words which bring out the personal and historical conflict between the sexes and generations:

> Many a man ere now in dreams hath lain
> With her who bare him. He hath least annoy
> Who with such omens troubleth not his mind.[26]

Freud quotes this passage, emphasizing the first sentence with italics, and adds, "Today, just as then, many men dream of having sexual relations with their mothers and speak of the fact with indignation and astonishment. It is clearly the key to the tragedy and the complement to the dream of the dreamer's father being dead."[27] In

Freud's German there is a contradiction between the "indignation and astonishment" of the men who recount this dream and the expression he uses which suggests they are "granted" (*zuteil werden*) the dream, rather than the more expected are "visited" or "plagued" by it (*heimsuchen*). It is almost as if Freud expected the dream, which seems to him (or to his patients?) like a gift from heaven. With the choice of that verb, we cannot help feeling the doctor has a slight tendency to prejudge the issue.

The tragedy of Oedipus, then, lies in the fact that he interprets that dream, remorselessly, right to the end. By interpreting he sets his tragic fate in motion. He brings into consciousness something which was already present as a premonition in his unconscious. The scales do not fall from his eyes; rather, it is he who tears the blinkers from his eyes himself. His self-confidence shattered, he despairs of man and the gods. Thus, step by step, he uncovers the truth about himself and his unconscious. He, who at the beginning had addressed his people as his children, now starts behaving like a tyrant, though his brutality is not really directed either at the two messengers, who help him reveal his fate, or at Creon and Tiresias, whom he suspects of having designs on being the next tyrant and his minion; it is not even directed at Jocasta, who had born him and lain with him and therefore must die, whose lifeless body he takes down from the noose in a gesture which is as final as it is conciliatory. In the final analysis, the merciless brutality with which he tracks down the truth is directed at himself and the revelation of his own identity. This process of discovery is an *actus tragicus,* and since it consists in the interpretation of dreams which his mother begged him to leave in darkness, it is the interpretation itself which becomes a tragedy. In the catharsis of the tragedy, he offers himself as a sacrifice, so that his blindness about himself can be healed.

The price he has had to pay for this healing is high: his people and crown lost, his wife and mother dead, he himself blinded by his own hand. But now his eye can see and his voice has taken on a new tone: tenderness. His farewell to his daughters, who are at the same time also his sisters, has a new intensity and is imbued with an hitherto unknown, appreciation for him of the world and its realities:

> ... For where
> Can ye find fellowship, what civic throng
> Shall ye resort unto, what festival,
> From whence, instead of sight and sound enjoyed,

Ye will not come in tears unto your home?
And when ye reach the marriageable bloom,
My daughters, who will be the man to cast
His lot with yours, receiving for his own
All those reproaches ...[28]

He has woken up and become consciously aware of himself. He has experienced for himself how fragile we humans are in the face of reality. Now he is "most wise" but wise in a different sense from that used by the chorus in their final stasimon: his wisdom is knowledge of himself. It may well have been the tragedy inherent in any interpretation which is concerned with the essential nature of human beings and their minds which made Freud go pale and his voice tremble when on the occasion of his fiftieth birthday he read that inscription again.

The unconscious fantasy the student Freud was "granted" in the Arcade Quadrangle of Vienna University gripped the consciousness of the mature Freud with a vengeance. It might even be that he suddenly became aware, with startling clarity, of his relationship to the tragic figure of Oedipus, a relationship he believed he had put behind him and the name of which he had irrevocably associated with the complex of infantile neuroses. In that case, he would, to use Thomas Mann's expression, have "confused himself mythically" with Oedipus, the king. Thus, the formula of myth, "I am he," would then, at the moment his disciples quoted the Greek tragedy, have laid claim to the figure of Freud and the tragic nature of his interpretations. The "mythic identification" would have been complete; he would have come full circle.

III

For Freud, Shakespeare's *Hamlet* had its roots in the same soil as Sophocles' *Oedipus*. "But," as he says in his interpretation of the later play which follows immediately on his analysis of the Greek tragedy, "the changed treatment of the same material reveals the whole difference in the mental life of these two widely separated epochs of civilization: the centuries-old advance of repression in the emotional life of mankind. In the *Oedipus*, that child's wishful fantasy that underlies it is brought into the open and realized as it would be in a dream. In *Hamlet*, it remains repressed; and just as in the case of neurosis, we only learn of its existence from its inhibiting consequences."[29]

What Freud is referring to by "inhibiting consequences" is the hero's inability to avenge his father. While the King of Thebes lives out his unconscious urges unconsciously, the Danish prince lives by the repression of his infantile neurosis, and dies from it. "Just as in the case of a neurosis," the Oedipus complex from which Hamlet suffers remains concealed from him until it rises to consciousness, with murderous and suicidal consequences, in the massacre of the last act, burying both protagonist and antagonist beneath it. For, as Freud continues in his interpretation, "Hamlet is able to do anything—except take vengeance on the man who did away with his father and took that father's place with his mother, the man who shows him the repressed wishes of his childhood realized."[30]

What Hamlet *can* do, though, is interpret the world. The deed, which is such a burden on his mind, is replaced by the word. Consequently, his neurosis is interminable: since it confines itself to playing with words, it can only be healed by death. Hamlet does not act because for him reflection replaces action, relieving him of the necessity of acting. His tragedy does not develop in an analytical process of revelation, but overtakes him at the very point when he believes he has finally got to the bottom of the way the world works. While Oedipus is a full-blooded male, Hamlet is from the very beginning sicklied over with the pale cast of death.

> ... To die: to sleep;
> No more; and, by a sleep to say we end
> The heartache and the thousand natural shocks
> That flesh is heir to; 'tis a consummation
> Devoutly to be wished. To die, to sleep;
> To sleep: perchance to dream: ay, there's the rub;
> For in that sleep of death what dreams may come
> When we have shuffled off this mortal coil,
> Must give us pause.[31]

The tragedy of Oedipus runs its inevitable course as it would, to use the expression Freud applied to it, "in a dream." Hamlet craves the dream, hoping it will relieve him of his duty to avenge his father. The further a character moves away from the mythic origins of its childhood dreams, the more marked is its loss of substance. Hamlet is more "grown up" than Oedipus; we can imagine him as a student in

Wittenberg but not as a child. The separation from the dreams of childhood appears in Hamlet as melancholy. In the true sense of the expression, he loses himself in his discussions with himself.

He also loses himself in his soliloquy at the beginning of Act III, the axis of his tragedy. He imagines himself dead and shrinks back in horror from the dreams that might accompany death. Oedipus still believed in the reality of the existence of Apollo; Hamlet does not even believe in life after death. What follows in his soliloquy is a list from our life here on earth, a catalog of the sins of the human condition, seen from the perspective of an end that is irrevocable. He torments himself with thoughts of the baseness surrounding him. Humanity is a disaster and the dream of it a nightmare; as he observes this nightmare unfolding before him, Hamlet interprets it. He interprets it by going through the life of man, point by painful point. As he lists them, his criticism is directed at society. What he rejects is:

> ... the whips and scorns of time,
> The oppressor's wrong, the proud man's contumely,
> The pangs of dispriz'd love, the law's delay,
> The insolence of office, and the spurns
> The patient merit of the unworthy takes[32]

Something similar is expressed in Shakespeare's sixty-sixth sonnet, again viewed from the threshold of our end: "Tir'd with all these, for restful death I cry." While the sonnet, however, finishes with a highly formalized bow to the beloved—"Save that, to die, I leave my love alone."[33]—Hamlet sums up his account of the life of man: "Thus conscience does make cowards of us all."[34] "Conscience"? Is it not rather *consciousness* that prevents Hamlet from taking up his sword and avenging his mother's disgrace? Freud himself sees conscience as a kind of superego. Accordingly, Hamlet's conscience ought to be putting all the more pressure on him to act after his father's ghost has appeared and his superego has implored him to take revenge for his murder.

Hamlet, however, knows too much. He thinks too much, like Cassius, from whose "lean and hungry look"[35] Caesar could tell he was dangerous, dangerous for the state, in which there is always something rotten, as there is in the state of Denmark. An older word for conscience is *inwit*, inward knowledge. Knowledge lies deep within Hamlet's consciousness; when it collides with the outside world, the sparks of his wit start flying, making him forget the sword he should have drawn. His consciousness does, of course, function as a conscience, namely as the guilty conscience of the others, of the adulterers and murderers, whose crimes he has played out before them, whom he hunts down and harries and routs—with words. But what makes him a coward is his *consciousness*, his consciousness of what he is and of the task his superego, his father's ghost, has given him. Is he mad? Or is he just playing the madman? We never find out. What we do see and hear, though, is the way he seesaws between illusion and reality, playing with words he has drawn, distilled from his unconscious. "Drop a word before the young Lord Hamlet," Erich Heller said about the Danish prince's wordplay, "and he will, as if it were a mouse and his mind the cat, chase it through all the chambers of consciousness, corner it, take it with a cunning smile between his teeth, let it go, be after it with graceful leaps, encircle it with the paws and claws of his brain and, having thus prepared for his intellectual meal, blink with feigned indifference into vacuous space as if in all the world there were no words to feed the truth."[36]

The picture Heller paints is very much in Hamlet's spirit, but it lacks the intensity of Hamlet's play with words. In Hamlet's wordplay the umbilical cord linking word, whim, and wit with his unconscious has not yet been cut. The young prince would surely suffocate if he could not measure reality with words and rub its nose, again and again, in its own vileness, if he did not see it, unaware of itself as it is, in all its awfulness, interpret it and then play with his interpretation, like a juggler with his balls. But these balls bear inside them their own poison, the poison of consciousness. His ability to interpret the world paralyzes him when it comes to action.

> And thus the native hue of resolution
> Is sicklied o'er with the pale cast of thought,
> And enterprises of great pith and moment
> With this regard their currents turn awry,
> And lose the name of action.[37]

The pale cast of thought. Thought as such is pale; that is what infects action, renders it sickly until it proves its own pointlessness and is not carried out.

Freud's commentary—"the loathing which should drive him on to revenge is replaced in him by self-reproaches, by scruples of conscience, which remind him that he himself is literally no better than the sinner whom he is to punish"[38]—only takes account of one side of Hamlet's character. There is another. The Prince of Denmark is one of the first, perhaps even the very first, of those sensitive types who not only consider themselves just as bad as all other sinners but also as considerably better, and that thanks to that very consciousness which both paralyzes and protects them at the same time. They have come to see clearly the reality of what the others, the men of the world, the men of action, the realists, do and have interpreted the sinners' deeds as misdeeds; and it is their consciousness that stops these scrupulous characters from joining in. That, as the end of the tragedy shows, they end up entangled in the net created by these misdeeds after all does not surprise these sensitive types in the least; they knew it from the start, that was the finding of their interpretation. Their consciousness feeds on the misdeeds, real and imagined, of the world around until it is full to bursting.

These sensitive types (Freud calls them "hysterics"[39]) are what you might call the aristocracy of those whose suffering is self-inflicted. Their hypertrophic consciousness raises them above the general mass (the "general" who do not appreciate caviar, perhaps). They understand the so-called real world; they understand it only too well and they exhaust their energies interpreting this real world. Therefore, they seek kindred souls, as Hamlet is compelled to seek Ophelia, whom they destroy because of that kinship, until they finally come face to face with their Laertes, Ophelia's more robust brother, who kills the Prince. Can we say that Hamlet has foreseen this too? His provocative words to Laertes at Ophelia's grave, "this is I,/ Hamlet the Dane,"[40] suggests that is the case. Whether it is or not, his consciousness also contains "The undiscover'd country from whose bourn/ No traveler returns."[41] Since his encounter with his father's ghost, he has been on the threshold of that country and interprets the hectic activity of the world around from that perspective.

He also acts, or at least gives the appearance of acting. Freud was not the first to observe "that Hamlet is far from being represented as a person incapable of taking any action. We see him," Freud goes on, "doing so on two occasions: first in a sudden outburst of temper, when he runs his sword through the eavesdropper behind the arras, and secondly in a premeditated and even crafty fashion, when, with all the callousness of a Renaissance prince, he sends the two courtiers to the death that had been planned for himself."[42] If, however, Freud's theory holds true and Hamlet's unconscious forbids him to slay the man who is his father's murderer and his mother's husband, then there must also be an inner voice telling him that the eavesdropper behind the arras cannot possibly be the man from whom he is to exact vengeance. The fact that he kills Polonius, the father of Ophelia and of his future killer, is more like a well-aimed Freudian slip than an autonomous action. Sometimes our unconscious makes us clairvoyant. But sending the two courtiers, Rosenkrantz and Guildenstern, into the trap Claudius has set for him is not an action but a murderous game, like the representation of his father's murder by the actor.

It is, in fact, a hallmark of Hamlet's character that the world has been sublimated into a stage on which he can practice his wordplay. This sensitive type reflects the world, refracts it in the lens of his irony. Since he knows he is unable to cope with the world as it is, he breaks it down into iridescent reflections, thus shattering it. This, and not the murder of the king, is Hamlet's revenge.

In Hamlet's case, the "centuries-old advance of repression in the emotional life of mankind" of which Freud has spoken is paired with a noticeable loss of vitality. His own mother calls him "fat and scant of breath,"[43] though he is scant of breath only when it comes to the duel; his soliloquies are well-nigh inexhaustible as they take flight on the twin wings of his eloquence: self-abasement and the death wish. Hamlet has been subjecting the world and his own self to interpretation for so long that both the world and his self have slipped from his grasp. Thus, he deprives Claudius of his victory and not only by dragging both the king and the queen down with him. Laertes only kills what is mortal in Hamlet, leaving Hamlet's irony with its final triumph.

IV

It is only one step, and a short one at that, from Hamlet's contempt for the real world to Tonio Kröger's "nausea that comes from knowledge." Thomas Mann's story appeared three years after Freud's *Interpretation of Dreams* and is as far removed from psychoanalytical knowledge as Lübeck is from Vienna. The "nausea" that comes from knowledge is, in Tonio Kröger's words, "a state of mind in which a man has no sooner seen through a thing than so far from feeling reconciled to it he is immediately sickened to death by it. This was how Hamlet felt, Hamlet the Dane, that typical literary artist."[44]

Hamlet a literary artist? What Tonio Kröger has in mind is the artist as *décadent*. "Can one even say that an artist *is* a man?" he asks his friend, the painter Lisaveta Ivanovna, and answers the question himself: "Let Woman answer that! I think we artists are all in rather the same situation as those artificial papal sopranos ... Our voices are quite touchingly beautiful. But—."[45] "Get thee to a nunnery,"[46] Hamlet, the *décadent* before his time, tells Ophelia.

It is not mere chance that the Prince of Denmark says this to Ophelia immediately after he has interpreted himself and seen his lack of action as a result of his awareness of death. He has interpreted himself; the only question is: has he understood himself? Far from being an "Oedipus unbound," which Erich Heller accuses his psychoanalytical critics of making Hamlet,[47] he becomes more and more of a puzzle to himself the longer he continues to interpret himself in his soliloquies, until he is lost not only to the world but to himself as well. In other words, the farther away we moderns move from our original dreams, the less transparent we become to ourselves. For Hamlet, there is no Delphic oracle he can misunderstand and then, in an abrupt, dramatic about-turn, understand. It is only his father's ghost that speaks to him, a wisp of cloud that has taken on form and voice on the platform at Elsinore.

For the *décadent* that is Tonio Kröger, the primal conflict has evaporated into thin air; for him, it is merely a matter of atmosphere, of impressions. And yet the contrast between his parents creates a beat that runs through the whole story in an oscillating diminuendo. Thomas Mann observes, with scrupulous impartiality, "Tonio loved his dark, fiery mother, who played the piano and the mandolin so enchantingly, and he was glad that his dubious standing in human society did not grieve her. But on the other hand he felt that his father's anger was much more dignified and *comme il faut*, and though scolded by him, he basically agreed with his father's view of the matter and found his mother's blithe unconcern slightly disreputable."[48]

The old gods have withdrawn, nor are there any ghosts haunting the alleys of the cramped old seaport of Lübeck. What remains is the southern fire and musical mystery of his mother and the anger of his Nordic father, what remains are the scoldings, and it is not even made clear whether they are directed at him, Tonio, or, ultimately, at his mother's "disreputable" behavior and her failure to bring him up properly. This uncertainty contains a final element, the merest suggestion, of mutual understanding between Tonio and his mother.

What also remains is the "dubious standing"—of the boy who writes poems—"in human society," the ordinary world he both admires and sees through, and whose very transparency causes him suffering.

The boy bequeaths these doubts to the man. Apart from matters of sex, Tonio, who has remained a *décadent* and become a writer, intends these doubts to be taken socially. To the verdict of his friend, Lisaveta Ivanovna—"You are a bourgeois who has taken the wrong turning, Tonio Kröger—a bourgeois manqué"—he replies, "*I have been eliminated*,"[49] meaning, "Now *you've* seen through *me*" or "Now you've solved the riddle of my sphinx."

But the doubts he suffers from do not leave Tonio in peace. He decides to go to Denmark, a decision he announces to Lisaveta with the words: "I want to stand on the battlements at Kronborg, where the 'spirit' came to Hamlet, and brought anguish and death to that poor, noble youth ..."[50] Self-pity shows through his characterization of Hamlet; the "literary artist" has been turned into his father's victim; it is the father who is to blame for the anguish and death into which the Prince is plunged. Here Tonio Kröger succumbs to a transference, a fraud, in order to shift onto his own father the burden of blame for the fact that he has become a bourgeois and gone astray. At the same time, by going to the north he is tempting fate: he is throwing out a challenge to the ghost of his father to appear to him. Despite all her friendship, all her artistic sensitivity, Lisaveta has not managed to solve the riddle of who he is.

He goes in search of his origins first of all to his home town of Lübeck, then to Denmark. Is it not as if he were retracing the line of a "pre-lived biography" back to the ghost of *his* father and then beyond him to that ghost whose "mythic formula" Tonio had forgotten and repressed so thoroughly that Oedipus does not even seem to disturb him in his dreams? Tonio Kröger, the *décadent*, has a Hamlet complex; an Oedipus complex is beyond him—or, if one takes the intellectual career of his creator into account, lies ahead of him.

The further the evolution of civilization progresses, the deeper the layers affected by repression. This evolution, Freud says in *Civilization and its Discontents*, "must present the struggle between Eros and Death, between the instinct of life and the instinct of destruction, as it works itself out in the human species. This struggle is what all life essentially consists of, and the evolution of civilization may therefore be simply described as the struggle for life of the human species."[51] *Civilization and its Discontents* appeared in 1930. It reveals a scientist whose researches have made him conscious of the tragic War of the Giants between the two primary forces affecting human existence: love and death.

Hamlet, as he says himself, had gone over to the side of death. The carnage of the fifth act takes place with the inevitability of a natural catastrophe. Tonio Kröger escapes unscathed. He does not meet a ghost in Denmark, but he does encounter the phantoms of his own youth. He boldly determines to face up to them, in the course of which he comes to the aid, out of pity and surreptitious tenderness, of one who has not been spoiled by "the bliss of the commonplace."[52] At a dance, he helps a skinny girl to her feet.

It is from Aalsgard that he also writes a letter to Lisaveta Ivanovna in Munich in which he repeats, almost in the manner of a leitmotiv, the things his creator knew about him at the beginning of the story and at that point had to say for him: "My father, as you know, was of a northern temperament: contemplative, thorough, Puritanically correct, and inclined to melancholy. My mother was of a vaguely exotic extraction, beautiful, sensuous, naive, both reckless and passionate, and given to impulsive, rather disreputable behavior."[53]

With these words of self-knowledge, Tonio Kröger puts himself on the side of life. He has become conscious of things of which, as a child, he was not conscious, thus freeing himself from all kinds of fears, doubts, and inhibitions. In the course of this, the past has been subjected to some severe revision: the balance of memory has shifted against his mother. Now Tonio's father comes first, his fits of anger, gone and forgotten, have given way to a quiet melancholy. Above all, however, as he writes the letter Tonio is trying to understand his father, in the way people at the turn of the century had learned to understand others: from their family background and their environment. (The spirits of Charles Darwin and Hippolyte Taine presided over the birth of Tonio Kröger.) Consul Kröger's temperament has been formed by the north, his meticulousness by extreme Protestantism. And what is sauce for the gander is also sauce for the goose: his wife's dark, southern fire is forgotten, along with the mystery of music with which she used to surround herself. Her family background is "vague," though "exotic," giving the whole figure a certain gypsy touch; her slightly disreputable "blithe unconcern" has turned into passionate sensuality and recklessness. With this shift, a moral undertone has crept in, a puritanical undertone. Tonio is starting to see his mother through his father's eyes. The split in his psyche seems to have healed: "for if there is anything that can turn a *littérateur* into a true writer, then it is this bourgeois love for the human and the living and the ordinary."[54] For Tonio, Hamlet was a *littérateur*; the image of his own father has blocked out the ghost that drove

Hamlet to anguish and death. By acknowledging his profession as a writer, the artist has made peace with the bourgeois who dwells within him. The only questions is, for how long? We do not know where his journey through life will take him—the novel ends with his letter.

However, the fact that Tonio Kröger is to a large extent a portrait of his creator, and the conflict in his family background a determining split in Thomas Mann's own psyche as well, suggests that the inner peace his hero finds is nothing to write home about. What is certainly true is that the older Tonio's creator grew, and the more wideranging his oeuvre, the more committed a supporter of Freud's teachings he became.

V

In his speech on the occasion of Freud's eightieth birthday,[55] Thomas Mann quoted the psychoanalyst's words, "Where *id* was, there *ego* shall be," and, recalling Freud's following sentence: "It is a work of civilization, rather like draining the Zuiderzee," went on to compare "the distinguished gentleman whose life we are celebrating" with Goethe's Faust who, in his old age, believed himself to be "standing on free soil, among a people free," concluding, "It is the people of a future freed from fear and hatred, ripe for peace."[56]

But apart from the fact that Thomas Mann, "the ironic German,"[57] closed his eyes to the irony in which Goethe had bathed the end of his Faust drama—Faust, blind like Oedipus, takes the noise of the lemurs digging his grave for the sound of spades reclaiming the land—the comparison with the Zuiderzee is and was flawed from the moment Thomas Mann levered it out of its context. The Zuiderzee has actually been drained, while an ego completely freed of its id is totally inconceivable in the individual, not to mention the collective sphere. It is, rather, in a polemic sense that Thomas Mann's comparison is to be understood: at the time it was being made in Vienna in 1936, over the border in Germany the "dismal ... figure" with the "fateful psychology"[58] was arming himself for that terror which, with its unique mixture of hysteria and aggression, was to demonstrate the power of the id, the unconscious, when, with a highly developed technology at its disposal, it crossed the border.

There is, anyway, something precariously hubristic about Freud's statement, "Where id was, there ego shall be." To understand it aright, we must read it in context. It appears when Freud, at the end of the thirty-first section of his *New Introductory Lectures on Psychoanalysis* of 1932, returns to the relationship between superego, ego, and id and, warning against drawing too sharp a distinction between them, goes on, "It is easy to imagine, too, that certain mystical practices may succeed in upsetting the normal relations between the different regions of the mind, so that, for instance, perception may be able to grasp happenings in the depths of the ego and in the id which were otherwise inaccessible to it. It may safely be doubted, however, whether this road will lead us to the ultimate truths from which salvation is to be expected. Nevertheless, it may be admitted that the therapeutic efforts of psychoanalysis have chosen a similar line of approach. Its intention is, indeed, to strengthen the ego, to make it more independent of the super-ego, to widen its field of perception and enlarge its organization, so that it can approach fresh portions of the id. Where id was, there ego shall be."[59]

As a practicing therapist, Freud was aware of his limitations. He could not expect to uncover the whole of the mystery of mankind; he could not hope, to stick to his image, to reclaim the whole of the Zuiderzee, only gradually to win back some solid ground from the sea, to strengthen the ego vis-à-vis the forces of conscience and the unconscious. The American critic, Stanley Edgar Hyman, understood this correctly when, in his essay of 1956, "Psychoanalysis and the Climate of Tragedy," he remarked, "For Freud, the aim of human existence is the reclamation of some cropland of ego from the 'Zuyder Zee' of id, and the limited victory in this bitter struggle is achieved primarily through the traditional philosophic means of self-knowledge. Man's animal nature is to be controlled and channeled in the least harmful direction possible, not changed or abolished, and cure lies not in extirpating animality but in facing it and living with it."[60]

What the American critic refuses to accept, however, is that as a *thinker* Freud was possessed of a rebelliousness that was nothing short of Promethean. He took Virgil's defiant words, with which he had prefaced his *Interpretation of Dreams*, literally. He genuinely believed he had got at the truth about the unconscious. In 1929, at the beginning of his book *Civilization and its Discontents*, he answered a letter from Romain Rolland, who had asked him, admittedly in somewhat naive fashion, whether he could not find within himself "a feeling which he would like to call a sensation of 'eternity,' a feeling as of something limitless, unbounded—as it were 'oceanic,'"[61] with the words, "If I have understood my friend rightly, he means the same thing by it as the consolation offered by an original and somewhat eccentric dramatist to his hero who is facing a self-inflicted death. 'We cannot fall out of this world.' That is to say, it is a feeling of indissoluble bond, of being one with the external world as a whole.... From my own experience, I could not convince myself of the primary nature of such a feeling. But this gives me no right to deny that it does in fact occur in other people."[62]

Giving himself "no right to deny" its existence is the farthest this died-in-the-wool empiricist will allow himself to go in acknowledging the mystery. It is with regard to religion alone that Freud refused to accept the self-imposed restriction of this "no right to deny." He called Heinrich Heine his "fellow-unbeliever"—a pun worthy of the Viennese satirist Karl Kraus—and, like the poet, left Heaven "to the angels and the sparrows."[63] *The Future of an Illusion* unmasked God as "the figure of an enormously exalted father."[64] He treated this figure with much less consideration than he showed his patients. As with his patients, however, he measured the divine being—for him a pure fantasy, a marvelous blend of collective nightmares and pious hopes—against the yardstick of empirical reality. And yet he was superstitious. It was superstition that convinced him he would die in February 1918. When that month had passed and he was still in the land of the living, he said, "That shows what little trust one can put in the supernatural."[65]

The harshness with which he treats God suggests there is some deep-seated emotion behind it. "We are supposed to believe because our fathers believed," he says at one point. "But these ancestors of ours were far more ignorant than we are. They believed in things we could not possibly accept today; and the possibility occurs to us that the doctrines of religion may belong to that class too. The proofs they have left us are set down in writings which themselves bear every mark of untrustworthiness.... It does not help much to have it asserted that their wording, or even their content only, originated from divine revelation; for this assertion is itself one of the doctrines whose authenticity is under examination, and no proposition can be a proof of itself."[66] At another point, when the discussion touched on the battle between the primal forces of Eros and Thanatos for the soul of mankind, he exclaimed, again with an allusion to Heine, "And it is this War of the Giants that our nursemaids try to appease with their lullaby about Heaven."[67]

What he overlooked in all this was the fact that the mythical War of the Giants was directed against the very Heaven from which the nursemaids and ministers of appeasement in their pulpits obtained their "lullaby." In general, Freud went to the Greek myths because of the difficulties he had with his Jewish heritage and the painful treatment he suffered from the Christians around him. A further tragic element lies in the fact that, clearly quite early on, he discovered within himself "a streak of paternalism,"[68] becoming not only the head of a school but a patriarch of disciples which, in terms of depth psychology, is more or less the same.

Sigmund Freud belongs in the great tradition of Jewish scholarship. Even where this tradition turns against its God, it still retains its characteristic of "clarifying," the sharp-eyed exegesis of the scriptures and Talmud. Freud's interpretations have all the insistent searching and probing, all the relentless logic and rigor of the Jewish belief in the importance of words. Where his ancestors sought God, he searched for the truth about the unconscious. Like his ancestors, he pursued his researches by the means of interpretation. He was what one might call a secularized rabbi of the enlightenment,[69] of the enlightenment of mankind about itself. It was medicine that led him to the interpretation of dreams, but his urge to clarify the mystery of mankind itself was so powerful that ultimately the whole range of human knowledge came within his compass.

For all that, he was enough of a cultured Viennese to go in awe of art, as if it were in some way taboo. It is perhaps this awe that explains why Freud, who was a born and accomplished writer, decided to "give preference to the scientist,"[70] as he wrote to Arthur Schnitzler, who had gone the opposite way, from doctor to writer. He could even, as he wrote in his letter to Yvette Guilbert of March 8, 1931, talk of the "beautiful mystery" of art, adding, "But one knows so little about it all."[71] But there are some things we do know, and we know them since Freud and through Freud. The development from Oedipus to Tonio Kröger has shown how a primal conflict can retreat to the furthest recesses of the unconscious. At the end of Sophocles' second Oedipus drama, the gods take the hero up into their midst. Hamlet and Tonio Kröger confront their fate with the irony of self-reflection. This cannot save Hamlet from the tragedy that is more a sentence carried out than a destiny fulfilled. With Tonio Kröger, tragedy has withdrawn, or so it appears; irony has set up its mirrors round his story, but Thomas Mann's novella, too, is the story of a journey of self-discovery, of a self-analysis. Although the end is anything but tragic, it is still uncertain.

Tonio Kröger's state of consciousness, watered down, as it were, with self-knowledge, corresponds to the psychological material Freud found in his patients. Of course, none of them shared Tonio Kröger's propensity for ironic self-illumination, but what they did have in common with the figure created by Thomas Mann's highly refined art was the distance separating them from the mythic primal conflict, for which Freud had made Oedipus the tragic model. Freud knew exactly why he had designated the theory of repression one of the cornerstones of his system which no psychoanalyst was to dare to call into question. As an analyst, Freud pierced the pale, flat surfaces of the minds his patients presented to him by first of all interpreting the symbolism of their dreams, then releasing their psychological energy. Interpreting human psyches was, to put it mildly, a bold venture, containing as it did the danger of destroying the mind which had opened up to the doctor in the hope of being healed, a danger that was all the greater the more delicate and sensitive, the more decadent and weak-willed the patients were who had put themselves in his hands.

Every interpretation is, by its very nature, dialectical. It serves to illuminate an object which the interpreter is convinced cannot be illuminated in its entirety. Thus, psychoanalysis can never hope to achieve a complete cure.[72] All we can ever do is approach the mystery, surround it; that reduces the mystery, but also compresses it, so that a mass of potentially explosive material piles up. A world that has been exhaustively interpreted is a world that is in danger of becoming fixed on its own consciousness, a mind that has been exhaustively interpreted of becoming the mind of an automaton.

In Rilke's first *Duino Elegy* are the lines:

> ... Ah, whom can we ever turn to
> in our need? Not angels, not humans,
> and already the knowing animals are aware
> that we are not really at home in
> our interpreted world. [73]

Rilke had had enough contact with the theory of psychoanalysis[74] to understand by this "interpreted world" a world which has lost its dreams. Anyone who inhabits such a universe is exposed to the void. They see through everything, with the result that everything is so transparent that they cannot see the wall they are banging their heads against.

The suggestion of tragedy tingeing Freud's statement, "Where id was, there ego shall be," comes from the fact that this dictum, taken out of context and thought through to its logical conclusion, relates to a consciousness that is no longer fed by the springs of the unconscious. This tragic aspect is already suggested by the paradox that it is only after he has put his eyes out that Oedipus can see himself. His catharsis is purchased at the price of a huge loss of sensory stimulation. When, however, we see him again at Colonos, he is almost his old self: rash, impetuous, his vitality unbroken. Even he has failed to sacrifice the whole of his physical urges to his consciousness of himself. The suffering his own self causes him is never ending; his tragedy continues until the gods themselves put an end to it, which, whatever else it may be, is an ending *ex machina*. But Oedipus was immortal even before the gods took him up into their midst. Immortality is a blessing of conscious humanity.

VI

The expectations with which Freud approached the world were titanic, the epigraph he placed over *The Interpretation of Dreams* the gesture of a revolutionary. At the end he knew better. Two years before his death, he published an essay, *Analysis Terminable and Interminable*. In this very late work he says, "Only by the concurrent or mutually opposing action of the two primal instincts—Eros and the death-instinct—never by one or the other alone, can we explain the rich multiplicity of the phenomena of life. How parts of these two classes of instincts combine to fulfill the various vital functions, under what conditions such combinations grow looser or break up, to what disturbances these changes correspond and with what feelings the perceptual scale of the pleasure principle replies to them—these are problems whose elucidation would be the most rewarding achievement of psychological research. For the moment we must bow to the superiority of the forces against which we see our efforts come to nothing."[75] The conditional "would be"—or should we perhaps read it as an optative?—once more opens the gate to the mystery of the unconscious in the human mind. It reveals the countless interpretations which can be derived from the "concurrent or mutually opposing action of the two primal instincts—Eros and the death-instinct," as well as from the "rich multiplicity of the phenomena of life." To a large extent, the resignation behind that conditional denotes Freud's acknowledgment that his theory cannot be limited to one single interpretation.

But that means that by its own light this theory, which is based on interpretation, becomes tragic, along with its creator, who scarcely had an equal in the art of interpretation.

Laius and Oedipus: Freud's Fainting Fits

In his tragedy *Ödipus und die Sphinx*, Hugo von Hofmannsthal had the murder of the father, the sight of which Sophocles had spared his Athenian audience, happen onstage. It is the first play to treat the son's struggle with his father with insight into the dynamics of the Oedipus complex, a theme the Expressionists were to deal with in ever cruder variations some ten years later. But Hofmannsthal was writing in 1905, when interpreting parricide in terms of depth psychology was new. At the time, Hofmannsthal, from Vienna himself, was influenced by Freud's theories[76] but had a low opinion of that influence and tried to conceal it,[77] even calling the creator of psychoanalysis, "an absolute mediocrity, full of narrow-minded, provincial conceit."[78] This misjudgment is as revealing as it is grotesque; the aggression is so evident it suggests that, somewhere deep within his unconscious, Hofmannsthal, insofar as he identified with his character of Oedipus, had worked his own hostility towards Freud into the murder of Laius.

However, Hofmannsthal was enough of a dramatist to allow the father's voice to be heard as well. When Oedipus provokes him:

> Your voice is hatred and torment. You have never had a child, you are one of the barren ones,
> your sad wife, dust in her hair,
> prostrated herself night and day before the gods—
> no blessing will come upon your house.

the old man replies:

> Boasting as well?—Grasp him, bring him here.
> I will make him drink the bitter juice in my heart.
> I have been drinking it for years, I have had enough—
> we'll make him drink it down in a single draught.[79]

Here it is the emotions of the father, in which those of his son are mirrored,[80] that find tragic expression. What is torment for the one sounds like boasting to the other. The son proclaims the old man's barrenness, and yet the tragic irony is that he is himself living proof that Laius is not barren. He himself has only just confessed to his servant, "I have never touched a woman."[81]

The old man, on the other hand, makes a boast of the bitterness in his heart. The two of them are caught up in a contest of suffering, which can only be decided by the "Oedipus act." But can it ever be decided? Laius lies slain, but his son is "overcome" with the "awful madness"[82] of the truth; he almost believes the man he has killed is his father.

Here Hofmannsthal has intuitively grasped what Erik K. Erikson, who was close to the Freud family, recently called the "Laius complex," which he claimed the founder of psychoanalysis suffered from.[83] Thus, the son's desire for independence would correspond to the profound distrust the father shows towards his son. It is no coincidence that it was in the context of the relationship between Freud and Carl Gustav Jung that Erikson brought up the "Laius complex."

In her letter of November 6, 1911, Emma Jung reminded Freud of their first conversation on the morning after he arrived at their house: "You said then," she wrote, "that your marriage had long been 'amortized,' now there was nothing more to do except—die. And the children were growing up and then they became a real worry, and yet this is the only true joy. This," she went on, "made such an impression on me and seemed to me so significant that I had to think of it again and again, and I fancied it was intended just for me because it was meant symbolically at the same time and referred to my husband."[84]

It is an astonishing confession for the fifty-five-year-old Freud to have made to a colleague, who was almost twenty years younger, and his wife. But it has the ring of truth, filtered through the feelings Frau Jung had for her husband. What Freud said about his marriage is confirmed by the choice of the word "amortized." The root syllable of the word is death, which Freud's libido had suffered with regard to his wife Martha and which foreshadowed his own death. By borrowing a word from the vocabulary of banking and mortgages to speak of the death of his love, he expresses his skepticism about the world of feeling as a whole. His patients had taught him what emotions mean and how easily they pass. This hidden pun was of the very essence of Freud's language; the Jungs, the Swiss couple, could never have invented it.

As far as his own children were concerned, Emma Jung goes on in her letter, on that morning Freud said he did not have the time to analyze his children's dreams because he had to earn money so that they could go on dreaming,"[85] a remarkable statement if one calls to mind the eminence his daughter Anna was later to achieve as a psychoanalyst. But in 1911, Anna Freud, the youngest of six children, was only sixteen. She was, as youngest children often are, her father's declared favorite and because of that she inherited, as one might say, his psychoanalytical bent. Or did her father love her because she was a difficult child, and he took her neurosis as evidence of her ability to become an analyst? We do not know. Beyond that, on that morning in Zurich, Freud displayed an embitterment which induced Emma Jung to take his words "symbolically" and interpret them as aggression directed towards her husband, who was twenty years younger and inwardly incapable of sharing Freud's embitterment.

The Oedipal ambivalence determining the relationship between Freud and Jung started before they even met face to face in Vienna in February 1907. Jung, as he recognized early on, labored under a father complex which, in Freud's view, derived from his concept of infantile sexuality, that is the Oedipus complex itself. As early as his book *The Psychology of Dementia Praecox* of 1906, Jung announced his reservations in the preface: " If I ... acknowledge that dreams and hysteria contain the mechanisms of complexes, that does not mean that I attribute to the infantile sexual trauma the exclusive importance that Freud apparently does."[86]

When, three years later, they met again in Vienna there was a very serious discussion between them which is recorded in Jung's *Memories, Dreams, Reflections* in the following words: "I can still recall vividly how Freud said to me, 'My dear Jung, promise me never to abandon the sexual theory. That is the most essential thing of all. You see, we must make a dogma of it, an unshakable bulwark.' He said that to me with great emotion, in the tone of a father saying, 'And promise me this one thing, my dear son: that you will go to church every Sunday.' In some astonishment, I asked him, 'A bulwark—against what?' To which he replied, 'Against the black tide of mud'—and here he hesitated for a moment, then added—'of occultism' .... This was," Jung goes on, "the thing that struck at the heart of our friendship. I knew that I would never be able to accept such an attitude. What Freud seemed to mean by 'occultism' was virtually everything that philosophy and religion, including the rising contemporary science of parapsychology, had to tell us about the psyche."[87] Even before this 1910 meeting in Vienna, Jung had been struck by the fact that "Freud was emotionally involved in his sexual theory to an extraordinary degree. When he spoke of it, his tone became urgent, almost anxious, and all signs of his normally critical and skeptical manner vanished. A strange, deeply moved expression came over his face, the cause of which I was at a loss to understand. I had a strong intuition that for him sexuality was a sort of *numinosum*."[88]

However vivid Jung's memory may have been, it remains a memory of something that had happened almost forty years previously. In addition, it is even more blurred by the fact that the editor, Aniela Jaffé, has, as she notes, incorporated into the "Sigmund Freud" chapter of *Memories* a number of excerpts from a seminar Jung delivered in 1925.[89]

It is hardly surprising, then, that the words Jung puts into Freud's mouth do not sound like Sigmund Freud. The phrase, "an unshakeable bulwark against the black tide of mud, of occultism" was not said by Freud. It comes from the dictionary of banalities which Nietzsche inveighed against in *On the Genealogy of Morality*: "Actually, a psychologist today shows his *good* taste, if he shows any at all (others might say his integrity), by resisting the scandalously *over-moralistic* language with which practically all modern judgments about men and things are smeared."[90] The "unshakeable bulwark against the black tide of mud" Jung himself could not get away from[91] is "bad taste" and "over-moralistic." Whenever Freud made personal remarks—and he could make very personal remarks—he let his wit (of which he was more than conscious of its connection with his own unconscious) do the talking. Mostly, however, he contented himself with hints, as in the passage quoted above from the *New Introductory Lectures on Psycho-analysis* of 1932, which is probably still directed against Jung: "It is easy to imagine, too, that *certain mystical practices* may succeed in upsetting the normal relations between the different regions of the mind ...."[92]

When Jung talks about himself, however (or his devoted editor talks about him) it sounds authentic. The sentence, for example, in which he describes sexuality as a *numinosum*—that is something ineffably holy—for Freud, applies in reverse to Jung himself. Freud's sexual theory did truly invade the world of the ineffably holy, which was a distinctive feature of the Protestant Jung's makeup and remained so until his death. It is a piece of self-analysis when Jung in his *Memories* goes on to say, "Just as the psychically stronger agency is given 'divine' or 'daemonic' attributes, so the 'sexual libido' took over the role of a *deus absconditus*, a hidden or concealed god. The advantage of this transformation for Freud was, apparently, that he was able to regard the new numinous principle as scientifically irreproachable and free from all religious taint. At bottom, however, the numinosity, that is, the psychological qualities of the two rationally incommensurable opposites—Yahweh and sexuality—remains the same."[93] The linking of the opposing "numinosities," Yahweh and sexuality, indicates a deep-seated thread of anti-Semitism woven into Jung's psyche. That helps make the political attitude of the German-Swiss psychologist during Hitler's thousand-year Reich more understandable; at the same time, however, the parallel drawn between the Jew's God, whose name Jung could not bring himself to pronounce, using instead the tautology "I am that I am," with which God identified Himself to Moses from the burning bush, and the sex drive, which was for Jung equally taboo, means that Freud's theory of infantile sexuality was bound to meet with a resistance from his younger colleague which was deeply rooted within his character. It was Jung who deified the sex drive, not Freud, whom he demonized by that very apotheosis. To use an image: the Oedipus complex was the forked goad with which, at the crossroads where they met, Laius/Freud seemed to threaten Oedipus/Jung, but it was also the implement with which this Oedipus took a big swing to rid himself of his Laius for good.

From the very outset, neither Freud nor Jung was unaware of the fact that the encounter between them was dangerous both for himself and for the other. The only question is: why did they still pursue their relationship with open eyes, what did they expect of each other, and why, despite their awareness of themselves and the other, did they manage to get each other so completely wrong?

In a letter from the early period of their relationship (October 28, 1907), Jung felt obliged to explain to Freud why he did not write to him more frequently: "Actually—and I confess this to you with a struggle—I have a boundless admiration for you both as a man and a researcher, and I bear you no conscious grudge. So the self-preservation complex does not come from there; it is rather that my veneration for you has something of the character of a 'religious' crush. Though it does not really bother me, I still feel it is disgusting and ridiculous because of its undeniable erotic undertone. This abominable feeling comes from the fact that as a boy I was the victim of a sexual assault by a man I once admired." A little further on comes the sentence Jung underlined: "*I therefore fear your confidence.*"[94]

Jung can hardly be accused of not wearing his unconscious on his sleeve. He reveals the mixture of love and hatred he feels towards Freud in all its tangled complexity. He is aware of the religious nature of his ambivalence as he is of the taint of homosexuality attaching to that very ambivalence. Is he not saying to the older man, "Once before, when I was a boy, I admired a man the way I admire you, and how did he reward me for it? With an attack on my virtue!" Here Freud appears in the guise of a seducer, an abuser of young boys, and there is a certain irony in the fact that, as will be shown later, Freud too was prey to similar obsessive ideas. In his letter, Jung expresses his fear of the man he admired invading his world, which seems to him childlike and innocent. In addition, he fears the trust, which, as he very well knows, Freud is about to place in him; he fears it like sin itself, and yet he goes ahead and accepts it.

In January 1908, Dr. C. G. Jung, lecturer in psychology, called the first congress on Freudian psychology in Salzburg—Chairman: Herr Professor Dr. S. Freud. The invitations were sent out from Burghölzli Mental Hospital in Zurich.[95]

About four weeks later, Freud offered the younger man his friendship. He did it by deleting the last two words of the set greeting—"Dear Friend and Colleague"—at the beginning of his letter of February 17, 1908. It is a long letter, dealing with Freud's work, the preparations for the Salzburg congress, the possibility of a translation of Freud's and Breuer's studies on hysteria, and finally with psychiatric studies, especially of paranoia. The idea of a "homosexual element" in that mental illness is mentioned. It sounds like an echo of the homosexual assault Jung had told Freud about the previous October. Then a sentence is slipped in which Jung could not but see as a scarcely veiled threat: "My one-time friend Fließ developed a dreadful case of paranoia after throwing off his affection for me, which was undoubtedly considerable."[96] Wilhelm Fließ (1858-1928) was almost the same age as Freud and they were such close friends that Freud's decisive letters about his self-analysis were addressed to him.[97] The break came when Fließ accused Freud of borrowing the idea of human bisexuality from the Viennese philosopher, Otto Weininger. In fact, however, Freud suspected Fließ of having an "undoubtedly considerable" homosexual affection for him. Implicit in his letter of February 1908 was a warning to Jung not to follow in Fließ's footsteps.

Jung was aware of the break with Fließ and the reasons for it since he took up Freud's coded language in his reply of February 20: "The undeserved gift of your friendship is one of the high points in my life which I cannot celebrate with big words. The reference to Fließ—surely not accidental—and your relationship with him impels me to ask you to let me enjoy your friendship not as one between equals but as that of father and son."[98] Translated out of the coded language of the letters, his reply is roughly as follows: I have understood ("The reference to Fließ—surely not accidental"); to what do I owe this honor? ("The undeserved gift of your friendship"); I am not the same age as you ("not as putting himself in the role of the boy who had fallen victim to the temptation of a man he had previously admired).

Translated into mythological terms, Oedipus was offering himself to Laius. Even as late as March 11, 1909, Jung was still writing to Freud, "You may rest assured, not only now but for the future, that nothing Fließ-like is going to happen."[99]

The inevitable came to pass—Freud designated Jung heir apparent of the psychoanalytical movement. Ernest Jones presumes it was Jung's vitality, the liveliness of the younger man, that attracted Freud and, above all else, his unrestrained imagination. "This," he notes, "was a quality that seldom failed to captivate Freud ... It echoed something of great significance in his own personality, something over which his highly developed capacity for self-criticism had to exercise the strictest control."[100] What drew the enlightened Viennese Jew to the Zurich Protestant was the latter's superabundant imagination, and the fact that the downside of Jung's easily stimulated imagination was a certain muddleheadedness clearly did nothing to diminish Freud's fatherly affection. Jones reports that a schoolmate of Jung's had noticed this muddleheadedness, adding, with meaning, "I was not the only person to observe this"[101] in the adult Jung.

A further reason for designating Jung his heir was that for Freud the Swiss psychiatrist embodied the decisive breakthrough of his theories outside Austria. It is true that his correspondence with Eugen Bleuler, Jung's teacher and superior, had started in 1904,[102] and in the English-speaking world, psychiatrists of the standing of Havelock Ellis, James J. Putnam, and Morton Prince had begun to take notice of him;[103] but England was a long way away, America even farther and from the very beginning filled Freud with unease, and his feelings towards Jung's superior in Zurich were ambivalent. Even while he was preparing the first congress in Salzburg together with Jung, he could write, "the prospect of Bleuler's presence rather confuses me, I have mixed feelings towards him ... Don't you think it would be a good idea to offer him the chairmanship? My Viennese will be much better behaved with him, and by providing the battle cry, I play enough of a role."[104] There are two things that strike one about that last sentence; firstly, that Freud assigns to himself the role of battle cry. "Battle cries" are only raised when a castle or town is being stormed. But whom does the castle or town symbolize? Clearly Bleuler who, with his air of academic superiority and neutrality, "rather confused" Freud, to put it mildly. Secondly, who was it who would make "my Viennese" behave better, the chairman or the "battle cry"? Whatever the answer to that, the possessive article in "my Viennese" has a definite proprietorial note. At the same time, it is impossible not to hear a certain undertone of disparagement toward "his" fellow countrymen in the clause as a whole. It was not only Jung who saw the regular members of the "Wednesday Psychology Society," which had been meeting in Vienna since 1902, as a "medley of artists, decadents, and mediocrities,"[105] Freud too, as his correspondence with his "son and heir" shows, sometimes viewed his disciples with a fair amount of skepticism. As long as the psychoanalytical society remained limited to Vienna, it was inevitable that it should appear to the extremely self-critical Freud, who had no religious ties with Judaism, like a kind of secularized rabbinical school. Behind Freud's preference for his Swiss colleague there lies a strong desire to differentiate himself from his Viennese disciples. Burghölzli Mental Hospital was untainted by the atmosphere of Vienna, and it was definitely in Freud's personal interest that the invitations to the first psychoanalytical congress were sent out not from Vienna but from Burghölzli in Zurich. The undeniable distrust with which Freud viewed his Viennese colleagues did not prevent him from taking the chair in Salzburg after Bleuler had "waved it away with a smile,"[106] nor did it stop him falling back on Jewish mythology when he wrote to Jung, on January 17, 1909, "if I am Moses, then you are Joshua and will take possession of the promised land of psychiatry, which I shall only be able to glimpse from afar."[107] One can imagine the look on the Swiss psychologist's face at this reference to the Old Testament.

How was it possible that two men, of which the younger had acquired so much insight into the teachings of the older that he used his vocabulary even when it went against the grain, that two doctors who were well versed in the treatment of psychological problems, that two types who were as aware of the differences between them as Freud and Jung were could be so unaware of the psychological and human constellation presiding over their relationship that they even avoided reading between the lines of their letters to each other? They will have been like other ordinary mortals, their conscious convictions and prejudices covering up the secret motives which from the very beginning had filled their unconscious with distrust of each other. It is also possible they deliberately sought the friction between them for the sparks it would set off.

It is easier to understand Jung than Freud. He was barely thirty-one years old, a non-salaried university lecturer, who, however, as he occasionally hinted to Freud, had the ear of his superior, when he received his first letter from Freud. Also he had publications to show which indicated a mind that was both independent and critical. He had, as Jones observed, a "commanding presence and soldierly bearing,"[108] qualities which presuppose a healthy self-regard, indeed, are impossible without it. In addition, he was daring and full of the zeal of the believer. "If what Freud says is the truth, I am with him. I don't give a damn for a career if it has to be based on the premise of restricting research and concealing the truth,"[109] he recalled having written in 1906. It was the boldness, not without religious, protestant undertones, of a man professing his faith. Also, he must have hoped he had secured his position vis-à-vis his older colleague through the objections and reservations about Freud's theories that he had expressed from the very beginning. That he was permitted, young as he was, to contradict Freud, whose greatness he recognized, at least in general outline, without bringing down an immediate anathema on his head, bolstered his self-confidence. When, in 1910, Freud entrusted him with the chairmanship of the International Psychoanalytic Association, he became its president; the Association had its headquarters in the president's place of residence: Zurich. But Jung continued to reply to Freud's letters, which were addressed "Dear Friend," with a formal "Dear Herr Professor."

On the other hand, Freud, in designating Jung his heir apparent and assigning the chairmanship of his association to him, seemed above all to be concerned with securing the future of the international psychoanalytical movement. "Just rest easy," he wrote on March 6, 1910, four weeks before he installed Jung as president, "just rest easy, dear son Alexander, I will leave you more to conquer than I myself have managed, all psychiatry and the approval of the civilized world, which regards me as a savage."[110] Here he has transferred the Moses-Joshua motif into the world—doubtless much more acceptable to Jung—of ancient Greek history. At the same time, it is worth noticing that Freud exploited the transfer to Greek mythology to yield to what was obviously a long-held wish and addressed his "son Alexander" by the familiar *du*. Admittedly, though, he could only fulfill this wish of his unconscious after he had given his "son" due warning: "Believe me, there are no further misunderstandings between us, nor do I regard you as 'vacillating.' I am neither so forgetful, nor so touchy, and I know how closely we are united by personal sympathy and by pulling at the same cart. I am merely irritated now and then—I may say that much, I trust?—that you have not yet disposed of the resistances arising from your father-complex.... "[111]

At that time, Freud must have seen the younger man's more robust and less apprehensive temperament as representing the psychoanalysis movement's best chance of survival, which explains his willingness to withdraw in favor of Joshua/Alexander. It also explains why he was willing to close his eyes to the threat of the tragic dilemma he felt gathering within him. On April 16, 1909, he wrote to Jung, "It is strange that on the very same evening when I formally adopted you as eldest son and anointed you—*in partibus infidelium*—as my successor and crown prince, you should have divested me of my paternal dignity, which divesting seems to have given you as much pleasure as I, on the contrary, derived from the investiture of your person. Now I am afraid of falling back into the father role with you... Accordingly I put my fatherly horn-rimmed spectacles on again and warn my dear son to keep a cool head, for it is better not to understand something than make such great sacrifices to understanding. I also shake my wise head over psychosynthesis and think: Yes, that's how the young people are, the only places they really enjoy visiting are those they can visit without us, to which we with our short breath and weary legs cannot follow them."[112] His unconscious was seething and bubbling, and the effects were only too clear on the surface, but still Freud preferred to retire behind a patriarchal irony which does not sound quite genuine. "In the end we are dependent/On creatures we've ourselves created"[113] —Mephisto's lines from *Faust* sound a warning.

It was the future of his theories which made Freud close his eyes to the better judgment of his unconscious. He subordinated his personal interest to the cause. Paul Roazen put forward the rather daring proposition that Freud indulged in the fantasy of having brought himself up, that is basically of being his own father. This hypothesis sounds less implausible if one remembers that Freud believed that he had overcome his father through his self-analysis. Roazen goes on, "Freud had to create a whole new family, the psychoanalytic movement, to make up for the family he denied. Freud could not finally become his own father until he could have his own sons. Natural born sons would not do; they had to have the qualities of immortality associated with genius. So Freud made symbolic sons of his most promising pupils. But of course Freud's quarrels with his pupils constituted the tragedy of his public life."[114]

Roazen's argument was taken up by Ernest Becker: "The uniqueness of the genius also cuts off his roots. He is a phenomenon that was not foreshadowed; he doesn't seem to have any traceable debts to the qualities of others; he seems to have sprung self-generated out of nature .... Ergo, Freud had to create a whole new family—the psychoanalytic movement—that would be his distinctive immortality-vehicle. When he died the genius of the movement would assure his eternal remembrance and hence an eternal identity in the minds of men and in the effects of his work on earth."[115]

A number of facts might be adduced to counter these abstractions and aphorisms. The sections of *The Interpretation of Dreams* or *New Introductory Lectures on Psycho-analysis* where Freud reviews the latest research, for example, contradict Becker's assertion that the genius "doesn't seem to have any traceable debts to the qualities of others." On a more fundamental level, the simple fact that his youngest daughter, Anna, was for decades the focal point of the psycho-analytical movement up to her death in 1982 runs counter to Freud's fantasy that he was fatherless and that he had to recruit his sons from among his flock of disciples. It is surely not the intention of the authors who indulge in these speculations to deny Anna Freud's eminence because she was not a son but a daughter? But it is a fantasy, not facts, we are talking about, and even though it is not really possible to deduce the daydreams of a great man with the degree of certainty Roazen and Becker show, the immense concern Freud felt for the psychoanalytical movement and a certain distance and resignation toward his own children suggest that he invested the movement as such with the libido of a father and used it in an attempt to transcend his limitations as a mortal. The squabbles, which were inevitable in his collaboration with his disciples, were not "naturally" the tragedy of his public life, as Paul Roazen assumes, but reflect tragedy on a personal level.

This tragedy takes us straight to the heart of the conflict between Freud's conscious mind and his subconscious. He wanted immortality (and who does not?), and he wanted to achieve it by overcoming or at least domesticating the unconscious. At the same time, he was fascinated by the unconscious, which attracted him as strongly as it repelled him. Of course, the unconscious loomed ever larger in his writings, namely in the form of the death principle. In this sense, the death principle is nothing other than the ultimate escalation of the "id," which Freud wanted to overcome by setting the conscious mind against it, as far as he was able. For him, death became the sphinx, whose riddle had been so easy for Oedipus to solve. The solution to that riddle was man, but the riddle did not only end with man; it started all over again. It was particularly in the relationship of man to the death principle that the sphinx continued to hold the scientist and thinker in its claws. Only the solution to this second riddle, the riddle of man as such, promised immortality.

But now Freud found that his unconscious played more than one trick on him. What other explanation could there be for the break with Jung, who eventually stepped down from the throne Freud had prepared for the younger man, than that his unconscious had outsmarted his conscious mind? And his conscious mind was one that was highly developed: the self-awareness of a doctor whose training was firmly grounded in the nineteenth century's empirical attitude to reality so that he was profoundly suspicious of Jung's occult and parapsychological leanings;[116] the self-awareness of the ironic Jew who was not easily fooled, who had no equal in the art of interpretation and who presumably did not take the younger man at his—admittedly sometimes fantastical—word, as the latter had a right to expect; the self-awareness, finally, of a spoiled and cultivated Viennese who complained that he could not get his beloved wild strawberries in America,[117] who liked to go to the theater to see the agonies and episodes his patients suffered from acted out, and who was bound to feel superior to the less sophisticated Jung in matters of civilization, comfort, and luxury. (The air in Burghölzli Mental Hospital in Zurich was not only richer in ozone, it was also free of the intellectual germs that were a significant component of the atmosphere in Vienna and from which a unique late culture developed after the turn of the century.)

The failure of Freud's affection for Jung, which was as complex as his own temperament and as fathomless as the complex which, in his interpretation, obtains between fathers and sons, had the inevitability of a natural catastrophe. If, however, a true tragic character emerges from the tragedy a greater figure, we can say that Freud came out of the drama of his encounter with Jung, if not unscathed, then with his stature enhanced, his nature enriched.

A clear irruption of the unconscious into a person's everyday existence is a fainting fit. Two cases are known where Freud fainted in Jung's presence. Of the first Jung says, "It was provoked—indirectly[!]—by my interest in 'peat-bog corpses.' I knew that in certain districts of northern Germany these so-called bog corpses were to be found. They are the bodies of prehistoric men who either drowned in the marshes or were buried there .... Having read about these peat-bog corpses, I recalled them when we were in Bremen, but, being a bit muddled, confused them with the mummies in the lead cellars of the city. This interest of mine got on F's nerves. 'Why are you so concerned with these corpses?' he asked me several times. He was inordinately vexed by the whole thing and during one conversation, while we were having dinner together, he suddenly fainted."[118]

This was in August 1909 when Freud and Jung were in Bremen, preparing to embark for America, where they had both been invited to speak at the celebrations for the twentieth anniversary of the founding of Clark University in Worcester, Massachusetts. The first question Jung's report prompts is: why did the peat-bog corpses occur to him in the first place? And the second: why did he insist on continuing to talk about them when he must have noticed that it "provoked"[119] Freud, who was the one paying for that particular meal?

The common explanation for this fainting fit is that it was brought on by jealousy. Freud's pride, it is maintained, had been wounded because Jung had been invited to America on the same terms as he had.[120] Also, he had been invited because of his own publications and not as a disciple of Freud. Jung's recollection that, "Afterwards he said to me that he was convinced that all this chatter about corpses meant I had death-wishes towards him,"[121] fits in with that. The version given by Ernest Jones, who, together with Alexander Ferenczi, was at the meal in the Essighaus in Bremen, is more innocuous: "after some argument he [Freud] and Ferenczi persuaded Jung to give up his principle of abstinence and to join them in drinking wine. Just after that, however, Freud fell down in a faint."[122] That Jung, who, though certainly not drunk, had, like many non-drinkers, become more talkative and more aggressive after having taken wine, should insist on talking about the excavation of the peat-bog corpses, is comprehensible; Freud's fainting fit remains unexplained.

The second faint happened in November 1912 in Munich. Jung had returned from America at the beginning of the month, and in his name Franz Riklin had called the presidents of the various European branches for a meeting on the 24th. The topic under discussion was Freud's dissatisfaction with Wilhelm Stekel as editor of the *Zentralblatt für Psychoanalyse.* Jones says, "The matter was quickly and amicably settled, but as we were finishing luncheon (in the Park Hotel) he [Freud] began reproaching the two Swiss, Jung and Riklin, for writing articles expounding psycho-analysis in Swiss periodicals without mentioning his name. Jung replied that it was unnecessary to do so, it being so well known, but Freud had sensed already the first signs of the dissension that was to follow a year later. He persisted, and I remember thinking he was taking the matter rather too personally. Suddenly, to our consternation, he fell on the floor in a dead faint. The sturdy Jung carried him to a couch in the lounge, where he soon revived. His first words as he was coming to were strange: 'How sweet it must be to die'— another indication that the idea of dying must have had some esoteric meaning for him."[123]

Three years separate his two fainting fits, but they have three things in common: that they happened during a meal (although presumably this time Jung had abstained from wine), that Jung was the cause (although on this occasion it was Freud who seems to have been the more obstinate), and that in both cases there is a wide divergence between Jones's and Jung's accounts. Jung's memory of the second faint is as follows: "Someone had turned the conversation to Amenophis IV. The point was made that as a result of his negative attitude towards his father he had destroyed his father's cartouches on the steles, and that at the back of his great creation of a monotheistic religion there lurked a father complex. This sort of thing irritated me, and I attempted to argue that Amenophis had been a creative and profoundly religious person whose acts could not be explained by personal resistances towards his father. On the contrary, I said, he had held the memory of his father in honor, and his zeal for destruction had been directed only against the name of the god Amon, which he had everywhere annihilated; it was also chiseled out of the cartouches of his father Amon-hotep. Moreover, other pharaohs had replaced the names of their actual or divine forefathers on monuments and statues by their own, feeling that they had a right to do so since they were incarnations of the same god. Yet they, I pointed out, had inaugurated neither a new style nor a new religion. At that moment Freud slid off his chair in a faint."[124]

On the surface, Jones's account is incompatible with Jung's memory of the incident. Either Freud collapsed after he had given the two Swiss a good telling-off, or Freud's faint came after they had been discussing the rather abstruse subject of the behavior of a long-forgotten historical figure. In both accounts, though, it is basically the same topic that was being discussed, with the important difference that the loyal Jones, much to his own dismay, has to accord Freud the active role, while Jung seizes the opportunity to deliver what amounts to an *apologia pro vita sua*, with particular reference to his father problem. Jones does not say who brought up the subject of Amenophis IV, but the passive "The point was made"—the point that by founding a monotheistic religion the pharaoh was basically working off his father complex—doubtless veils the active intervention of Jung's superego, Freud, and not only because it expresses ideas the latter published in *Moses and Monotheism* twenty-five years later. "This sort of thing irritated me," Jung adds, and what follows is an attempted justification which was intended both as a defense of the pharaoh and as a counter to the accusation that he had knowingly and intentionally omitted mention of Freud's name in his publications. Looked at in this light, Jung's memory can be seen as complementing Jones's account. Amenophis, Jung went on, had been a profoundly religious person, but that had not stopped him from erasing the name of the god Amon even where it was merely part of his father's name, Amonhotep, on the cartouches. Translated into the language of the Freud/Jung relationship, Jung is saying: it was for the sake of the psychoanalytical movement as a whole that I suppressed the name of Freud in my publications. Supplementing this "translation" is a letter Jung wrote to Freud from America in 1912 in which he informs the older man "that his [Jung's] modifications of psycho-analysis had overcome the resistances of many people who had hitherto refused to have anything to do with it."[125] But, Jung continues in his *Memories*, Amenophis had held the memory of his father in honor, and anyway, replacing one's ancestors' names with one's own was customary in ancient Egypt, even when it was not a monotheistic society. *Così fan tutte*.

Later on, Jones corrected himself. There had indeed been "a little discussion about Abraham's recent paper on the Egyptian Amenhotep"—which makes it likely that it was Abraham who brought the conversation round to his own work—"with some difference of opinion;"[126] only then, he said, had Freud started to criticize the two Swiss. That clears up the sequence of events at the Munich meeting: first the "amicable settlement" of Freud's concerns about Stekel and his editing of the *Zentralblatt* (all the more amicable, given that Stekel was absent), then the discussion about Amenhotep, finally Freud's complaint about the two Swiss not mentioning his name. The meeting, then, had a general theme of the sons breaking away from the father of the movement. Jung does not recall Freud's criticism, even though his faint came after it. Who can say why? Perhaps he felt Freud's remarks were too trivial to be worth mentioning, or he simply wanted to give greater weight to his own comments on Amenhotep? Perhaps he had repressed them.

The meeting in Munich took place at the time when Freud was preparing *Totem and Taboo*. The chapter *The Return of Infantile Totemism* had appeared in the second volume of *Imago*; there it says, "One day the brothers who had been driven out came together, killed and devoured their father and so made an end of the patriarchal horde. United, they had the courage to do and succeeded in doing what would have been impossible for them individually."[127] Freud saw the totem meal as his own original contribution to Darwin's hypothesis of the primeval horde. This makes it entirely possible that during the meal with his disciples in the Palasthotel in Munich he was struck by the analogy between his situation and that of the primal father at the totem meal. After all, it was not just that Freud, as Jones observed, already sensed "the first signs of the differences of opinion" that were to precede the break with Jung the following year; rather, Freud was already aware of the break. Ten days before the Munich meeting, he wrote to Jung, "I greet you on your return from America, no longer as affectionately as on the last occasion in Nuremburg—you have successfully broken me of that habit—but still with considerable sympathy, interest, and satisfaction at your personal success. Many thanks for your news of the state of affairs in America. But we know that the battle will not be decided over there. You have reduced a good deal of resistance with your modifications, but I shouldn't advise you to enter this in the credit column because, as you know, the farther you remove yourself from what is new in $\Psi\alpha$ the more certain you will be of applause and the less resistance you will meet."[128] Freud's use of the term "modifications" suggests that this is his answer to Jung's letter from America.[129] Moreover, this is the first letter which no longer has the usual salutation of "Dear friend" but a reserved "Dear Dr. Jung."[130]

From this point onward Freud's letters to Jung are reticent, concerned to keep their dealings on an impersonal level, whereas after the fainting fit Jung's take on a superior, occasionally even "mocking"[131] tone. He himself gives the psychological reason in his memory of Freud's faint: "Everyone clustered helplessly around him. I picked him up, carried him into the next room, and laid him on a sofa.

As I was carrying him, he half came to, and I shall never forget the look he cast at me. In his weakness, he looked at me as if I were his father."[132] The symbolic fact that it was he who laid Freud on the couch did not escape him.[133] He had seen his father in his physical weakness and could not forget it; their roles were reversed; he was now the doctor, Freud the patient, bound to him by transference, and it was up to him whether he allowed or denied him the counter-transference. The first letter he wrote to Freud after the latter's return to Vienna sounds as if it is written to a sick man ("I have been very worried about how you got back to Vienna."[134]). He assures him of his continuing loyalty ("Now you can rest assured that I shall not give up our personal relationship."[135]), but the opening has the tone of a declaration of independence: "I am glad we were able to meet in Munich, as this was the first time I have really understood you. I realized how different I am from you. This realization will be enough to effect a radical change in my whole attitude."[136] Emma Jung had written to Freud on November 6, 1911, when the first clear signs of the crisis had begun to appear, "And do not think of Carl with a father's feeling: 'He will grow, but I must dwindle,' but rather as one human being thinks of another, who like you has his own law to fulfill."[137] That Freud could not accept this advice from a loving heart shows the tragic depths to which his unconscious had been stirred by Jung's defection, his "modifications." That now made it easy for the latter to diagnose Freud's fainting fits as "the fantasy of father-murder."[138]

One thing he did not record, however, was Freud's sigh, "How sweet it must be to die." That Freud was at times *weary* unto death he had admitted to the Jungs in their Zurich house the previous year.[139] That it would be *sweet* to die, however, presumably presupposes—given the stoic character of Freud, whose actual death twenty-seven years later was anything but sweet—a cause for which one is sacrificing oneself. It is not impossible that here Freud's unconscious is quoting in the manner of famous last words,[140] quoting the well-known line from Horace, "Dulce et decorum est pro patria mori."[141] Now it was certainly not the Habsburg monarchy Freud had in mind, even though Jones records him as saying, in the days following the outbreak of the first World War, "All my libido is given to Austria-Hungary."[142] It would be Vienna for which it was sweet to die or, to be more precise, the Viennese school of the psychoanalytical movement, which was his cause, identical, unmistakably one with him. Despite that, it was possible, even desirable to seek a neutral center for the school and to install the Swiss—Jung—as the president of the international movement. Freud's feelings toward Vienna and his Viennese school were ambivalent, especially in the way the school appeared to the outside world as represented by his Viennese disciples. When, however, this same Swiss, this same president, turned against Freud and against the city he represented, proposing his "modifications," Freud stood by his cause and his school, and his unconscious spoke for him when it sighed that it was sweet to die for them.

Both faints are linked to the image Freud had formed of America. One happened in Bremen, where Freud and Jung had gone to embark for the New World, and one happened when Jung, this time alone and independent, reported from America that his modifications had "overcome the resistances of many people." When he and Jung were in America, Freud's impressions had been, to put it mildly, mixed. Among Freud's anti-American prejudices, Jones mentions, "a lasting intestinal trouble brought on, so he very unconvincingly asserted, by American cooking, so different from what he was accustomed to."[143] Bladder problems, too, were blamed on America: "'They escort you along miles of corridors and ultimately you are taken to the very basement where a marble palace awaits you, only just in time.'"[144] Even his handwriting, he maintained, had deteriorated since his visit to America. More profound were his difficulties with the American language. Freud had always been touchy when it was a matter of understanding others and making himself understood. "I recollect an occasion," Jones said, "when one American asked another to repeat a remark he had not quite caught. Freud turned to Jung with the acid comment: 'These people cannot even understand each other!'"[145] All of this was later to lead to the colossal generalization, "America is a mistake; a gigantic mistake, it is true, but none the less a mistake."[146]

On the other hand, America had a part to play in the way Freud saw his movement developing: it was a kind of transatlantic Switzerland. Just as his correspondence with Eugen Bleuler and his collaboration with Jung served to break out of the isolation of Vienna and turn the psychoanalytical movement into a real movement, so the recognition he found on the other side of the Atlantic was confirmation that it had spread over the whole world. When the honorary doctorate was conferred on him at Clark University, he replied, visibly moved, "This is the first official recognition of our endeavors."[147] And in his *Autobiographical Study*, when the memory had had sixteen years to mature, he even went so far as to write, "my short visit to the New World encouraged my self-respect in every way. In

Europe I felt as though I were despised; but over there I found myself received by the foremost men as an equal. As I stepped on to the platform at Worcester to deliver my Five Lectures on Psycho-Analysis it seemed like the realization of some incredible daydream: psycho-analysis was no longer a product of delusion, it had become a valuable part of reality."[148]

Memory has the effect of rose-tinted spectacles. What Freud actually experienced when he stepped onto American soil for the first and only time was the culture shock familiar to all European immigrants, even to Americans visiting Europe or immigrants returning there. Brought on by the American way of life, which is at the same time both turbulent and regimented, it can quite often, as in Freud's case, result in psychosomatic disorders. Jones is surely right when he comments on Freud's 1909 visit, "He was a good European with a sense of dignity and a respect for learning which at that time were less prominent in America."[149]

In his 1914 *History of the Psychoanalytic Movement*, Freud put into words what he had in 1909 intuitively seen as a "gigantic mistake" in the American way of life and what in 1912 he had found deeply disturbing about Jung's "modifications" to his theories. He says, "with Jung, the appeal is made to the historic right of youth to throw off the fetters in which a tyrannical age with its hidebound views seeks to bind it."[150] America is indeed the land of youth, of sudden change, of the generation gap; according to its constitution, it is the nation where happiness is pursued and the life force comes first; it is the land where spring explodes with violence and autumn is afire with incredible colors. Winter, though, is a scarcely veiled embarrassment and even wisdom dons youthful garb to compete with the impetuous young. Reforms are good, complete change better; fashions vary from generation to generation, only to come full circle with the old in a new guise. The land of boundless opportunity is, at least in its official declarations, proud of its utopian optimism which, in an unfavorable political climate, can easily be reduced to indifference and fear of the very violence which is also a symptom of vitality. Freud, on the other hand, for all the upheaval he, as he was well aware, had caused, was conservative, ironic, skeptical. His individualism took offence at the only superficially broad-minded pluralism of the country. Anyway, his stay in the United States neither lasted long enough nor took him far enough to give him even the faintest idea of the complex intertwining of all the mixed and transitional forms, all the nuances of American life. The fact that it was from America of all places that Jung announced his modifications of his theories, that he emphasized its effectiveness there of all places, must have hit Freud particularly hard. Ambivalence was piled on ambivalence; one trauma tore open another.

Freud easily got over his Munich faint. On November 29, he wrote to Jung, "Many thanks for your friendly letter, which shows me that you have dispelled various misconceptions about my conduct.... Believe me, it was not easy for me to reduce my demands on you; but once I had succeeded in doing so, the swing in the other direction was not too severe, and for me our relationship will always retain an echo of our past intimacy. I believe we shall have to invest a fresh capital of benevolence for one another, for it is easy to see that there will be controversies between us in matters of scientific fact...."[151]

Conciliatory words, noble sentiments, but still they conceal unconscious barbs. The phrase "an echo of our past intimacy" was one that could not fail to irritate Jung. Apart from his initial declarations of belief in psychoanalysis, he had always taken great pains to keep his distance. A more deeply concealed and even sharper irritant is contained in the fact that in the brief first paragraph of his letter Freud twice uses commercial expressions, which do not normally suit his style: the "capital of benevolence" that they have to "invest" for each other, as if their relationship was that of a savings bank; and it comes close to being a "Freudian" slip when he says his "demands" have not been "moderated," but "reduced." That, especially in the German word "ermäßigt," is the language of the clearance sale. There is something strained about Freud's noble sentiments. Was he stressing what he called the new "scientifically matter-of-fact" tone that would determine their relationship from now on, and overdoing it? Was he, in this awkward situation, retreating behind the language of his father, who had been a wool merchant? Was he regressing? Or was he hinting at the other's anti-Jewish feeling by emphasizing the commercial element that even then Jung probably unconsciously objected to in his "Jewish science" of psychoanalysis. Or was he accusing Jung himself of acting with commercial acumen? Six days later, he wrote to him in reproachful tones, "You yourself have no doubt become familiar while in America with the principle that a man who is out for profit must take a good look at the persons and conditions on which his chances of profit depend."[152]

Jung and America—his unconscious was trying to kill two birds with one stone. As Freud was by then well aware, slips, like dreams, have a multitude of different motives and possible interpretations.

As far as possible, he tried to minimize the significance of what happened to him in Munich. His letter to Jung of November 29, 1912, goes on, "My attack in Munich was no more serious than the similar one at the Essighaus in Bremen" (with which he himself admits the link between the two fainting fits); "my condition improved in the evening and I had an excellent night's sleep. According to my private diagnosis, it was migraine (of the ophthalm. type), not without a psychic factor which unfortunately I haven't time to track down now." (This was pure prevarication; in fact, Freud devoted a considerable amount of time looking into the reasons for his faint.) "The dining room of the Park Hotel seems to hold a fatality for me. Six years ago I had a first attack of the same kind there, and four years ago a second. A bit of neurosis that I ought really to look into."[153] (Again, the conditional "ought to" says he would pursue the matter if only he had time to do so.)

He did have the time. Nine days later, on December 8, he wrote to Jones, "I cannot forget that 6 and 4 years ago I suffered from very similar though not so intense symptoms in the same room of the Parkhotel; ... I saw Munich first when I visited Fließ during his illness ... and this town seems to have acquired a strong connection with my relation to this man. There is some piece of unruly homosexual feeling at the root of the matter. When Jung in his last letter again hinted at my 'neurosis'[154] I could find no better expeditive than proposing that every analyst should attend to his own neurosis more than to the others'."[155]

Like Jung, Freud suspected he had a homosexual drive as part of his makeup. In a letter to Alexander Ferenczi of January 10, 1910, he mentioned that overcoming his "homosexuality" had "brought him greater self-dependence."[156] The first of the *Three Essays on the Theory of Sexuality* of 1905 had been devoted to what Freud, following the moral taste of the time, called "the sexual aberrations" and a footnote names Fließ as one of the first to "suggest bisexuality as an explanation of inversion." The footnote ends with the remark, "In lay circles the hypothesis of human bisexuality is regarded as being due to O. Weininger, the philosopher, who died at an early age and made the idea the basis of a somewhat unbalanced book (*Geschlecht und Charakter* [Sex and Character],1903). The particulars which I have enumerated above will be sufficient to show how little justification there is for the claim."[157]

Jones has pointed out that it was the argument about Weininger's claim to precedence that sealed the break between Freud and Fließ, hinting that the subject of bisexuality was clearly a sore point in relations between the two,[158] quite apart from the fact that in his irritation Freud did the dead Weininger a terrible injustice. (Under different circumstances, Freud would have had greater understanding for the case of Otto Weininger, perhaps even for his genius.)

For Freud, the subject of his homosexuality, both in theory and in his experience, was initially bound up with Fließ. At first, though, he assumed he had overcome the "aberration" with the ending of his relationship with his old friend.[159] The bit of "neurosis" which he confessed to Jung, and which corresponds (linguistically in the German) to the "piece of unruly homosexual feeling" he admitted to Jones, taught him otherwise. Jones recalls that Freud repeatedly mentioned the "feminine side of his nature," adding that not only his relationship with Fließ and Breuer but also that with Jung and Adler indicated a certain dependence and corresponding overestimation of the other person. Where his ambivalence got in the way, Jones concluded, the father of psychoanalysis was a poor judge of men. "Presumably these attitudes came from some impairment of self-confidence."[160]

How could it have been otherwise? He had such a wealth of creativity that his character naturally included a feminine component as well. That he was not only a scientist who could be strict with himself but also, as his style alone proves, a highly gifted artist, suggests that his character was mixed in a way that he refused to acknowledge but that differentiated him from less complex characters such as Breuer, Fließ, and Jung. What was feminine about him was his less inhibited relation with his unconscious, the aspect which made him liable to moods, whims, prejudice, irony and, paradoxically, to petty tyrannies and "patriarchism," and which also prompted him to admit to them, as he had done to Jung and his wife. That he then opposed his unconscious with all the force of his conscious mind shows how powerful the activity of the former seemed to him, how much he felt oppressed and endangered by it. And however much he was determined by the public sexual morality of his time and his city (almost as much as he undermined that morality with his discoveries), the fact remains that it was mainly men who bore the brunt of his ambivalent attitudes and that he believed he understood women better. It was women who had been his first patients; the first dream he interpreted was dreamt by an Irma. At times, and much against his will, Herr Professor Freud revealed characteristics of the Viennese family doctor of the old school, who had learned how to care for his patients from his nurses. In brief, he possessed to a marked degree that "dual nature" which the "more perfect angels" in Faust's ascent to heaven call indissoluble once it is united but whose elements are "not pure."[161] All in all, he was not only a contradictory person, but one gifted with the tensions between many opposites, including the male-female. He was not an abstract intellect but a character with all its creative interplay and inconsistencies. That is where his weaknesses and mistaken conclusions have their roots, his hubris and his tragedy.

And it is a very human trait that he, whose faints, as well as the causes behind and beneath them, gave him no peace, should end up transforming them into evidence of his power. Once more, the main testimony for this transformation comes from Jones, and since his biography is not only the most comprehensive but also what one might call the official life of Freud, we are justified in assuming that, with minor distortions, it more or less reflects Freud's own thinking.

As far as Freud's fainting fit in Bremen is concerned, in the second volume of his *Life* Jones revises the version on which both he and Jung had concurred, namely that Freud had collapsed after the argument over the peat-bog corpses. There Jones says Freud had won a "little victory" over Jung by persuading him to take alcohol, which was contrary to the spirit of abstinence ruling in the Burghölzli clinic. "He succeeded in changing Jung's previous attitude towards alcohol—incidentally with serious after-effects on the relations between Jung and Bleuler."[162] Even though the struggle between the two "fathers" for the soul of the "son" and Freud's triumph at Bleuler's defeat must have been considerable, this "victory" was by no means of sufficient proportions to obscure Freud's irritation at Jung's thoughts of death, which he took personally, and to produce a paradoxical faint.

The second "victory" was connected with the so-called "gesture of Kreuzlingen," which Jones himself calls "mysterious." Kreuzlingen, near Konstanz, was where the Swiss psychoanalyst Ludwig Binswanger lived. On May 23, 1912, Freud had sent word to both Binswanger and Jung that he would visit them the following day; he hoped Jung would find the time to come to Binswanger's house on Lake Constance. It was Whitsuntide and Jung, who was not in Zurich that weekend, got the letter too late. The Austrian postal service probably also played its part.[163] That did not stop him writing to Freud on June 8, "The fact that you felt no need to see me during your visit to Kreuzlingen must, I suppose be attributed to your displeasure at my development of the libido theory."[164] At the meeting of prominent colleagues in Munich, the two of them went for a two-hour walk before lunch and Freud, not unreasonably, asked Jung why he had not looked at the date franked on the letter in question, or asked his wife when it had arrived, before writing to him with reproaches. According to Jones, Jung was "extremely contrite," admitting "the difficult traits in his character." But Freud also "let off steam" and insisted on giving the younger man "a good fatherly lecture." Jung accepted the criticism entirely and promised to mend his ways.[165]

That does not sound at all like the language Jung was already adopting toward Freud. The "modifications" letter from America had long been written. Or was he bolder in his letters than when face to face with Freud? However that may be, his apology referred solely to the "gesture of Kreuzlingen" and not to disagreements regarding methodology. Freud must have understood it in that sense too when, after his fainting fit in Munich, he wrote to him that he was glad that he had "dispelled various misconceptions about [his] conduct."[166] About his conduct, not his theory.

Freud was visibly in good spirits when they sat down to eat in the Palasthotel. With his intimate knowledge of Freud's character, Ferenczi, whom Freud "loved like a son"[167] and who had also been present in the Essighaus, foresaw another faint. As we know, he was right; whether, however, his prediction was based on Freud's mood, as Jones assumes, is not known. And it was Ferenczi to whom Freud admitted, after he had analyzed his reaction to his faint, that all these fits derived from the impression the death of his younger brother had made on him when he himself was nineteen months old. Jones goes on, "It would therefore seem that Freud himself was a mild case of the type he described as 'Those Wrecked by Success,' in this case the success of defeating an opponent,—the earliest example of which was his successful deathwish against his little brother Julius. One thinks in this connection of the curious attack of obfuscation Freud suffered on the Acropolis in 1904, one which, when he was eighty-one years old, he analyzed and traced to his having gratified the forbidden wish to excel his father. In fact Freud himself mentioned the resemblance between the experience and the type of reaction we are considering."[168]

In the essay *Those Wrecked by Success* of 1905, that is three years after Munich, Freud had expressed his amazement at what he had found in his medical practice, namely that "one makes the discovery that people occasionally fall ill precisely when a deep-rooted and long-cherished wish has come to fulfillment. It seems then," he added, "as though they were not able to tolerate their happiness; for there can be no question that there is a causal connection between their success and their falling ill."[169] That a nineteen-month-old child could count the death of an eight-month-old child as such a "success" does not seem all that likely; that a person should later become conscious of it is, of course, within the bounds of possibility, but it does incorporate all the dangers of a simplistic interpretation.

Finally, the lapse of memory on the Acropolis, which Freud analyzed twenty-five years after his second faint, also had something to do with his infantile feelings of guilt, "with a child's criticism of his father, with the undervaluation which took the place of the overvaluation of earlier childhood. It seems as though the essence of success was to have got further than one's father...." The word "success" crops up here, but Freud now, with the wisdom of old age, sees the lapse as a whole as "*a feeling of filial piety.*"[170]

All this is a series of variations on a kind of relationship between father and son with which we are no longer familiar. As an attempt to "save" Freud, that is to present his faints as a "victory" over Jung, it is inadequate. Despite his protestations, Jung did harbor death wishes toward Freud, and despite Freud's consequent attempts to claim he had intercepted them and overcome them with ease, his faints remain faints, that is, his unconscious announcing the abdication, however brief, of his conscious mind. It is therefore not very convincing when Ernest Becker, who is all too aware that Jones "shaped" his biography to give a "heroic image"[171] of Freud, attempts for his part to see the faints as demonstrating Freud's strength. "It is reasonable," Becker argues, "to broaden the burden placed on Freud beyond that of a reaction to Jung alone. After all, he [Freud] supported on his shoulders one of the great iconoclastic movements of human thought, against all competition, all hostility, all denigration, all the other more 'spiritual' ('occult') meanings that mankind held so sacred, all the other minds who thought such sublime thoughts, insisted on such widely-held truths, enjoyed so much support and acclaim throughout the ages.... Would we dare to imagine that one can support this superordinacy easily, without superhuman powers on which to lean? How to take a stance toward all this impersonal and historical, as well as personal, concrete, and physical transcendence: the pyramids, the peat-bog corpses, one's own new religion? It is as if one's whole organism were to declare: 'I can't bear it, I haven't the strength to stand up to it.' Admittedly, the strong and large figure of Jung, an original thinker, standing independently and even arguing and opposing Freud, adds to all this; but Jung's concrete presence is only one aspect of a general power problem. In this sense, even to finally win out against Jung was for Freud to put the whole weight of the psychoanalytic movement squarely on his own shoulders. We can see how apt the 'wrecked-by-success' insight is, though not according to the specific dynamics that Freud had in mind."[172]

Sympathetic words, especially in what they say about Freud. The only question is, why does Becker try to reduce the part Jung played in Freud's faints, at the same time building up Jung into such a formidable figure as an adversary? It is also surprising that, for all the recognition he accords Freud's achievements, he adopts the theory that Freud had become conscious of his being wrecked by this success at the very moment when he took refuge in his unconscious. Becker then crowns this piece of muddled thinking with the claim that this retreat into the unconscious represented his victory over an opponent whose defeat, he assures us, had not been the decisive reason for celebrating that victory, thus celebrating a victory over an opponent who was by no means Freud's only opponent. The answer to these questions presumably lies in the fact that Becker closes his eyes to the power, as elemental as it is symbolic, of the meeting between son and father, to the Oedipus complex. Giving priority to an existentialist interpretation leads him to grant the terror of death, as the sole decisive power behind all repression, the right to create myths which he refuses to the *agon*, the tragedy dominating relationships between the generations. That is the reason for his partial elimination of Jung from the controversy with Freud; that is the reason for the game—as brilliant as it is confused—he plays with the victory Freud gained by being wrecked by his success, even if not "according to his own dynamics."

Freud did fail with Jung, and his faints prove that he was at first unconscious of the tragedy of that failure, later becoming conscious of it. More than Breuer and Flieẞ before him, more than Viktor Tausk[173] after him, Jung was involved in a dialogue with Freud in which protagonist and antagonist played themselves. But dialog, if the characters are capable of it and the time is ripe for it, belongs to the essence of tragedy just as much as the hero's flaw, *hamartia*. Hamartia is an expression derived from archery: a person aiming at the bullseye and missing commits hamartia. Freud committed it when he wooed Jung, circling round his target, aiming at it from all sides, seeing and yet not seeing, getting his timing wrong by appointing the younger man son and heir before he had proved himself and dispatching the arrow from the bowstring even though he must have noticed at least one thing, namely that the target was unstable and wobbling. Like Oedipus, he knew and was ignorant, he saw and was blind. Jung was correct when both faints threw up in him the association of parricide fantasies, however it was not Laius who harbored these fantasies but the Oedipus inside Freud that could never rest. It was his unconscious that sought immortality for himself and for his movement; but striving for immortality is a tragic enterprise and, like all tragedy, bound to a paradox. The distinction between father and son disappeared when he appointed his son "heir" and president of the movement; his conscious mind advised it on rational grounds; his unconscious also advised it, but for the opposite reasons. One can only become immortal by dying; Freud's faints were the foretaste of a death that promised such immortality. This gives the sigh, "How sweet it must be to die," an even clearer urgency. A prerequisite of tragedy, on the other hand, is the hamartia of its hero, and Freud committed such a tragic mistake when he fell in love as a father with Jung as his son. Freud's fainting fit in Munich is not a victory but catharsis; it is only as catharsis that it becomes a victory. As long as the recipient allowed it, that is, until Jung's withdrawal from the International Psychoanalytic Association in August 1914, the few letters Freud sent to Jung seek to continue the collaboration. But their tone is dry, the impatience well concealed, the communications matter-of-fact to the point of self-irony, the feeling gone.

When Jung laid Freud on the couch he had fundamentally misunderstood him. The thought really did arise within him that he had overcome his father. That alone can explain the tone of his subsequent letters, which is distorted by an "uncontrolled rage."[174] Only a man who wants to avenge himself for something the other has *not* done to him can write like that.

In his letter of December 3, 1912, he says, "I hope you will not be offended by my Helvetic bluntness. One thing I beg of you: take these statements as an *effort to be honest* and do not apply the depreciatory Viennese criterion of egoistic striving for power or heaven knows what other insinuations from the world of the father complex. That is just what I have been hearing on all sides these days, with the result that I am forced to the painful conclusion that the majority of $\Psi\alpha$ misuse $\Psi\alpha$ for the purpose of devaluing others and their progress by insinuations about complexes (as though that explained everything. A wretched theory!) A particularly preposterous bit of nonsense now going the rounds is that my libido theory is the product of anal eroticism. When I consider *who* cooked up this 'theory' I fear for the future of analysis."[175] The underlining of *who* and the quotation marks round the word *theory* point the finger at Freud as the "inventor" of anal eroticism.[176] And Jung goes on, "The pity of it is that the wretched Ψα are just as supinely dependent on Ψα as our opponents are on their belief in authority. Anything that might make them think is written off as a complex. This protective function of Ψα badly needs unmasking."[177]

At first it was the tone that created the dissonance—Helvetic bluntness rubbing up against egoistic Viennese striving for power. Now it was Jung who was bringing the geographical argument into play. Expressions such as the repeated "wretched" and "a preposterous bit of nonsense" cannot simply be explained away as Swiss earthiness, nor is the "Helvetic bluntness" rendered any less offensive by Jung admitting to it. Equally, a letter is rendered no less "brazen" by the fact that the writer describes it in his preamble as "brazen."[178]

The ostensible cause of Jung's loss of self-control was a remark of Freud's in his letter of November 29, 1912, which, though not as harmless as it sounds, simply cannot have provoked the downright hysterically shrill tones of Jung's reply. It concerned a criticism by Ferenczi of Jung's *Psychology of the Unconscious* (1912). Freud had written, "I am gradually coming to terms with this paper... and I now believe that in it you have brought us a great revelation, though not the one you intended. You seem to have solved the riddle of all mysticism, showing it to be based on the symbolic utilization of complexes that have outlived their function."[179]

Jung repeats this last sentence in his reply, underlining every word and adding, "My dear Professor, forgive me again, but this sentence shows me that you deprive yourself of the possibility of understanding my work by your underestimation of it. You speak of this insight as though it were some kind of pinnacle, whereas it is at the very bottom of the mountain. This insight has been self-evident to us for years."[180]

It was not. It was only in May 1911 that Jung had informed Freud that he regarded the term "libido" "merely as a designation of *general* tension."[181] In her letter of November 6 of that same year Emma Jung wrote to Freud, "If I talked about *Symbols* it was chiefly because I knew how eagerly Carl was waiting for your opinion; he had often said he was sure you would not approve of it...."[182]

Jung foresaw that the last chapter of the book in particular would cost him Freud's friendship: "For I planned to set down in it my own conception of incest, the decisive transformation of the concept of libido, and various other ideas in which I differed from Freud. To me incest signified a personal complication in only the rarest cases. Usually incest has a highly religious aspect."[183] The concept of the libido itself was another such symbol of higher ideas. In the early chapter that was to provide the title for Jung's book, he says, "the will to suppress or repress the natural instincts ... derives from a spiritual source; in other words the determining factor is the numinous primordial images.... Even the authority of the father is seldom powerful enough to keep the spirit of the sons in permanent subjection. This can only happen when the father appeals to or expresses an image which, in the eyes of humanity, is numinous."[184]

These, then, were the "modifications" Jung imposed on Freud's theories. One cannot imagine that Freud, who was convinced that "the common man cannot understand this Providence otherwise than in the figure of an enormously exalted father"[185] and who had written in *Civilization and its Discontents*, "The whole thing is so patently infantile, so foreign to reality, that to anyone with a friendly attitude to humanity it is painful to think that the great majority of mortals will never be able to rise above this view of life,"[186] was delighted at this elevation of the Oedipus complex into the realm of the numinous.

With regard to Jung's concept of the libido, Edward Glover gives a precise summary of the difficulties that had cropped up between Freud and Jung. "Although ready to concede that the Freudian libido played *some* part in the development of adult neuroses, he came to the conclusion that the Freudian libido theory did not explain the ego repressions and delusional products of dementia praecox (schizophrenia). One cannot but surmise from this that Jung had never really grasped Freud's concept of the libido and that he continued wittingly or unwittingly to equate it with the energy of adult sexual instincts. Only on this assumption can we account for Jung's blindness to the facts of infantile sexuality and his total neglect of the concept of narcissistic libido. A moment's consideration should have shown that the conflict present in dementia praecox necessitated an expansion rather than a contraction of the Freudian libido concept."[187]

Naturally, Glover follows Freud's views, as his book follows the abstractions of his theories. But it is precisely the technical nature of the book that clearly reveals, even after the forty years between the conflict of 1912 and the appearance of Glover's book, how devastated Freud was at the defection of his heir apparent.

The Viennese ax that was about to descend on the Swiss blunt instrument was finely honed and exceedingly polite. "Dear Dr. Jung,"

Freud wrote on December 5, 1912, "You mustn't fear that I take your 'new style' amiss. I hold that in relations between analysts as in analysis itself every form of frankness is permissible. I too have for some time been disturbed by the abuse of Ψα to which you refer, that is, in polemics, especially against new ideas. I do not know if there is any way of preventing this entirely; for the present I can only suggest a household remedy: let each of us pay more attention to his own than to his neighbor's neurosis."[188] And he closes his letter of December 9, 1912, with the words, "I follow you with interest through all the variations of the lyre that you play with such virtuosity."[189] This is not a helpless father speaking, one who has let himself be laid on the couch by his son, the new "father"; this is a man who has overcome his father-son complex, this is Laius who has escaped Oedipus by his own clarity of mind and power of judgment.

Freud's self-control was more than Jung could take. His reply of December 18, 1912, is down-to-earth, not to say coarse: "I would, however, point out that your technique of treating your pupils like patients is a *blunder*. In that way you produce either slavish sons or insolent puppies (Adler-Stekel and the whole insolent gang now throwing their weight about in Vienna).... You go around sniffing out all the symptomatic actions in your vicinity, thus reducing everyone to the level of sons and daughters who blushingly admit the existence of their faults. Meanwhile you remain on top as father, sitting pretty. For sheer obsequiousness nobody dares to pluck the prophet by the beard and inquire for once what you would say to a patient with a tendency to analyze the analyst instead of himself. You would certainly ask him: '*Who's* got the neurosis?' — You see, my dear professor, so long as you hand out this stuff I don't give a damn for the symptomatic actions; they sink to nothing in comparison with the formidable beam in my brother Freud's eye. I am not in the least neurotic—touch wood! I have submitted *lege artis et tout humblement* to analysis and am much the better for it. You know, of course, how far a patient gets with self-analysis: *not* out of his neurosis—just like you."[190]

The German of the letter is not without interest. The "*wurscht*" (= "I don't give a damn for"), especially in the Austrian spelling with "ch," is a blow aimed at "the whole insolent gang now throwing their weight about in Vienna." The "*unberufen*" (= touch wood) is short for "*unberufen toi, toi, toi*" (= Hebrew "*tow, tow, tow)* and thus floats on anti-Semitic undertones, like an oil slick on the clear waters of Lake Zurich. The full version of the saying of Jesus to which Jung alludes is "Thou hypocrite, first cast out the beam out of thine own eye; and then shalt thou see clearly to cast out the mote out of thy brother's eye."[191] The whole letter points towards the theme of hypocrisy, which, however, is never played in full, though its resonance is clearly audible underneath the verse from the Bible. Moreover, using that quotation makes it possible for Jung to address the other as "my brother Freud," which is less extreme than the "son" on the sofa of the Palasthotel in Munich; it also allows him to pluck the father/prophet by the beard and present himself as a prophet. The foreign phrases, "*lege artis*" and "*tout humblement*" clearly smack of one-upmanship. Furthermore, every neurotic child is familiar with the strategy of calling his brother neurotic and himself healthy or, to use Jung's phrase, cured by analysis "and ... much the better for it." The sideswipe at Freud's self-analysis is unfair for the simple reason that without it there would not have been any analysis at all—and therefore no analysis of Jung. Jung was beside himself when he wrote that letter, as he still was in 1934, when he published an article on psychotherapy in the *Zentralblatt für Psychotherapie,* in which he wrote, "In my opinion it has been a grave error in medical psychology up till now to apply Jewish categories—which are not even binding for all Jews—indiscriminately to Germanic and Slavic Christendom. Because of this the most precious secret of the Germanic peoples—their creative and intuitive depth of soul—has been explained as a morass of banal infantilism, while my own warning voice has for decades been suspected of anti-Semitism. This suspicion emanated from Freud. He did not understand the Germanic psyche any more than did his Germanic followers. Has the formidable phenomenon of National Socialism, on which the whole world gazes with astonished eyes, taught them better? Where was that unparalleled tension and energy while as yet no National Socialism existed? Deep in the Germanic psyche, in a pit that is nothing like a garbage-bin of unrealizable infantile wishes and unresolved family resentments."[192]

Jung was beside himself because inside him was the Oedipus complex, which he refused to accept, at least in the form in which Freud understood it. And yet Jung knew enough about the human mind and the interpretation of myth to admit to himself that there was something particular about the tragic contest between fathers and sons which he had experienced himself, and given permanent expression to, in that letter of December 18, 1912.

At the end of his life, Jung seems to have recognized the true meaning of Freud's faints. Even in his later years, he refused to budge an inch on his conception of the libido. And yet he found some generous things to say about Freud. In his *Memories* he says, "He remained the victim of the one aspect ['mere sexuality' or 'psychosexuality'] he could recognize, and for that reason I see him as a tragic figure; for he was a great man, and, what is more, a man in the grip of his daimon."[193] It is a worthy epitaph. In the end, Jung had become conscious of the tragic role that had fallen to him in the tragic conflict between Laius and Oedipus.

The Death Principle

The most astonishing thing the young Freud wrote is in his letter of July 3, 1899, to Wilhelm Fließ. His friend's pregnant wife and his mother were both ill. Freud wrote, "It is frightening when the mothers wobble; they are the only ones who stand between us and our demise."[194]

It was the year at the end of which *The Interpretation of Dreams* was to appear. The Oedipus complex had been formulated and with it the sentence, "Today, just as then, many men dream of having sexual relations with their mothers, and speak of the fact with indignation and astonishment."[195] In his letter to Fließ the figures of the mothers are not only radically demythologized, they are also given greater mythological depth since they are the only ones who stand between a person and death.

It is all the more surprising then that these mothers can "wobble;" the word is neither appropriate to an academic stripping away of the veil of mystery, nor does it, in its graphic physicality, do justice to the shudder men feel when seized by the fear of death. But it is precisely the graphic grotesqueness of the wobbling primal figures that arouses a sense of the uncanny in the reader. "An uncanny experience," says Freud in an essay from 1912, "occurs either when infantile complexes which have been repressed are once more revived by some impression, or when primitive beliefs which have been surmounted seem once more to be confirmed."[196] Here we come full circle: the uncanny nature of the mothers, who have started to wobble, points back to that infantile sexuality which Freud postulated when he articulated the idea of the Oedipus complex. Wobbling mothers are no longer able to love their sons; therefore, they arouse uncanny feelings. In his essay on the uncanny, he goes on, "Concerning the factors of silence, solitude and darkness, we can only say that they are actually elements in the production of the infantile anxiety from which the majority of human beings have never become quite free."[197] Silence, solitude, and darkness, however, are attributes of death. The wobbling mothers have the poetic force of a child's drawing. Born of the child's fear, they tremble and wobble with the grownup's fear of death.

So vivid is this fear that Freud cannot even bring himself to use the word "death." The euphemism corresponds to the infantile language of the wobbling mothers. What *Ablöse*, the German word Freud uses [translated above as "demise"] immediately suggests is the changing of the guard, which brings relief and a well-earned rest to the guard on sentry duty. But this image recedes when we recall how, from very early on, Freud was concerned to guard the only thing he thought worth guarding, namely the psychoanalytic movement: what difficulties that caused him and how much he therefore feared being relieved. It was his ambivalence that made him turn to the euphemism. Even if we take *Ablöse* in its root meaning of "abstraction," "detaching," thus probably coming closer to Freud's intention, it is but a short step to "dissolution," "dispersal." Schur, who brought the passage to our notice, mistakenly translates "Ablöse" as "redemption."[198] Nothing was further from Freud's mind than the religious concept of redemption. But even Goethe's definition of aging as a "step-by-step withdrawal from the world of appearances"[199] was not binding for him, despite his reverence for Germany's great classical writer. Until shortly before his end, he was still jealously making sure his mind and his personality did not withdraw. He only bowed to what was absolutely inevitable: it was only when his chow could not stand the smell of decomposition from his cancer lesion and started to avoid him that he accepted what could not be reversed.[200] He was so determined to be immortal that, even as early as the letter to Fließ, he took care to drape a veil over the word "death." In later academic articles he did use it, even though he feared death as much as he knowingly and deliberately hastened its approach. Underlying all this was the same ambivalence which characterized his attitude to the mothers and to the Oedipus complex.

The mothers do not sway, they do not waver, they do not threaten to lose their balance; they wobble. The aggressive undertone is unmistakable. For the writer of this early letter, the idea of the mothers with their balance disturbed is not only uncanny, it sounds as if he feels guilty of having given the first push that started the wobbling. It is the sons who desire their mothers' fall. They see their mothers, at least in their dreams, as giving themselves to them; it is they who sin against their mothers and they shift the blame onto them. Since, moreover, their mothers are the only ones who stand between them and death, the sons, when they see their mothers wobbling, desire their own demise. Death is an irrevocable denial of love. This early image of the "wobbling mothers" combines infantile sexuality and the death wish toward the woman who denies us her love. "The Mothers! Mothers! — It sounds so strange."[201] They don't even need to wobble.

Thus, it was mainly the thought of his own mother that kept Freud from suicide, whatever his personal situation. On May 29, 1918, he wrote to Karl Abraham, "My mother will be 83 this year and is now rather shaky. Sometimes I think I shall feel a little freer when she dies, because the idea of her having to be told of my death is something from which one shrinks back."[202] In the thought he is expressing here, mother fixation and the death wish are inextricably interwoven. Freud only enjoyed the freedom to which he was alluding for the last nine years of his life. Amalia Nathanson Freud died in 1930, at the age of 95.

Freud's "personal physician," Max Schur, assures us that the thought of suicide never entered Freud's mind.[203] That is highly unlikely. Albert Camus calls the process of thinking itself the basis of suicide: "To start to think is to start to be undermined."[204] The idea of suicide cannot have been foreign to a man who thought such undermining thoughts as Freud, who stirred up the black waters of the river of the underworld as he did, who was professionally exposed to the outpourings of the unconscious in the way the founder of psychoanalysis was. His intransigence toward suicides such as Otto Weininger and Viktor Tausk reveals the defense mechanisms he had set up and indicates how vulnerable he was himself.

See him sitting there, covered in blood, on a kitchen chair in a drafty vestibule of the Hajek Clinic after he had undergone his first operation for cancer. Afterwards, he was placed in a small room he shared with a cretinous dwarf, who was to prove his savior. When Freud had a hemorrhage, he tried to ring for help, but the bell did not work and the dwarf got up, dashed out of the room, and brought help.[205] It was a scene worthy of Goya's most somber gouaches. Freud would not have been human if he had not thought of suicide at moments like that.

Freud had been prepared for his cancer crisis. Both his experience of life and the development of his thought had brought him to the point where he was ready to confront the question of whether it was better to go on living or not.

In his own personal experience, it was the death of his grandson Heinele, his daughter Sophie's son, who herself had died in 1920. On June 11, 1923, he wrote to Katja and Lajos Levy, "We brought here from Hamburg Sophie's younger son, Heinele, now aged four and a half. My eldest daughter Mathilde and her husband have almost adopted him and have fallen in love with him to an extent that couldn't be foreseen. He was indeed an enchanting little fellow, and I myself was aware of never having loved a human being, certainly never a child, so much. Unfortunately he was very weak, never entirely free of a temperature, one of those children whose mental development grows at the expense of its physical strength.... This child fell ill again a fortnight ago, a temperature between 102 and 104, headaches, no clear local symptoms, for a long time no diagnosis, and finally the slow but sure realization that he has a miliary tuberculosis, in fact that the child is lost. He is now lying in a coma with paresis, occasionally wakes up, and then he is so completely his own self that it is hard to believe.... I find this loss very hard to bear. I don't think I have ever experienced such grief; perhaps my own sickness contributes to the shock. I work out of sheer necessity; fundamentally everything has lost its meaning for me."[206] Heinele died on June 19, 1923, six days after the letter.

Freud's letter has the ring of severe depression and it is only thanks to his extreme self-discipline that the word "suicide" did not slip out. With the death of Heinele, all his pleasure in life, of which he never had an inordinate amount anyway, was gone. Even in 1926, he was still writing—to Ludwig Binswanger, who had lost an eight-year-old son—that all his interest in his grandchildren and all his joy had vanished. "This is also the secret of my indifference—it was called courage—toward the danger to my own life."[207]

We can only guess at what it was that made Heinele so dear to his grandfather that his loss was more than he could bear. The fact that the oedipal threat is absent from a grandson is not sufficient explanation; Freud had other grandchildren. The possibility that dark feelings of guilt going back to his own childhood were involved cannot be discounted: his brother Julius died when he was eight months old and Freud nineteen months. It was in 1897 that Freud admitted to Fließ "that I greeted my one-year-younger brother ... with adverse wishes and genuine childhood jealousy; and that his death left the germ of self-reproaches in me."[208] Heinele's death seems not to have reawakened these feelings of guilt, at least not in Freud's conscious mind. Both as doctor and as grandfather, though, Freud must have been moved by the strange magic of decadence emanating from the child ("one of those children whose mental development grows at the expense of its physical strength.") And the Viennese *fin de siècle* had its effect. Although Freud's psyche rested on the more robust foundations of a mid-nineteenth-century Jew from the Bohemian countryside, he was still susceptible to the combination of charm and sickliness, especially when he encountered it in a helpless child. Five years later, on March 11, 1928, he could still write to Jones, whose little daughter had died, "He, too, was of superior intelligence and indescribable spiritual grace, and he repeatedly said he would die soon! How do these children come to know these things?"[209]

Max Schur was one of the first to remark on the "uncanny" way in which Freud's description of Heinele foreshadows the description of the elfin child Echo in Thomas Mann's *Doctor Faustus* of 1947. Echo dies of meningitis. That Mann was influenced by Freud is hardly likely, that the combination of factors was similar more so. From the very beginning, Thomas Mann was familiar with the fascination of "dying in beauty." In his *Die Entstehung des Doktor Faustus* [*The Genesis of Doctor Faustus*] he says, "I depicted the frail little boy in all his elfin charm. I took the tenderness of my own heart and transformed it into something no longer entirely rational, endowing the child with a loveliness which was somehow divine, so that people felt him as a visitor from some high and faraway realm, an epiphany."[210] And in the novel itself, he says, "And yet there was something here ... which put it out of one's power to believe in time and time's common work, or its power over this pure and precious being. Such was the impression it gave of its extraordinary completeness in itself; the conviction it inspired that this was a manifestation of 'the child' on earth; the feeling that it had 'come down to us' as, I say it again, an envoy and message-bearer; all this lulled reason into dreams beyond the claims of logic."[211]

The response of Thomas Mann's hero, the German composer Adrian Leverkühn, to the child's death, is to "take back" Beethoven's Ninth Symphony and go insane; he eliminates himself, helped, it is true, by an early syphilitic infection.

Freud did not need to revoke Schiller's *Ode to Joy*, with which the Ninth Symphony ends; he had long since broken it down into the pathological nuances from which it had been derived.[212] But it is quite possible that in Heinele he encountered a *pre*analytical phenomenon, a being beyond all oedipal fixations, that increased the tenderness of his heart "until it was no longer quite rational." We get the impression that in his encounter with this child, Freud suspended the law of infantile sexuality. Heinele must have appeared to him as the embodiment of a purity which, as he well knew, did not exist in reality. The death of the child restored reality and confirmed the correctness of Freud's theory.

Why then the depression? With reference to Echo, Thomas Mann had talked of an "epiphany." Epiphanies were foreign to Freud, the scientist and rabid agnostic, and yet he had been overwhelmed by a feeling he took good care *not* to analyze. Whatever we know of Freud's inner life, tenderness did not figure on the palette of his emotions. But for this child he harbored a feeling of unalloyed tenderness. He did not believe in paradise, and certainly not in the paradise of childhood, but Heinele taught him that it was a paradise lost, doubly lost, since death took him away.

After the death of Heinele's mother, Freud wrote to Ferenczi, "*La séance continue.*"[213] Even after the death of the boy, he continued to treat his patients, six patients a day in 1924 ("I work out of sheer necessity.") But something had gone. Three years later he wrote to Binswanger, "You are young enough to surmount your loss; as for me, I don't have to any more."[214] He had made his decision to remain alive, and it is this that led to his emotional devastation and his decision, not the earlier outbreak and (delayed) diagnosis of his fatal illness; his own illness was preparation, but it was only with Heinele's death that he was confronted with the certainty of death: "I don't think I have ever experienced such grief." The words, "fundamentally everything has lost its meaning for me," are to be taken literally; among other things, "everything" included the psychoanalytical movement.

Even though Freud successfully managed to repress the idea of suicide, he was still by no means free of destructive urges. The first operation on his jaw took place on April 20, 1923; on May 10, 1923, he wrote to Karl Abraham, "I can again chew, work, and smoke."[215] He knew, and his doctors constantly emphasized the fact, that his beloved cigars were probably what had caused his fatal illness and that after his operation they were, according to Schur, "a constant irritation of the area and provided the stimulus for the formation of new leukoplakias."[216] But after more than thirty operations for his cancer, he could still write to Marie Bonaparte, from England on June 1, 1938, "Your cigars are certainly harmless, even if not very tasty. So far I have not found anything similar here."[217] The well-meaning Princess had sent him some nicotine-free cigars but, although the last stages of his illness were approaching, he still did not find them acceptable. He soon found some that were to his taste in England.[218]

Every passionate lover of Dame Nicotine knows that she brings twofold pleasure: the sensual pleasure of taste and smell, and a heightening of the intellectual powers, a state of sober intoxication that sees through dreams and all other illusions. It is characteristic of Freud that the sole reason he would allow for his addiction was the heightening of his capacity for creative work.[219] What he said in his letter of December 22, 1897, to Wilhelm Fließ had been repressed: "The insight has dawned on me that masturbation is the one major habit, the 'primary addiction,' and it is only as a substitute and a replacement for it that the other addictions—to alcohol, morphine, tobacco, and the like—come into existence."[220] Sensuality, even that of masturbation, had to take a back seat before the work ethic of his labors in psychoanalysis. It was only when the disease began to spread, becoming more and more unbearable, that he felt guilty about it and tried to escape from his dependence. To Max Eitingon on May 1, 1930: "For six days now I have not smoked a single cigar, and it cannot be denied that I owe my well-being to this renunciation. *But it is sad.*"[221] And to Max Schur on September 9, 1930: "My condition is on the whole satisfactory; no cardiac symptoms. On the debit side: one cigar daily; since yesterday, two."[222] To Eitingon again, one of his main suppliers: "Your question about the cigars induces me to confess that I'm smoking again. Considering my age and the amount of discomfort which I have to bear day after day, abstinence and the prospect which it involves do not seem justified to me."[223]

The prospect linked to abstinence is nothing other than the chance of a cure or at least of a stabilization of his condition. Looked at from the other side, it cannot have been old age and its discomforts which excused his continued smoking, given the amount of willpower Freud displayed in putting up with his suffering. Cigars were certainly a palliative, but he himself admitted that smoking was an area where he could not establish the "dominance of the ego."[224] Where the ego (and quite obviously the superego) abdicates responsibility, the unconscious opens up. It seems reasonable to suppose that Freud's intense will to suffer corresponded to a similarly pronounced will to extinction. "*The aim of all life is death,*" he says in *Beyond the Pleasure Principle* and, "*inanimate things existed before living ones.*"[225]

Survival (*pace* Rilke) is not everything. There is a tragic quality in the fact that Freud did not allow his suffering—and above all his grief at the loss of Heinele—to tempt him to commit suicide, but lived on through the torment of another sixteen years and thirty-three operations, with ever increasing difficulty in speaking. But tragedy also requires the tragic flaw of the hero. It is this flaw that gives the play its tension, its irony. The accommodation Freud came to with the death wish, as embodied in nicotine, creates a dialectic the synthesis of which forms a physical representation of tragedy as personified in the figure of the aging Freud.

Freud was conscious of this tragic dialectic. As has often been pointed out,[226] the title of his book, *Beyond the Pleasure Principle,* has echoes of Nietzsche's *Beyond Good and Evil.* And it is in Nietzsche that we find the classic anticipation of the pleasure principle: "What is done out of love always takes place beyond good and evil."[227] Freud went beyond this in his assertion "that instinctual life as a whole serves to bring about death." And he goes on, "What we are left with is the fact that the organism wishes to die only in its own fashion. Thus these guardians of life, too, were originally the myrmidons of death. Hence arises the paradoxical situation that the living organism struggles most energetically against events (dangers, in fact) which might help it to attain its life's aim rapidly—by a kind of short-circuit. Such behavior is, however, precisely what characterizes purely instinctual as contrasted with intelligent efforts."[228]

"Short circuit" is one of the many plays on words that show Freud to be a genuinely literary writer. Just as when there is a short circuit, the light goes out and darkness falls, so it is dangers which "help" (the choice of that word is revealing) the organism attain the goal of life, i.e. death. The shortest of circuits and the most urgent of "events" is suicide. When Freud goes on to describe the organism's resistance to its end as "purely instinctual as contrasted with intelligent efforts," then the man who taught us about our instincts is bowing to the rule of the irrational. What he has to thank his "intelligence" for (though "thank" is probably not the word he would have used) is the decision to go on living. His organism wanted "to die only in its own fashion" and that excluded the short circuit of suicide. But he loosened the grip of his stoic will to live with the death instinct which placed the cigars between lips already bearing the mark of his end.

To quote Nietzsche's *Beyond Good and Evil* once more, "The sense of the tragic increases and decreases with sensuousness."[229] Nietzsche's aphorism is wittily ambiguous. And yet it can be seen to operate in the case of Freud. As his letters to his fiancée show, he was never afflicted with excessive sensuality and by 1911 his marriage had long since been "amortized"[230]; the outbreak of his illness and, above all, the death of Heinele, erased what sensuality was left in him; Freud's last two decades were—there is no other word for it—unsensual and therefore highly tragic. His face was gradually transformed into a tragic mask combining the goat song (the literal derivation of "tragedy"), wisdom, pride, and trance of the scapegoat.

Freud was quite justified in his fear that his disclosure of the death instinct, which came in his 1920 book *Beyond the Pleasure Principle*, would be understood as autobiographical. Although 1923 was the real year of catastrophes, his daughter Sophie had died in 1920. When Fritz Wittels attempted a biographical explanation of the death instinct in his book, *Sigmund Freud: His Personality, His Teaching, His School*,[231] and submitted the manuscript to Freud, he received the following correction: "Beyond question, if I had myself been analyzing another person in such circumstances I should have presumed the existence of a connexion between my daughter's death and the train of thought presented in my book *Beyond the Pleasure Principle*. But the inference that such a sequence exists would have been false. *Beyond* was written in 1919, when my daughter was still in excellent health. She died in 1920. In September 1919, I had sent the manuscript of this little book to be read by various friends in Berlin.... *What seems true is not always the truth*."[232] Freud even asked the Berlin-based psychiatrist, Max Eitingon, to confirm in writing that he had read the completed book before January, at a time, that is, when Sophie appeared to be in good health.[233]

Freud's concern was unfounded. It is an attempt to cover his tracks. As the letter of July 3, 1899, to Fließ[234] shows, death was always with him. The dreams that Freud reports on as his own in his *Interpretation of Dreams* of 1899 are full of death, war, and homicide. There is, for example, the so-called *non vixit* dream, which the interpreter himself describes as "a fine specimen." This dream moves toward the following climax: "Fl. spoke about his sister and said that in three-quarters of an hour she was dead, and added some such words as, 'that was the threshold.' As P. failed to understand him, Fl. turned to me and asked me how much I had told P. about his affairs. Whereupon, overcome by strange emotions, I tried to explain to Fl. that P. (could not understand anything at all, of course, because he) was not alive. But what I actually said—and I myself noticed the mistake— was, '*NON VIXIT*.' I then gave P. a piercing look. Under my gaze he turned pale; his form grew indistinct and his eyes a sickly blue—and finally he melted away. I was highly delighted at this and I now realized that Ernst Fleischl, too, had been no more than an apparition, a 'revenant,' and it seemed to me quite possible that people of that kind only existed as long as one liked and could be got rid of if someone else wished it."[235]

It is, to quote the title of one of Hofmannsthal's poems, a dream of great magic. Its subject is the ability of the dreamer to reduce the

figure he has dreamed up to nothing, to make it fade away, that is to
kill it. Appropriately, the key words *non vixit* are in a *dead* language.
Max Schur had given us the key to the names in this dream. "Fl." is of
course Wilhelm Fließ; his sister, who died young, was called Pauline,
as was Fließ's daughter; Ernst Fleischl von Marxow was a teacher at
Ernst Brücke's Physiological Institute, in the laboratory of which
Freud had begun his scientific career. Freud dreamed the dream in the
autumn of 1898; Fleischl died in 1891; a bust in his honor was
unveiled in the Arcade Quadrangle of the University of Vienna on
October 16, 1898. (In one of the young Freud's *day*dreams, a decisive
role was played by a similar bust in his own honor in the same
quadrangle;[236] it must be counted as part of the spill-over from this
dream into his daytime existence.) Finally, P. is Josef Paneth, Freud's
successor at Brücke's institute; Paneth had been impatient for Fleischl
to die so that he could take his position, but he had died a year before
Fleischl. Freud had borrowed money from both Fleischl and
Paneth.[237]

One strange aspect is that Freud spends a significant part of his
Interpretation of Dreams on his use of the expression "he did not live"
(*non vixit*) rather than "he is no longer alive" (*non vivit*), thus extending
the death sentence he passes, the "judgment" he "passed,"[238] to the
very denial of the existence of the man concerned. Clearly Freud could
not get the dream out of his mind; he returned to it, though his
interpretation is mainly concerned with tracking down the spillover
into his daytime existence and the emotions that it aroused. Part of
that, though, is an operation Fließ underwent, which brings in, at least
potentially, the motif of death. "After all, I reflected, was not having
children our only path to immortality?" In his interpretation, Freud is,
of course, speaking of his own children, in whom his immortality is
grounded: "I had insisted on their names being chosen, not according
to the fashion of the moment, but in memory of people I have been
fond of. Their names made the children into *revenants*."[239] In the dream
itself, on the other hand, Fließ talks of his sister, after whom his
daughter has been named, thus being also a "revenant." Immortality is
therefore the "threshold" the dream-Fließ had in mind when he talked
of his sister; what he was really talking about was death. "Revenants"
haunt the dream, the rather banal conclusion of which is "that the
revenants will only exist for just so long as one likes."[240] But ghosts,
whether one can exorcize them or not, are the spirits of the dead.

Thus, it is death into whose empty eyesockets we find ourselves
gazing at the end of this dream. Freud gives the interpretation himself:

"The central feature of the dream was a scene in which I annihilated P. with a look. His eyes changed to a strange and uncanny blue and he melted away. This scene was unmistakably copied from one I had actually experienced. At the time I had in mind I was a demonstrator at the Physiological Institute and had to start work early in the mornings. It came to Brücke's ears that I had arrived late a few times at the students' laboratory. One morning he turned up punctually at the hour of opening and awaited my arrival. His words were brief and to the point. But it was not they that mattered. What overwhelmed me were the terrible blue eyes with which he looked at me and by which I was reduced to nothing—just as P. was in my dream, where, to my relief, the roles were reversed. No one who can remember the great man's eyes, which retained their striking beauty even in his old age, and who has ever seen him in anger, will find it difficult to picture the young sinner's emotions."[241] These feelings must have been not unrelated to those through which Freud, in the dream itself, tried to inform Fließ that Paneth was dead or, if one accepts the preterite *non vixit*, had never lived.

Underlying these emotions is the Oedipus situation. Metaphorically speaking, the "young sinner" being "reduced to nothing" on that early morning in the Physiological Institute before the "terrible" gaze of his spiritual father, whom, according to the academic custom of the time, he called "Master," is a castration scene, the murder of the son by the father. The dream takes the metaphor literally and swaps the roles around. Now Freud is the master, if only because he is the one who has survived; the living survivor is always right. If the "*non vixit*" of the dream is saying that anyone who is in thrall to death has never existed at all, then the fact that the dreamer is dreaming proves the immense superiority of the living man over the dead. I dream, therefore I am. Now it is the survivor who "passes judgment" on the dead man and causes him to "melt away." (The German word for "to melt away"—"*auflösen*"—has an echo of the word "*Ablöse*" translated as "demise" in the letter to Fließ.) What is not clear from Freud's interpretation is why it is poor Paneth who falls victim to the dreamer's look. Even the language of the dream veils the fact: Paneth "melts away" more or less of his own free will. He was a year younger than Freud,[242] so from a chronological perspective he cannot have played the role of either father or son. Of course, the fact that Freud, who was extremely touchy in matters of money, was in debt to him, may have fitted him for the role of the older man. In connection with the *non vixit* dream, Freud further remarked, "how my warm friendships as well as my enmities with contemporaries went back to relations in childhood with a nephew who was a year my senior; how he was my superior, how I early learned to defend myself against him, how we were inseparable friends, and how, according to the testimony of our elders, we sometimes fought with each other and—made complaints to them about each other. All my friends have in a certain sense been reincarnations of this first figure ..., *revenants*."[243]

Freud's life was a search for time past, both in his own memories and in those of his patients. It is hardly surprising then that so haunted was he by these apparitions that his only means of keeping them at bay was by a drastic reinterpretation of the *revenants*. In his professional capacity, he illuminated the past, childhood, and he found there the love of his mother and the death of his father. In dreams he repeatedly saw his father dead, but no more made the link between the child's oedipal wish and the death wish than he did in the dream of the "breakfast ship," which he claimed to have subjected to "the most exhaustive analysis."[244] At the beginning of this dream, which resounds with the tumult of war and is imbued with the fear of death, the authority figure, the governor, falls down dead.[245] The dreamer feels guilty: "No doubt I had put unnecessary strain upon him with my questions."[246] But is it really simply the case, as Freud says in his interpretation, that he is the governor who suddenly dies: "The dream-thoughts dealt with the future of my family after my premature death"?[247] At another point in *The Interpretation of Dreams*, he himself talks of the fact that "dreams generally have *more than one meaning*."[248] Could it not be that the figure of his own father, whom he had already criticized as a child (dream of the trip to Rome), *also* contributed to the authority figure of the governor?[249] His assertion that "the dream-thoughts dealt with the future of my family" almost suggests that.

In the final analysis, is not the myth of Oedipus itself the myth of love and death, of Eros and Thanatos? It is indubitable that Freud, in his discovery of infantile sexuality, invested the dream of sexual intercourse with one's mother with the libido of his passion as a scientist. It is "the key" to Sophocles' tragedy, and when he goes on to say it is also "the complement to the dream of the dreamer's father being dead,"[250] then the censorship he exercises over his dreams and their interpretations inverts the relationship and makes the hatred of the father the "complement" to the desire for the mother. The reason for this presumably lies in his personal situation. In the preface to the second edition of his *Interpretation of Dreams* (1908), he says that the book turned out to be "a portion of [his] own self-analysis, [his] reaction to [his] father's death—that is to say, to the most important event, the most drastic loss, in a man's life."[251] In the letter from late in his life to Romain Rolland (*A Disturbance of Memory on the Acropolis*) he talks of "*filial piety*" as being what "interfered with our enjoyment of the journey. It must be that a sense of guilt was attached to the satisfaction in having gone such a long way: there was something about it that was wrong, that from earliest times had been forbidden. It was something to do with a child's criticism of his father, with the undervaluation which took the place of the overvaluation of earlier childhood."[252] Filial piety, a virtue that is both Jewish and bourgeois, must, despite his occasional criticism of his father, have obscured the motives of hatred for his father and the death wish. This Oedipus was not pleased to see Laius lying slain at the crossroads. It was the memory of his mother, who was only twenty-one years older than he himself, that prevailed, and thus the pleasure principle closed his eyes to the manifestations of aggression, hatred, and death, which he had repressed under the seal of filial piety. But images of death, including those of his dead father, abound in his dreams; the *interpretations* of those dreams, on the other hand, suppress or veil the fact of death, of parricide, which is inevitable according to the "eye-for-an-eye" principle underlying the Oedipus complex. Of the tragic elements of the Greek play, it is above all the pleasure principle of infantile sexuality that is emphasized in *The Interpretation of Dreams*.

It was only after he had transformed himself, not least through the success of *The Interpretation of Dreams*, into a father figure of international repute, and after he had realized from his disciples, above all from his "crown prince," Carl Gustav Jung, just how difficult being a father is, that death increasingly began to beleaguer him. "How sweet it must be to die," he sighed in Munich in 1912 when he awoke from one of his faints on the couch where Jung had laid him.[253] In *The Interpretation of Dreams*, he had coined the phrase, "Love and hunger ... meet at a woman's breast,"[254] a typically Oedipal statement which was provocative for its time. The more he developed, through statements such as this, beyond *The Interpretation of Dreams* into the father of psychoanalysis, the further he left Oedipus as a role model behind him, and the more he began to experience the fate of Laius for himself, the more unchallenged the position of Thanatos as an equal partner with Eros became for him. People grow older, and Freud started to grow old early. Now that he was himself a father—and being father of the psychoanalytic movement promised more certain immortality than any amount of real fatherhood—the urges, which his filial piety had kept veiled from his keen eye, now presented themselves to him more and more urgently as undeniable.

In 1912, he had sighed, "How sweet it must be to die." The following summer he went for a walk with a "taciturn friend" and a "young but already famous poet" and discussed "transience"[255] with them. The piece is perfection itself, relaxed prose imbued with the warm summer air of the Vienna Woods. The sentences have a classicistic cadence in the style of Goethe's old age, and yet Freud has no difficulty integrating expressions such as "scarcity value" and "libido" into them.

The poet has clearly still not overcome the somewhat self-pitying melancholy of the Vienna fin de siècle. He "admired the beauty of the scene around us but felt no joy in it. He was disturbed by the thought that all this beauty was fated to extinction, that it would vanish when winter came, like all human beauty and all the beauty and splendor that men have created or may create. All that he would otherwise have loved, seemed to him to be shorn of its worth by the transience which was its doom."[256]

Freud's initial response to the young poet's *Weltschmerz* echoes some verses by his favorite poet, Heinrich Heine (indeed, it is surprising they did not occur to him):

> A maiden stood by the ocean
> And sighed a doleful sigh,
> So deep was her emotion
> As the sun sank in the sky.
>
> Cheer up, young miss, I told her,
> It's just a routine affair;
> It disappears over yonder
> And reappears back there.[257]

Freud says, "what is painful may none the less be true. I could not see my way to dispute the transience of all things, nor could I insist upon an exception in favor of what is beautiful and perfect. But I did dispute the pessimistic poet's view that the transience of what is beautiful involves any loss of its worth."[258] There now follows an excursus on mourning, which is "a great riddle" to psychologists, "one of those phenomena which cannot themselves be explained but to which other obscurities can be traced back,"[259] a phenomenon which he tried to decipher later on in his writings on the work of mourning, above all in the essay on *Mourning and Melancholia* (1917). Finally, he talks about the war (the essay was written in 1915); he is thoroughly patriotic and—what a rarity!—optimistic (clearly it was the memory of the air in the Vienna Woods which engendered such a sense of security): "We cannot be surprised that our libido, thus bereft of so many of its objects, has clung with all the greater intensity to what is left to us, that our love of our country, our affection for those nearest us and our pride in what is common to us have suddenly grown stronger. But have those other possessions, which we have now lost, really ceased to have any worth for us because they have proved so perishable and so unresistant? To many of us this seems to be so, but once more wrongly, in my view."[260] This essay was written at the request of the Goethe-Bund in Berlin, that is, for Austria's ally, and, although arising from psychoanalytical concerns, is of a quasi-official nature. Its final sentence runs, "We shall build up again all that war has destroyed, and perhaps on firmer ground and more lastingly than before."[261] It rings false. Not false in the sense of Hugo von Hofmannsthal's confident expectation of victory and his Prince-Eugene-of-Savoy syndrome; it rings false because we distrust words such as "build up," "firm ground" and "lasting" when they are used by a man who had made it his business to stir up the underworld.

Throughout his life, Freud was a masterly archeologist of the mind, stripping away the layers covering the dreams and illusions, which he recognized as the shaky ground of the neuroses his times had hatched. Freud as the custodian and assessor of the cultural heritage of humanity? Had he not long since seen them as the sublimation of the dark forces, of the unconscious? What makes this part of the essay a cliché, almost a journalistic platitude, is its complete lack of a sense of tragedy.

This lack was to be remedied through a lecture with the title *Thoughts for the Times on War and Death* which Freud gave to the Jewish B'nai Brith lodge, and which appeared in the same year as *On Transience*, 1915, but in the psychoanalytical publishing house of *Imago*. Once more, the title has echoes of Nietzsche. Whereas in his *Unzeitgemäße Betrachtungen* [Untimely Mediations], especially the piece on Richard Wagner, Nietzsche turns his back, though not without a touch of irony, on anything topical, Freud faces up to his subject—war and death—in all its immediacy. Nietzsche in 1873 had spoken of death, but it was the *Liebestod* of Tristan and Isolde, which he called the true *opus metaphysicum,* "of all art, a work upon which there lies the broken glance of a dying man."[262] Freud, too, spoke of the theater when, twenty-two years later, in the second year of the war, he said:

"It is an inevitable result of all this that we should seek in the world of fiction, in literature and in the theatre compensation for what has been lost in life. There we still find people who know how to die ... There alone too the condition can be fulfilled which makes it possible for us to reconcile ourselves with death: namely, that behind all the vicissitudes of life we should still be able to preserve a life intact .... We die with the hero with whom we have identified ourselves; yet we survive him, and are ready to die again just as safely with another hero." But, Freud goes on, "it is evident that war is bound to sweep away this conventional treatment of death. Death will no longer be denied; we are forced to believe in it. People really die; and no longer one by one, but many, often tens of thousands, in a single day. And," he adds, his anger scarcely contained, "death is no longer a chance event."[263]

From being an aesthetic phenomenon that can be experienced and repeated at will, filling a stage with all its décor and, in the case of Richard Wagner, the music washing over, death has become a reality from which it would be absurd, would be madness to avert our gaze. That is the tragic aspect of the times in 1915 which is bound to make even a tragedy such as Tristan's *Liebestod* "conventional." But is this new tragic aspect, unheard of for a man of the nineteenth century such as Nietzsche, still a tragedy? Tragedies are bound to individual destinies, however representative they are. But Freud is no longer talking of destiny but of chance, and denying its existence. "Death is no longer a chance event," he says, adding the comment, "To be sure, it still seems a matter of chance whether a bullet hits this man or that; but a second bullet may well hit the survivor; and the accumulation of deaths puts an end to the impression of chance. Life has, indeed, become interesting again; it has recovered its full content."[264] That last sentence has an echo of Charles Darwin and his "survival of the fittest," but it was something which, in view of the organized mass slaughter which the First World War developed with machine guns and all kinds of poison gas, could not last.

Freud was not yet ready to allow that war had taken on a mass character; for him, it remained a personal experience. The reason was that, despite the wounded and maimed to be seen in the streets of Vienna and whom Karl Kraus portrayed in their masses in *The Last Days of Mankind,* he was unwilling to deny death the individual character of a personal tragedy.

It was for the sake of its tragic aspect that Freud held on to the idea of death as a personal catastrophe, an idea he derived from anthropology when he referred to his book *Totem and Taboo*. Despite the masses of maimed and wounded filling the stations and streets of Vienna and which Karl Kraus used in *The Last Days of Mankind* as symptoms of what he saw as collective transience, Freud held on to the idea of death as a personal tragedy. "O Lord, grant each his own, a death indeed,"[265] Rilke had cried in 1903 in response to the modern phenomenon of death as a mass process. Freud insisted on each person having "his own death" and in precisely the same sense intended by Rilke, as the fulfillment of one's individual destiny.

It is no contradiction when in *Thoughts for the Times* he says, "His own death was certainly just as unimaginable and unreal for primeval man as it is for any one of us today."[266] It is only death as one's own property that comes into conflict with the imagination of the individual, whose "own" death remains his right. It is the adjective "own" that is ambiguous. Death can be our own property and yet beyond imagining. Even primeval man, to whom death was unimaginable, is seen as an individual. He had, said Freud, "a very remarkable attitude towards death.... On the one hand, he took death seriously, recognized it as the termination of life...; on the other hand, he also denied death and reduced it to nothing."[267] But there was, he goes on, one case in which the two basic attitudes to death collided and came into conflict. This case "occurred when primeval man saw someone who belonged to him die—his wife, his child, his friend—whom he undoubtedly loved as we love ours, for love cannot be much more recent than the lust to kill."[268] Here we can see beginning to emerge, even if only in the larval stage, the polarity of Eros and aggression, the life instinct and the destructive instinct, a logical consequence of Freud's discovery of the death principle. And he goes on, "then, in his pain, he [i.e., primeval man] was forced to learn that one can die, too, oneself, and his whole being revolted against the admission; for each of these loved ones was, after all, a part of his own beloved self."[269] One is immediately struck by the concentration on the ego, that is, death as a traumatic thrust to the ego's sense of self, to its narcissism. "But, on the other hand," Freud adds, "deaths such as these pleased him as well, since in each of the loved persons there was also something of the stranger. The law of ambivalence of feeling, which to this day governs our emotional relations with those whom we love most certainly had a much wider validity in primeval times.... Of this conflict of feeling psychology was the first offspring."[270] The psychology of the individual, the encounter with one's own death, and tragedy. The examples of Oedipus and Hamlet, which Freud had used in *The Interpretation of Dreams*, are models of this kind of murderous and suicidal ambivalence. In his late correspondence with Albert Einstein, *Why War* (1932), he asks, "Why do you and I and so many other people rebel so violently against war? Why do we not accept it as another of the many painful calamities of life?"[271] And his answer is "that we react to war in this way because everyone has a right to his own life."[272] And, we can add, to his own death. While during the First World War he could still say of the mass killing that Karl Kraus, in an untranslatable pun, called the *Diebstahlbad*: "It compels us once more to be heroes who cannot believe in their own death,"[273] seventeen years later he recognizes "that in its present-day form war is no longer an opportunity for achieving the old ideals of heroism and that owing to the perfection of instruments of destruction a future war might involve the extermination of one or perhaps both of the antagonists."[274] In his *Group Psychology and the Analysis of the Ego* of 1921 he compared the modern army with the church. Of both it is said that they are "artificial groups—that is, a certain external force is employed to prevent them from disintegrating and to check alterations in their structure. As a rule a person is not consulted, or is given no choice, as to whether he wants to enter such a group; any attempt at leaving it is usually met with persecution or with severe punishment, or has quite definite conditions attached to it. It is quite outside our present interest to enquire why these associations need such special safeguards."[275] Only one *safeguard* is identified and that not a social but a personal one. Just as the believer is bound to the church through the figure of Christ, so the libido of the common soldier is fixed on the figure of his superior officer. "Every captain is, as it were, the Commander-in-Chief and the father of his company, and so is every non-commissioned officer of his section."[276] The compulsion of the masses, which, in 1914, soon replaced the euphoria of the masses and led to the terrorization of the masses by men and machines, is still not recognized. The description of the captain as "father of his company" makes the common soldier the Oedipus of his superior officer. If Oedipus the soldier feels slighted, he will lose the war. Freud says, "Prussian militarism, which was just as unpsychological as German science, may have had to suffer the consequences of this in the [first] World War. We know that the war neuroses which ravaged the German army have been recognized as being a protest of the individual against the part he was expected to play in the army.... If the importance of the libido's claims on this score had been better appreciated..., the splendid instrument would not have broken in the hands of the German leaders."[277]

And the Austrian war machine? In *The Last Night*, the epilog to *The Last Days of Mankind*, which Karl Kraus completed in 1917, a "dying soldier" cries:

> Captain, call a drumhead court.
> I won't die for any Kaiser.
> Captain, you're the Kaiser's man.
> When I'm dead, I won't salute.
>
> When I'm up there with my Lord,
> I'll look down on the Kaiser's throne,
> Look with scorn on his commands.
> Where's my village? There's my son.
>
> When I'm resting in the Lord,
> They'll all read my last letter home.
> A cry! A cry! A cry! A cry!
> My love, my love, how deep it is!
>
> Captain, you must be a fool
> To send me to this place of death.
> My heart has burnt up in the fire.
> I won't die for the Fatherland!
>
> You can't force me, you can't force me.
> See how death breaks all the bonds.
> Put Death before your drumhead court,
> I won't die for any Kaiser.[278]

The end of the first line of the first verse contains the term signifying the extreme of military compulsion: "drumhead court," while the first line of the fifth verse rebels against this compulsion, bringing in death, mass death. The captain is not at all the "father of his company;" rather, he is the "Kaiser's man." Even in the Imperial and Royal Austrian Army there was no question of a "libidinous structure." Karl Kraus' soldier, probably a Slav or Hungarian peasant, does know of and acknowledge an authority figure, namely God. Twice he calls this figure the "Lord," the second time in the euphemistic cliché "to rest in the Lord." The relationship between this peasant and his God is the primitive agrarian relationship between a serf and his lord, a relationship based on faith and fealty, not on material ties. When Freud says a "democratic strain runs through the Catholic Church for the very reason that before Christ everyone is equal, and that everyone has an equal share in his love," then this soldier's gracious Lord is neither a "kind elder brother" nor a "substitute father."[279] The common soldier rebels not only against his captain and his Kaiser but also against the Creator himself. The creature and envoy of God is death, whom the soldier in a magnificent line, the most magnificent in this poem, summons to the drumhead court martial. But that means that death too is socialized, allegorically. It is no longer the friend and comforter of the individual; it has become anonymous, faceless, not associated with a personal destiny. There is no personal name attached to it, it is the collective death of wartime that is being called to account here; it is not the Last Judgment but the very latest, the twilight of God, where man, inflamed by war, sits in judgment on no less a figure than his God. God also has the last word in Kraus's inverted mystery play, *The Last Days of Mankind*: "I did not want it."[280] Whether one interprets this final statement, taken from the declaration of war of Kaiser Wilhelm II, as a theodicy or as a declaration of war on God, it is to be seen as both metaphysical and critical of the social order, and definitely as non-tragic. That is not to say that Freud was a less convincing pacifist than Karl Kraus. In *Why War?* he talks of the "lowering of aesthetic standards," which contributed as much to his revulsion against the massacre as its "cruelties."[281] That is precisely the same as Kraus's attitude towards the mass destruction of human life, the horrendous nature of which he deduced from the corruption of the language, which, for a man so sensitive to language, was first of all an aesthetic category and only then a moral one. While, however, Kraus opposed the war for social reasons, creating a phonographic record of the social catastrophe which he only gave mystical trappings at the end, Freud saw the war as a natural catastrophe, a catastrophe coming from human nature. And while Karl Kraus, whose political and religious attitude was, to put it mildly, one of vacillation, regarded a reform of human society as unavoidable if war was to be abolished for good, the only palliative for Freud was his trust in the process of the "evolution of civilization:" "Of the psychological characteristics of civilization, two appear to be the most important: a strengthening of the intellect, which begins to govern instinctual life, and an internalization of the aggressive impulses, with all its consequent advantages and perils."[282] The social reform of the antiwar Karl Kraus corresponded to the sublimation of the pacifist Freud. Sublimation, however, relates to the structure of the individual's libido; it is the individual's sex drive which is sublimated, the Oedipus situation, the tragedy. The letter to Einstein makes it clear that advances in the "evolution of civilization" differentiate between the elite and the masses, between the "pacifists and the rest" in the degree of sublimation: "And how long shall we have to wait before the rest of mankind become pacifists too?" Freud asks and answers his own question, "There is no telling. But it may not be Utopian to hope that these two factors, the cultural attitude and the justified dread of the consequences of a future war, may result within a measurable time in putting an end to the waging of war."[283] The following year Adolf Hitler became chancellor of the German Reich.

Of course, the First World War had made a decisive contribution to Freud's study of civilization: death had removed the mask with which its interpreter had succeeded in veiling it in his dreams and had become a reality with which individuals had to come to terms if they were to cope with the pain and joy of life. "Would it not be better," he says at the end of the lecture on *Thoughts for the Times on War and Death*, "to give death the place in reality and in our thoughts which it is due, and to give a little more prominence to the unconscious attitude towards death which we have hitherto so carefully suppressed?"[284] That is not a rhetorical question; the answer was something Freud had experienced in his own life. He does go on, as if to soothe himself and his audience, "This hardly seems an advance to higher achievement, but rather in some respects a backward step—a regression; but," he assures himself and his audience, "it has the advantage of taking the truth more into account, and of making life more tolerable for us once again. To tolerate life remains, after all, the first duty of living beings. Illusion becomes valueless if it makes this harder for us."[285]

Thus, when in 1920 Freud formulated death both as principle and instinct, he had little reason to take steps to prevent people from assuming there was a biographical reason for the formulation in the death of his daughter Sophie. Death had run through the stuff of his dreams like ore through the rock, he had simply refused to take note of it in his interpretation. In his lecture on *Thoughts for the Times on War and Death*, death had detached itself from the unconscious, appearing for the first time in one of Freud's titles, becoming as clear and visible as the principle of infantile sexuality. But it was the discovery of the polarity whose effect on his disciples Freud feared. And justifiably, as it turned out. This is all the more surprising as the dialectic between Eros and Thanatos is an arch-Romantic theme that was given the full treatment in the so-called Neoromanticism of the Viennese fin de siècle, for example, in the lines spoken by Death in Hugo von Hofmannsthal's allegorical dream play, *Der Tor und der Tod* [The Fool and Death]:

> Arise, cast off mankind's instinctive dread
> No horror I, no bony skeleton.
> Before you stands a great god of the soul,
> To Dionysus and to Venus kin.[286]

Here the triad of death, sexuality (Venus) and psyche (soul) is clearly expressed. It is Death that expresses it.

And almost all of Freud's disciples did indeed reject the death instinct, Carl Gustav Jung as well as Alfred Adler and Otto Rank. There seemed to be something indecent about death; roused from its sleep once, the unconscious was unwilling to be roused a second time. The most cautious approach was that of the Swiss pastor, Oskar Pfister, when he wrote to Freud on February 4, 1930, "I regard the 'death instinct,' not as a real instinct, but only as a slackening of the 'life force,' and even the death of the individual cannot hold up the advance of the universal will, but only help it forward."[287] Freud replied by return post, and his answer is revealing: "The death instinct is not something I have set my heart on in advance, it just seems to me to be an inevitable assumption on both biological and psychological grounds. The rest follows from that. Thus to me my pessimism seems a conclusion, while the optimism of my opponents seems an *a priori* assumption. I might also say that I have concluded a marriage of reason with my gloomy theories, while others live with theirs in a love-match. I hope they will gain greater happiness from this than I."[288]

There is something prophetic about the gloominess of which Freud speaks here. It is apparent in the very title of "*Beyond* the Pleasure Principle," which points to the death instinct as an element transcending the sex drive. Of course, the death instinct was not something Freud "had set his heart on"—is it for anyone?—and he rarely admitted openly that as he grew older the more the balance between Eros and Thanatos dipped on the side of death. That would have been contrary to his principle of scientific neutrality, which consciously followed the laws of biology and psychology. But unconsciously there were deeper forces beyond all rationality at work when he declared death an instinctual drive and, in the name of biology and psychology, ventured beyond the demands of the nineteenth-century's belief in science. Freud was not a happy person, and what he called his pessimism was more deeply rooted in his nature than his theories, thoughts, and reflections. Should we call his nature tragic? If so, then the death instinct reached down into the realms from which he had brought the myth of Oedipus.

If this were the case, then there would be no point in the opposition to the death principle which Ernest Becker, following in the footsteps of Otto Rank, formulated succinctly when he wrote, "how could psychoanalytic therapy *scientifically cure* the terror of life and death? But it could cure the problems of sex, which *it itself* posited."[289] That is the wrong answer to the wrong question. Was not psychoanalysis, at least since *The Interpretation of Dreams*, more than an attempt to cure neuroses scientifically? After that point, did not Freud's knowledge of mankind go hand in hand with visions which came dangerously close to literature? Did not his theory of love and death go into deeper levels of his personality than Freud himself was either able to perceive or willing to acknowledge? What is certainly true is that after *Beyond the Pleasure Principle* Freud extended his scope more and more, with the result that insights which had the appearance, at least on the surface, of scientific medical findings were replaced by interpretations that related to the history of culture and religion. What is also certain is that there is a tragic note to the compulsion of compulsions, the compulsion to repeat, "which overrides the pleasure principle,"[290] the compulsion, that is, to expose oneself, with one's eyes open and against one's better judgment, to experiences from the past, mostly from childhood, which, however, "include no possibility of pleasure, and which can never, even long ago, have brought satisfaction even to instinctual impulses which have since been repressed."[291]

The compulsion to repeat an action, which Freud first noticed among obsessional neurotics,[292] he also observed in the lives and characters of so-called normal people. "The impression they have is of being pursued by a malignant fate or possessed by some 'daemonic' power; but psychoanalysis has always taken the view that their fate is for the most part made by themselves and determined by early infantile influences."[293] Then he appends a list which reads like a cross-section of the tragic repertoire of human existence: "the benefactor who is abandoned in anger after a time by each of his *protégés*, however much they may otherwise differ from one another, and who thus seems doomed to taste all the bitterness of ingratitude; or the man whose friendships all end in betrayal by his friend; or the man who time after time in the course of his life raises someone else into a position of great private or public authority and then, after a certain interval, himself upsets that authority and replaces him by a new one; or again the lover, each of whose love affairs with a woman passes through the same phases and reaches the same conclusion."[294]

Freud appears to be answering the classic question of whether it is fate or character that decides the course a man's life takes in favor of character, in favor of those "early infantile" influences on which the psychoanalytic system rests. That is only logical. But he also says that the fate of those who act under compulsion is made by themselves "for the most part." What is the remaining part? Is it not that remainder that gives the compulsion to repeat its impression of "demonic" power? See, for example, Thomas Mann's *Doctor Faustus*, where Adrian Leverkühn, a man who is in the grip of compulsions anyway, tries to rid himself of his syphilitic infection and tragically manages not to meet doctor after doctor. The last doctor even dies. Early infantile influences on Adrian? It is the tiny remainder, what is left when the early childhood influences are taken away from the compulsion to repeat, that counts.

In his speech celebrating Freud's eightieth birthday, Thomas Mann managed the rather unorthodox feat of quoting "the intelligent, if somewhat ungrateful scion" of psychoanalysis, Carl Gustav Jung, who says in his introduction to the *Tibetan Book of the Dead*,[295] "It is so much more immediate, striking, impressive and therefore more convincing to watch it *happening* to me, than to observe myself *doing* it."[296] Between "doing," that is the self-determination of the individual through the experiences of early childhood and "happening to," the influence of the outside world, there is definitely an extremely delicate interplay, the "demonic" character of which cannot be put down to adverse developments of the libido alone.

Freud knew that. "It is evident, " said Schur, "that for Freud the attribute 'demonic' was a necessary steppingstone toward the formulation of the death instinct theory and the repetition compulsion as superordinated principles of mental functioning."[297] That was why in the compulsion to repeat as well Freud noted a phenomenon "which overrides the pleasure principle."[298] But even the compulsion to repeat cannot be defined by childhood experiences alone. There remains a small amount of the clay from which we are molded, embarrassing to bear, a dark crack opening up between childhood and the outside world which "happens" to us. It is through this crack that death appears as a principle.

Two years before his death, Freud wrote his essay *Analysis Terminable and Interminable*, in which he says, "Only by the concurrent or mutually opposing action of the two primal instincts—Eros and the death-instinct—never by one or the other alone, can we explain the rich multiplicity of the phenomena of life,"[299] an apparently impartial statement allowing equal scope to the troublemaker, the clamorous Eros, and the "mute" Thanatos.[300] But the title of Freud's essay acknowledges the fact that as well as terminable, there are interminable analyses. But when the analysis is interminable, the neurosis is incurable. The admission that there are neuroses which are absolutely incurable—neuroses which are only resolved with the death of the neurotic—was made a great deal easier by the fact that Freud had become aware of death as a principle.

In *Beyond the Pleasure Principle* Freud still spoke of the death instinct as an "often far-fetched speculation, which the reader will consider or dismiss according to his individual predilection."[301] Toward the end of that book, he subjects the "speculation" to the following consideration: "It may be asked whether and how far I am myself convinced of the truth of the hypotheses that have been set out in these pages. My answer would be that I am not convinced myself and that I do not seek to persuade other people to believe in them. Or, more precisely, that I do not know how far I believe in them. There is no reason, as it seems to me, why the emotional factor of conviction should enter into this question at all. It is surely possible to throw oneself into a line of thought and to follow it wherever it leads out of simple scientific curiosity, or, if the reader prefers, as an *advocatus diaboli*, who has not on that account sold his soul to the devil."[302] That sounds almost apologetic, especially when one compares it with the assertive confidence, the persuasive power with which he had expounded the theory of infantile sexuality in *The Interpretation of Dreams*. The man who had stirred up chaos, the man who had uncovered the unconscious, drew back in horror when he held the mask of an *advocatus mortis* over his face.

In order to confirm and clarify Freud's attitude to the death principle, this "speculation" needed to be grounded in psychological and biological understanding. Three years later, Freud had done this. In *The Ego and the Id*, he wrote "we have to distinguish two classes of instincts, one of which, the sexual instincts, or Eros, is by far the more conspicuous and accessible to study. It comprises not only the uninhibited sexual instinct proper ... but also the self-preservative instinct, which must be assigned to the ego.... The second class of instincts was not so easy to point to; in the end we came to recognize sadism as its representative. On the basis of theoretical considerations, supported by biology, we put forward the hypothesis of a death instinct, the task of which is to lead organic life back into the inanimate state; on the other hand we supposed that Eros, by bringing about a more and more far-reaching combination of the particles into which the living substance is dispersed, aims at complicating life and at the same time, of course, at preserving it.... The emergence of life would thus be the cause of the continuance of life and also at the same time of the striving towards death; and life itself would be a conflict and a compromise between these two trends. The problem of the origin of life would remain a cosmological one; and the problem of the goal and purpose of life would be answered dualistically."[303]

Freud is still writing in the conditional, the mood of doubt, of hypothesis. But he has postulated, even if in the conditional, the dualism of the two drives, Eros and Thanatos, and he will stick to this dualism right through to the last of his great works to examine cultural attitudes, *Civilization and Its Discontents*. (More of that later.) But he also notes that life is a "conflict and compromise" between the two drives. The word "conflict" could be replaced by the Greek word, *agon*, the conflict between two protagonists, which is the defining mode of tragedy. Here Freud touches on the polarity which is an innate part of our very existence. As far as Freud's own existence is concerned, he was not a man to compromise. The *agon* was his field.

It was as the psychological grounding of the death instinct that Freud came upon sadism or, as he called it a little later on, the instinct of destruction. "For the opposition between the two classes of instincts we may put the polarity of love and hate. There is no difficulty in finding a representative of Eros; but we must be grateful that we can find a representative of the elusive death instinct in the instinct of destruction, to which hate points the way."[304] But that is to give death, which Freud calls "an abstract concept with a negative content,"[305] both form and content. At the same time, it opens the way for the modern science of aggression on the biological level. Konrad Lorenz, the founder of the science of ethology and champion of "what we call evil,"[306] talked about the "greatness of Sigmund Freud" and said, "At a time when it never occurred to anyone to entertain even the slightest doubt about the absolute correctness of Sherrington's theory of reflex action or Pavlov's of the conditioned reflex, Freud clearly recognized that behavioral drives are not *re*-active, that they do not wait, like machines that are idle or like reflexes, for an external stimulus to set them in motion but that, on the contrary, it takes an active expenditure of energy to hold their effects in check, even for a while."[307] What Lorenz clearly has in mind is the interplay between the survival instinct, which from this point onwards Freud subsumes under the sex drive, and aggression (sadism). Lorenz goes on, "Only now did I sense that Sigmund Freud would be a great helper and ally in the struggle against the monopoly enjoyed by the ideology of the reflex and the conditioned reaction in explaining behavior."[308]

But it is not only the survival instinct which Freud sees as working against the death drive. Delving deep into physiology, he said in *The Ego and the Id*, "The ejection of the sexual substances in the sexual act corresponds in a sense to the separation of soma and germ-plasm. This accounts for the likeness of the condition that follows complete sexual satisfaction to dying, and for the fact that death coincides with copulation in some of the lower animals. These creatures die in the act of reproduction because, after Eros has been eliminated through the process of satisfaction, the death instinct has a free hand for accomplishing its purposes."[309] One of these "lower animals," for example, is the praying mantis, which Günter Eich came to see as a model of the Mother Nature whose innocent atrocities he abhorred: "But suddenly she's back, her mouth smeared with blood, and shows me her latest model. Everything split in two, she says, a stylistic principle, male and female. Can't you think of anything better, I ask. Come off it, old boy, she says. Here's the praying mantis. While his rear mates with her she devours his front. Pooh, I say, Mum, you're unappetizing. But think of sunsets, she titters."[310]

And what of the male praying mantis, which allows itself to be consumed while still living and loving? Obviously, we must include masochism as well as sadism among the instincts of destruction. Freud makes this clear as well. In *The Economic Problem of Masochism* (1924), he explains, "If one is prepared to overlook a little inexactitude, it may be said that the death instinct which is operative in the organism—primal sadism—is identical with masochism. After the main portion of it has been transposed outwards on to objects, there remains inside, as a residuum of it, the erotogenic masochism proper.... This masochism would thus be evidence of, and a remainder from, the phase of development in which the coalescence, which is so important for life, between the death instinct and Eros took place."[311] Here the "dualism" of libido and Thanatos has become a "coalescence" and the death instinct a blend of sadism and masochism. Max Schur's emphasis on the severe physical pain Freud had to endure while he was writing his work on masochism, and which made him entertain the wish to die himself,[312] is not as sentimental as it sounds. It was a unified theory of psychoanalysis, such as had been necessary since his awareness of the death principle, that Freud had been seeking as an antidote to his own mortality, as a desperate attempt to conquer his own death with this theory.

Once again, Freud had recourse to physiological speculation to find a basis for his sadism-masochism duality: "In (multicellular) organisms the libido meets the instinct of death, or destruction, which is dominant in them.... The libido had the task of making the destroying instinct innocuous, and it fulfills the task by diverting that instinct to a great extent outwards ... towards objects in the external world. The instinct is then called the destructive instinct, the instinct for mastery, or the will to power. A portion of the instinct is placed directly in the service of the sexual function, where it has an important part to play.... Another portion does not share in this transposition outwards; it remains inside the organism and, with the help of the accompanying sexual excitation..., becomes libidinally bound there. It is in this portion that we have to recognize the original, erotogenic masochism."[313]

Freud concedes that it is completely impossible for physiology to provide a basis for this speculation. As far as psychoanalysis is concerned, he talks of a "fusion" and a "*de*fusion" of the two classes of instincts. "How large the portions of the death instincts are which refuse to be tamed in this way by being bound to admixtures of the libido we cannot at present guess."[314] In *Analysis Terminable and Interminable*, he is still saying, "even the way a psychical influence is exerted on simple masochism presents a great challenge to our abilities."[315]

The only thing that these reflections have in common with Freud's aim of curing neuroses scientifically is the general direction. They are, and Freud was aware of this, a large-scale prolegomenon to an anthropology based on depth psychology. The sadism–masochism and Eros-Thanatos dualities are, so to speak, the horizontal lines of a system of coordinates in which the ego–id–superego triad forms the verticals. There is no end to the *fusions and defusions*.

The varied interplay of the pleasure principle and the instinct of destruction is evident on the surface of Freud's outline of the structure of the personality. As he grew older, however, and his illness more advanced, a further dimension became clearer behind that system of coordinates, a pessimistic, even tragic morality, which he was loath to admit to. As early as *Totem and Taboo* (1912/13), he had conjectured that the totem meal was "perhaps mankind's earliest festival," the origin "of social organization, of moral restrictions and of religion."[316] He takes up this idea in his essay on masochism, explaining, "In this way the Oedipus complex proves to be ... the source of our individual ethical sense (morality)."[317] Why Freud felt it necessary to give two words for morality, one apparently as an explanation, remains an open question. The reader would have been perfectly capable of understanding it without the addition in brackets. Was this "translation" intended to heighten the shock effect he was expecting? To tone it down? Was he slightly shocked himself? We do not know. And Freud goes on, "The course of childhood development leads to an ever-increasing detachment from parents, and their personal significance for the super-ego recedes into the background. To the imagos they leave behind there are then linked the influences of teachers and authorities, self-chosen models and publicly recognized heroes, whose figures need no longer be introjected by an ego which has become more resistant. The last figure in the series that began with the parents is the dark power of Destiny which only the fewest of us are able to look upon as impersonal. There is little to be said against the Dutch writer Multatuli when he replaces the Μοῖρα – [Destiny] of the Greeks by the divine pair Λόγος καὶ Ἀνάγκη – [Reason and Necessity]; but all who transfer the guidance of the world to Providence, to God, or to God and Nature, arouse a suspicion that they still look upon these ultimate and remotest powers as a parental couple, in a mythological sense.... In *The Ego and the Id* I made an attempt to derive mankind's realistic fear of death, too, from the same parental view of fate. It seems very hard to free oneself from it."[318] The last sentence could also be read as: "It is very hard to be a grown-up." As far as God is concerned, to the end of his life this enlightened urban Jew continued to deflate the image of God, as if it were a car tire. In *Civilization and its Discontents* he calls divine providence the "figure of an enormously exalted father," adding, "The whole thing is so patently infantile, so foreign to reality, that to anyone with a friendly attitude to humanity it is painful to think that the great majority of mortals will never be able to rise above this view of life."[319]

The idea of parents as the child's destiny, on the other hand, is a mythic and therefore tragic construct. Can anyone have seen the father who lives on in the son's superego more clearly than Franz Kafka who, in "The Judgment" makes old Bendemann drive his son, with his self-reproaches and unconscious feelings of guilt, to suicide? "You were an innocent child, to tell the truth—though to tell the whole truth you were the devil incarnate!"[320]

In terms of depth psychology, old Bendemann's condemnation makes sense insofar as it gives powerful linguistic expression to the son's superego; it is moral in the sense of that morality which regards the breaking away from the father, who is to be honored, as a break with morality. It has the force of an existential statement: that is what mankind is like, innocent and devilish at the same time. This is one more attempt by Kafka, that "religious humorist,"[321] to breathe life into the image of God.

As far as Freud's view of morality is concerned, he comes to the surprising statement that, *"Kant's Categorical Imperative is thus the direct heir of the Oedipus complex."*[322]

The Enlightenment as the heir to myth! Tolerance as the product of the bloody working-out of fate! When Freud was awarded the Goethe Prize of the city of Frankfurt in 1930, it was his daughter Anna who went to receive the prize and said, in his name, "In what is perhaps his most poetical creation, *Iphigenie,* Goethe shows us a striking instance of expiation, of the freeing of a suffering mind from the burden of guilt, and he makes this catharsis come about through a passionate outburst of feeling under the beneficent influence of loving sympathy."[323] It is Orestes of whom Freud is speaking here and not Iphigenie, Orestes, the matricide and obsessional neurotic, who is pursued by the Furies. Goethe did as much as he could to excuse his murder of his mother and avoid tragedy.[324] But what if Orestes' neurosis is interminable, and the Furies, lying in wait outside the sanctuary of the temple of Diana, get their hands on their prey?

It is at places like this that the tragic undertone of a piece such as *Analysis Terminable and Interminable* becomes almost painfully evident. Freud is better when talking of the existentially incurable nature of mankind than when he is pronouncing on morality, the stability of which he could not really bring himself to believe in. Prometheus cuts a dubious figure as a harbinger of peace. This is presumably what Philip Rieff had in mind when he said, "His moralizing is of the sort peculiar to our age, most effective when executed with a bad conscience. He set himself up as an amateur moralist, not in the pay of any system, a strict scientist in search of hard facts who, in passing, could not avoid throwing light on the dark corners out of which morality grows."[325]

What led Freud to this "amateur moralizing" was his conception of human happiness, which remained highly theoretical and came in unbroken descent from the Enlightenment. While in the preamble to the American Declaration of Independence the *pursuit of happiness* is declared a human right, and therefore almost a human duty, Freud says in *Civilization and Its Discontents* of 1930, "A person who is born with a specially unfortunate instinctual constitution, and who has not properly undergone the transformation and rearrangement of his libidinal components which is indispensable for later achievements, will find it hard to obtain *happiness* from his external situation, especially if he is faced with tasks of some difficulty. As a last technique of living ... he is offered the flight into neurotic illness.... The man who sees his pursuit of *happiness* in later years thwarted can still find consolation in the yield of pleasure of chronic intoxication; or he can embark on the desperate attempt at rebellion seen in a psychosis."[326] That is not without moralizing undertones: the "unfortunate instinctual constitution" (presumably the product of early childhood experiences and therefore the parents' fault) is a misfortune; neurosis, especially one that is not cured, is blamed on the patient, it is his fault. "Every new arrival on this planet," it says in a footnote from 1920 to the third of the *Three Essays on the Theory of Sexuality* of 1905, "is faced with the task of mastering the Oedipus complex; anyone who fails to do so is a slave to neurosis."[327] The phrase "is a slave to" contains the threat of a guilty verdict; the doctor takes on the role of judge, the verdict is interminable unhappiness. Psychoanalysis, on the other hand, contains the promise of the happiness man is duty bound to pursue. This promise explains the remarkable spread of the "Jewish Science" among Americans, who are driven by the urge to achieve happiness.

After Freud had completed *Civilization and Its Discontents*, he wrote to Lou Andreas-Salomé on July 28, 1929, from Schneewinkl, where he was on vacation, "It [the book] deals with civilization, sense of guilt, happiness and similar lofty topics, and strikes me, no doubt rightly, as very superfluous—in contrast to earlier works, which always sprang from some inner necessity. But what else can I do? One can't smoke and play cards all day, I am no longer much good at walking, and most of what there is to read doesn't interest me any more. So I wrote, and in that way the time passed quite pleasantly. In writing this work I have discovered afresh the most banal truths."[328]

It is telling that initially the word "discontents" in the title was to have been "unhappiness."[329] But did unhappiness pertain to the civilization alone, to which it seemed bound? Was it not inherent in the process Freud saw taking place within himself?

Freud was seventy-three when he wrote his letter to Lou Andreas-Salomé. The previous year, he had gone to Professor Schroeder in Berlin to have a new prothesis made for his palate. The relief it brought did not last. He must have had the feeling that he was beyond cure. Yet he still wrote about happiness in his book on "unhappiness" and toned his misery and bitterness down to "discontent." The personal undertone in this wide-ranging morphology of civilization is plainly evident. It is difficult to contradict him when he complains, in hypochondriac fashion, to Lou Andreas-Salomé that he no longer feels the same urge to work. And yet writing was a great comfort to him. He acknowledged his own apathy: most of the things he read did not appeal to him; he was tired and tormented; but stronger than torment and tiredness was his perseverance in the torment, an act of will requiring considerable discipline. The man who had once said of himself, "My usual way of going upstairs is two or three steps at a time,"[330] now had to admit that "I am no longer much good at walking."[331] He considered most people "trash"[332] and still declared his faith in "Eros, the builder of cities,"[333] the teacher of the doctrine of happiness. He was still smoking, of course, as he did not forget to inform Lou Andreas-Salomé; this brought, if nothing else, guilt and destruction, and the severe things he has to say about the unhappiness of neurosis, dependence, the compulsion to repeat and addiction sound strange in his mouth; that was, quite literally, the place where he was mortal. He discovered truths and called them "most banal." What a contradiction! He was still talking of the polarity of being, which is an old truth, certainly, but not in the least banal, and if from now on he seems to lean towards the death instinct, it was because his back had started to become noticeably bowed.

Civilization and Its Discontents is the first work of Freud's old age that he acknowledged; *The Future of an Illusion* he rejected. When, in 1928, a young student praised the latter book enthusiastically, he dismissed it: "This is my worst book! ... It isn't a book of Freud.... It's the book of an old man! ... Besides Freud is dead now, and, believe me, the genuine Freud was really a great man. I am particularly sorry for you that you didn't know him better."[334] Everything recedes, everything becomes transparent, nothing touches him any more because everything has already become slightly distant; tiredness, hovering between sadness and apathy, is the most effective of all sedatives and painkillers. He feels castrated by death. He is only half at home to the suffering that visits him. The pain he bears is both inside and outside him at one and the same time, a strange tension which indicates that he is no longer completely in possession of himself, is both sufferer and observer. Death opens up before him, the black hole out of which the waters of the underworld pour. But they do not bring oblivion, not yet.

It is only people who do not know better who hope they will get better. Freud was a doctor and knew what the outcome of his disease would be as soon as he had been given the diagnosis. Only the time left to him, the time the disease would take, remained open. In this, the fate of the aging Freud is no different from that of other people, even when they do not have cancer. What did differentiate him from other people was his inborn sense of tragedy. Whatever may have been the origin of that sense—his knowledge of myth, which he had subjected to a most radical secularization; his Jewishness, which he had robbed of its illusions and to which, two years before his death, he left a memorial of anti-prophetic lucidity in *Moses and Monotheism;* or simply his own vitality, which he had sacrificed to his work—it was that sense of tragedy which led him to accept old age as a matter of course, if superfluous. From its very origin, all tragedy is sacrifice. Delphi lies in the shadow of Mount Moriah. What Freud gained from the process of aging—which was and remained a sacrifice, precisely because he neither wanted nor knew it to be one, nor wanted to know—was detachment.

Civilization and Its Discontents is not only a work of Freud's old age, it is distinguished by a serene aloofness expressing itself in wit and the ability to see things whole.

Freud's sense of humor is attested right up to his last days. It was a particular humor, sharp and cutting, sometimes so sharp it cut itself. He was very fond of jokes, especially jokes of the Jewish persuasion. And yet Freud was too filled with a sense of the morality of his science to be able to enjoy jokes as a free, surreal interplay of absurd associations. Freud's mind had more of the spirit of Goethe than of Mozart, more of the spirit of Schopenhauer than of Nietzsche, more of the spirit of *Die Meistersinger* than of Verdi's *Falstaff,* and his love of Heine was a pragmatic love. He had a heavyweight mind. That did not change in *Civilization,* but suddenly there is a completely nonscientific sense of freedom, an ability to make associations.

At one point, he discusses the categorical imperative which, as we recall, he described as the "heir of the Oedipus complex." Now, however, he seems to have doubts about it, in which anti-Christian feeling may well have played a part. But his doubts had their limits. "Even so," he says, "the behavior of human beings shows differences, which ethics, disregarding the fact that such differences are determined, classifies as 'good' or 'bad.' So long as these undeniable differences have not been removed, obedience to high ethical demands entails damage to the aims of civilization, for it puts a positive premium on being bad. One is irresistibly reminded of an incident in the French Chamber when capital punishment was being debated. A member had been passionately supporting its abolition and his speech was being received with tumultuous applause, when a voice from the hall called out: 'Que messieurs les assassins commencent!' "[335]

The wit in this joke does not simply lie in its effect of "an economy in expenditure upon inhibition,"[336] that is, in the fact that murderers are invited to be the first to abolish the death penalty, but also in the integration of murderers into society, into very polite society, with the "*messieurs les assassins*" of the heckler. The murderers, it says, making the *politesse* inherent in the French language perform the most absurd somersaults imaginable, are gentlemen, like the deputies in the French parliament. "*Messieurs les assassins*" are murderers as a class, as a recognized status, a profession recognized and accorded rights by the authorities. That not only blunts the impact of the bloody trade these "gentlemen" follow, it blunts the guillotine, the abolition of which was the subject of the debate. The whole gravity is taken out of the situation by the play with words, the play on words, a surrealist meeting of opposites. It is in the spirit of that demonic linguistic sorcerer, Johann Nestroy,[337] and Freud, who quotes the one-liner in French without making any attempt to subject the joke to analysis, well knew how delightful that deadly play with words had been.

He brings himself back down to earth by defining the objective correlative of the joke: "The element of truth behind all this, which people are so ready to disavow, is that men are not gentle creatures who want to be loved, and who at the most can defend themselves if they are attacked; they are, on the contrary, creatures among whose intellectual endowments is to be reckoned a powerful share of aggressiveness. As a result their neighbor is for them not only a potential helper or sexual object, but also someone who tempts them to satisfy their aggressiveness on him .... *Homo homini lupus*. Who, in the face of all his experience of life and of history, will have the courage to dispute this assertion?"[338]

A pessimistic view of civilization? Secondhand Schopenhauer? What now follows is an exposition of civilization as tragedy, which is all the more relentless the more clearly the old man gets the death instinct in his sights, the better the grip he gets on it or, to be more precise, the more powerfully he is gripped by it: "The assumption of an instinct of death or destruction has met with resistance even in analytic circles; I am aware that there is a frequent inclination rather to ascribe whatever is dangerous or hostile in love to an original bipolarity in its own nature. To begin with it was only tentatively that I put forward the views I have developed here, but in the course of time they have gained such a hold upon me that I can no longer think in any other way."[339] His subconscious thought, we suspect, is: that I cannot think of anything else. It is only very late on, and in very ponderous language, that Eros appears beside death, to join it in carving up the world: "This aggressive instinct is the derivative and the main representative of the death instinct which we have found alongside of Eros and which shares world-dominion with it. And now, I think, the meaning of the evolution of civilization is no longer obscure to us. It must present the struggle between Eros and death, between the instinct of life and the instinct of destruction, as it works itself out in the human species. This struggle is what all life essentially consists of, and the evolution of civilization may therefore be simply described as the struggle for life of the human species."[340]

Here Darwin's *survival of the fittest* has been turned inward. The struggle for existence has become the existential struggle which Eros and Thanatos fight out within the self, which has the task of helping to determine the general evolution through its happiness or unhappiness, the curability or incurability of its neuroses. The jungle has been turned into civilization. Compared to Darwin's ideas, Freud's theory is a late theory. It sees sublimation as sacrifice, the struggle for existence as an *agon*. This is similar to David Riesman's view of the late Freud, when he says, "Genuine, lasting greatness is in general paid for with libidinal sacrifices. And indeed, the tragedy which is brought out in that statement runs through his last, long philosophical essay, *Civilization and Its Discontents*, in which he argues that there is no civilization imaginable which could meet the demands of human beings, since they are only happy in a state of idleness and sexual satisfaction: biological facts and civilization, both render it impossible. The reader is forced to the conclusion that the world is a trap."[341] The world as a trap—that is an existential image that would fit Kafka's *Castle*, for example, or Jean-Paul Sartre's *Huis clos*. However, existence as a "racecourse,"[342] the battleground of mankind, with civilization as a hurdle and the "biological fact" of death as the finishing line, would be more fitting. Unsurprisingly for an aficionado of Viennese theater, there is a good deal of self-representation in all this, both in the sense of playing a role and of being a sacrifice on the temple altar.

In 1929, *Civilization and Its Discontents* closed with the words: "Men have gained control over the forces of nature to such an extent that with their help they would have no difficulty in exterminating one another to the last man. They know this, and hence comes a large part of their current unrest, their unhappiness and their mood of anxiety. And now it is to be expected that the other of the two 'Heavenly Powers,' eternal Eros, will make an effort to assert himself in the struggle with his equally immortal adversary."[343]

Freud's expectation does not sound all that hopeful. When he looked around, all he could see was the economic crisis in the West and Communism in the East. Unlike most of his Viennese academic colleagues, he did not abhor Marxism, he just thought it psychologically unfeasible. He feared the repressed urges which would necessarily result from the transformation of a whole society and which indeed found expression in the Moscow show trials under Stalin. "I have no concern with any economic criticisms of the communist system .... But I am able to recognize that the psychological premises on which the system is based are an untenable illusion. In abolishing private property we deprive the human love of aggression of one of its instruments."[344] What disturbed him about Russia was what had disturbed him about America, the egalitarian, non-tragic character of society.

In addition to that, the modest material circumstances of his early years had left a serious trauma; now he saw the fruits of his labors threatened from both the East and the West; the biological uncertainty of advanced old age was compounded by the material insecurity of inflation. Austria, which had only been saved from becoming a soviet republic in the revolutionary situation of 1918 by the tactical skill of the Social Democrat deputy, Seitz, was at the dead center of the storm of economic crisis and revolution. It was the situation of W. B. Yeats' "Second Coming:"

> Things fall apart; the centre cannot hold;
> Mere anarchy is loosed upon the world,

The blood-dimmed tide is loosed upon the world, …
The best lack all conviction, while the worst
Are full of passionate intensity.[345]

That was the mood in which Freud added to the final sentences of *Civilization* the following words, "But who can foresee with what success and with what result?"[346] He could, and he was right.

Unlike most of his academic colleagues, he did abhor Hitler. The feeling was mutual. There is reason to believe that when he invaded Austria in March 1938 the anti-Semite Hitler saw Freud personally as "one of those very Jews whose extermination became his dedicated purpose."[347] When Anna Freud, who had herself been summoned to the Gestapo shortly after the Anschluss, asked him whether it would not be better if they all committed suicide, he countered, "Why? Because they would like us to?"[348] "They" were the mass hysterics, whose illness he regarded as incurable, despite—or perhaps because of—all their cries of "*Heil!*"[349] The eighty-two-year-old chose exile which, as he knew in his nerves, was harder than suicide.

He decided to give in to the urging of his disciples and friends and to leave Vienna. At the last meeting of the committee of the Vienna Psychoanalytic Association, he said, "Immediately after the destruction of the Temple in Jerusalem by Titus, the Rabbi Jochanan ben Zakkai asked permission to open the first Torah school in Jabneh." [350] This sentence also appears in his *Moses* of 1939, followed by a further one: "From that time on, the Holy Writ and intellectual concern with it were what held the scattered people together."[351] History as a means of making sense of what seemed senseless? Or tradition as a comfort as things fall apart? The only "Writ" the agnostic Freud can have had in mind that was sacred for *him* was his own doctrine, which, in an unheard-of act of self-stylization, he declared a sacred text. But so great was the catastrophe engulfing him and his doctrine, so overpowering his fear and so feeble his strength, that he roused himself one last time and, in a Promethean metaphor, compared his doctrine with the one he believed he had revealed to be an illusion. Of all the acts of hubris he permitted himself, this was at the same time the most outrageous and the most understandable.

When the Nazis made Freud's exit permit dependent on his appending his signature to a declaration that he had been treated by the Gestapo with all due consideration and respect, that he had been given all the support needed for his work and had no grounds for complaint, Freud signed the document without batting an eyelid, then asked the Gestapo officer on duty whether he should add, "I can heartily recommend the Gestapo to anyone."[352] The irony here is as evident as the courage of old age it required. Nor was it lacking in tragic undertones. There he was, in their eyes a poor, old Yid at the mercy of their fists and whips, and he faced up squarely to their revolution, even if it was only a "revolution of the janitors." All that was left him was the assertion of his human dignity, which at the time of the Enlightenment had also been a revolutionary principle, but which in the two hundred and fifty years since then had become a prerequisite of a civilized life. For all its questionable nature, his statement that "Where id was, there ego shall be"[353] was an assertion of reason against madness, whatever degree of murderous technological perfection the latter may have acquired. Thus, wit had literally become his sole refuge where he was secure. Irony showed his presence of mind, a superior mind which saw through the Gestapo officer and his system, and he made it plain to him; by exaggerating it, he nullified the lie that was intended to humiliate him, rendered impotent the superior power that now had no choice but to let him escape unscathed. On May 10, 1938, Freud and his entourage, a dozen people, left Vienna. (Only his personal physician had sent his excuses because of appendicitis.)[354] That was the manner in which, in better days, the great rabbis from the east had traveled to an Austrian spa.

There is a photograph from the stopover Freud made in Paris showing him in the company of the American ambassador, William C. Bullitt, who had once been his patient, and his former student, Princess Marie Bonaparte, with whom Bullitt wrote a controversial book about President Wilson. Those two, together with Ernest Jones, played the leading role in Freud's rescue. The Princess looks devastated; the American, with a flower in his buttonhole, is nonchalant enough. The two of them are looking down, while Freud's eyes are open and looking straight ahead. The Princess has taken his arm in hers; he is leaning on her arm, a poor old soul; his body has become so light, it no longer seems able to bear his head, which appears to be pushing itself forward and out of the picture. Were it not for the penetrating stare of his dark eyes, the head would appear to be an ageless mask. His beard, now snow-white, surrounds the mouth, an open wound, a grotesque sight, since it is a face from which all other marks of sexuality have been erased. Dying is always a catastrophe. Freud's eyes, behind the glasses in their dark frames, tell us that he was aware of the extent of that catastrophe in more than a biological sense. With the dialectic of tragedy, that awareness, those eyes, gave him immortality.

England gave him a warm welcome, but, as he wrote to Max Eitingon on June 6, 1938, "The emotional climate of these days is hard to grasp, almost indescribable. The feeling of triumph on being liberated is too strongly mixed with sorrow, for in spite of everything I still greatly loved the prison from which I have been released."[355] Besides his personal physician, it was above all his daughter Anna who assumed responsibility for his care. His eyes grew dull, his mind gradually clouded over. But he died in harness. A Nazi lawyer, who had used his Party membership to facilitate Freud's emigration,[356] visited him in London.

As Dr. Indra was taking leave before returning home, he was shocked when Freud said to him, "Now you are going back to... What is the name of the place?" Dr. Indra assumed it was the forgetfulness of old age.[357] Jones interpreted the old man's slip as "protective amnesia to convey his struggle to forget Vienna."[358] It was neither the one nor the other. Vienna was his mother town, a mother that had rejected him and driven him away, a mother he had suffered under as long as he was with her, he had been attached to her and had loved her, he spoke with her cadences, he lived his life in her style. Now Hitler had violated her, had degraded her to a provincial town, and yet Vienna remained the "Capital of the Movement"—not of the National Socialist movement but, on the contrary, of the psychoanalytic movement. In the words of Rabbi Jochanan ben Zakkai, the capital was destroyed, the temple lay in ruins. The news from Vienna ate away at Freud like his cancer. And here was a man who could return to that place of ruins. Although Freud could not call its name to mind, he did remember, and what he remembered was the lamentation of the exiles in Babylon: "If I forget you, O Jerusalem, let my right hand wither away."[359] His forgetting was a quotation: he could not remember the name of Vienna and his right hand, the hand he wrote with, was crippled. But his unconscious was still at work and from its depths emerged the words of the psalm to make a statement which consisted of silence. For Freud, even the infirmity of his old age was creative.

His end was stoical. When, at the end of 1928, Dr. Schur became his "personal physician" Freud said to him, "Promise me one more thing: that when the time comes you won't let me suffer unnecessarily."[360] On September 21, 1939, Freud said, "My dear Schur, I'm sure you will remember our first talk. You promised me then not to forsake me when my time comes. Now it's nothing but torture and

112

makes no sense any more." When the doctor indicated that he remembered his promise, he thanked him and added, after a moment's hesitation, "Tell Anna about this."[361]

In 1913, Freud had subjected the choice facing the three suitors in *The Merchant of Venice* to an almost poetic analysis. From Portia's three suitors he went on to the three daughters of King Lear, and said, "The relationship of a father to his children, which might be a fruitful source of many dramatic situations, is not turned to further account in the play. But Lear is not only an old man: he is a dying man .... But the doomed man is not willing to renounce the love of women; he insists on hearing how much he is loved. Let us now recall the moving final scene, one of the culminating points of tragedy in modern drama. Lear carries Cordelia's dead body on to the stage. Cordelia is Death. If we reverse the situation it becomes intelligible and familiar to us. She is the Death-goddess.... The dramatist brings us nearer to the ancient theme by representing the man who makes the choice between the three sisters as aged and dying .... We might argue that what is represented here are the three inevitable relations that a man has with a woman—the woman who bears him, the woman who is his mate and the woman who destroys him; or that they are the three forms taken by the figure of the mother in the course of a man's life—the mother herself, the beloved one who is chosen after her pattern, and lastly the Mother Earth who receives him once more. But it is in vain that an old man yearns for the love of woman as he had it first from his mother; the third of the Fates alone, the silent Goddess of Death, will take him into her arms."[362]

Oedipus, Oedipus! Freud's sense of tragedy was the real tragedy of the scientist.

Freud and Tragedy

On June 23, 1912, Freud wrote to his disciple, Sándor Ferenczi, "A single thought that will amuse you was that the introductory scene in Lear must mean the same as the selection scene in *The Merchant of Venice*. Three caskets are the same as three women, three sisters. The third is always the correct choice. But this third one is peculiar, she doesn't speak, or she hides (Cinderella!), she is mute.... With a few associations I came out with the idea that they are the three—sisters of destiny, the Fates, the third of whom is mute, because she—symbolizes death (Stekel). The compulsion of fate is transformed into a motif of selection. Cordelia, who loves and is silent, is thus actually death. The situation of Lear with Cordelia's corpse in his arms should be reversed, the old man in the arms of the Fate of death. The three Fates are woman in her three principal manifestations: the one who gives birth, the one who gives pleasure, and the one who spoils; or mother, lover and Mother Earth = death."[363]

The Theme of the Three Caskets appeared in 1913 in the second number of *Imago*. The first sentence of the essay is, "Two scenes from Shakespeare, one from a comedy and the other from a tragedy, have lately given me occasion for posing and solving a small problem."[364] The problem posed is not as small as Freud would have us believe. As far as I can tell, this is the first time Freud openly acknowledged the death instinct.[365] And with good reason. In 1912 and 1913, the break with Jung had become inevitable, thus leaving the position of his successor as leader of the psychoanalytic movement vacant. At stake was the empire Sigmund Freud had founded and which was dearer than life to him; an empire was being divided up, just as in *King Lear*.

The solution to the problem in the comedy *The Merchant of Venice* is a "tragic" solution, as Freud himself says.

The words with which Portia reveals her feelings to Bassanio before he makes his choice are a comic play with words:

> One half of me is yours, the other half yours,
> Mine own, I would say; but if mine, then yours,
> And so all yours.[366]

Freud, on the other hand, took these words seriously, declaring them a model slip of the tongue. Even as early as *The Psychopathology of Everyday Life,* he quotes them and the interpretation of his disciple Otto Rank: "The very thing which she would like to hint to him gently, because really she should keep it from him, namely, that even before the choice she is wholly his, that she loves him, the poet, with admirable psychologic sensitiveness, allows to come to the surface in a speech-blunder. It is through this artifice that he manages to allay the intolerable uncertainty of the lover as well as the like tension of the hearer concerning the outcome of the choice."[367]

Portia's slip of the tongue slips Bassanio the promise that she will be his regardless of the choice between three caskets her father's will has imposed on her. Freud was so taken with this slip of the tongue, in which language itself becomes transparent and the psyche expresses itself, that he repeated Otto Rank's interpretation word for word in his *Introductory Lectures on Psycho-analysis,* with the crucial addition of, "Observe, too, how skillfully Portia in the end reconciles the two statements contained in her slip of the tongue, how she solves the contradiction between them and yet finally shows that it was the slip that was in the right:

> … but if mine, then yours,
> And so all yours."[368]

It was the synthesis through which a woman bound by oath managed to overcome the contradiction between her duty as a daughter and her love as a woman which fascinated Freud the analyst and remained with him for a long time.

These are serious thoughts on a scene from a comedy. After the slip of the tongue with which Portia, with the full intent of her unconscious, promises Bassanio her hand, the choice of caskets proceeds in a rapid series of scenes. The Prince of Morocco chooses first, the black man chooses gold.[369] The Prince of Aragon selects silver and gets "as much as he deserves."[370] Thus, according to the laws of comedy, lead automatically falls to Bassanio, who is no prince, but a simple suitor, and the one who suits Portia. The rest of the scene trips along at a lively pace in a mood of exhilaration, just as the tone in which Freud writes about it is so relaxed that in the middle of his argument he can refer to Offenbach's *La belle Hélène.*

While Bassanio is racking his brains over the caskets, a song is heard. Mysterious voices, which no one can tell where they come from, sing:

> Tell me where is fancy bred,
> In the heart or in the head?
> How begot, how nourished?

All: Reply, reply.

> It is engender'd in the eyes,
> With gazing fed; and fancy dies
> In the cradle where it lies.
> Let us all ring fancy's knell
> I'll begin it, —Ding, dong, bell

All: Ding, dong, bell.[371]

A mysterious song, a somber song. Who ordered it? Surely not Portia, who has just assured her beloved:

> ... I could teach you
> How to choose right, but then I am foresworn;
> so will I never be: [372]

But is not this expression of her will, which is bound to her superego, to her father's mind—"but then I am foresworn" —contradicted by the rhyme of the first line of the song, "bred," which rhymes with "lead," thus subliminally suggesting the correct casket to Bassanio? One could well believe Portia's subconscious, which has just made the slip of the tongue interpreted by Rank, capable of sending such a secret message. If, however, that were the case, then Portia, afflicted with feelings of guilt toward her father, would have good reason to fear the end of their love, the death of a passion which had not yet had the chance of fulfillment.

However that may be, the ghostly song brings a tragic note to the comedy of the scene, and presumably Freud did not hear it, solely because, for reasons of structure—the contrast between comedy and tragedy—he did not *want* to hear it. At the same time, this deafness to the tragic note symbolized his general resistance, in his early works, to the principle of death. In asking ourselves how comic the scene, which

Freud chose as the title for his essay, actually is, we are, at the same time, asking what Freud, who was certainly not without wit himself, understood by comedy.

In general, it was Shakespeare's tragic figures which fascinated Freud. It is all the more remarkable, then, that in *The Merchant of Venice* he was not drawn to the figure of Shylock, the man "that hath no music in himself,"[373] the man who is beyond healing. So strong was his resistance to his "fellow-unbeliever,"[374] the Jew of Venice, that he made him taboo in all his writings.

This silence is Freud's invariable response when the tragic figure reminds him all too clearly of the tragedy he himself embodied, yet refused to acknowledge right to the end. The most striking example is the complete suppression of Sophocles' late work, *Oedipus at Colonos*. It is true that the play contains the apotheosis of the hero, but Freud was enough of a critical intellect to be able to measure the aesthetic truth of Oedipus' ascent to the gods against the famous, even infamous, line of the chorus: "Far best were ne'er to be."[375]

And indeed the tragedy demonstrates the compulsion to repeat, which is buried deep within the hero's psyche: just as he slew Laius, now he curses his own son, Polynices. He is beyond help, beyond healing. And since the overall aim of Freud's theories was helping and healing, he must have been horrified at the spread of the Oedipus complex from Thebes to Colonos. The site of Colonos is at the foot of the Acropolis; Freud does not mention it, even when he was staying in Athens with his brother in 1904.

In 1915, Freud wrote three essays under the general title of *Some Character-types met with in Psycho-analytic Work*. The middle one he called *Those Wrecked by Success,* referring to the phenomenon where a neurosis is brought on not by deprivation or renunciation but by wishes being fulfilled. The literary cases he cites are Lady Macbeth and Rebecca Gamvik from Ibsen's *Rosmersholm*, overlooking the Master Builder, Solness, even though the conclusion Freud comes to is nowhere so clearly demonstrated as in the story of the master builder and the female troll, the young hysteric who is his ruin. The concluding sentence of the short essay runs as follows: "Psycho-analytic work teaches that the forces of conscience which induce illness in consequence of success, instead of, as normally, in consequence of frustration, are closely connected with the Oedipus complex, the relation to father and mother—as perhaps, indeed, is our sense of guilt in general."[376] The reason why Ibsen's tragedy was taboo for him came from his identification with the builder, though this only appeared seven years later. In his diary entry for June 16, 1922, Arthur Schnitzler wrote, "At a late hour [Freud] walks home with me from Berggasse to my apartment.—The conversation grows warmer and more personal;—on growing old and dying;—he confesses to certain Solness feelings (which are completely alien to me)."[377] Here Freud drew back the veil from his repression: the "Solness feelings" of 1922 explain his blindness to Solness in 1915. Freud refused to allow literature to touch the most secret parts of his mind. It was this, paradoxically, that constituted the poetic side of his character and his style.

The silence in which he shrouded the figure of Shylock was a mixture of sympathy and shame. Both feelings were expressed by Heinrich Heine in his collection *Shakespeares Mädchen und Frauen* (Shakespeare's Girls and Women). Although Heine was one of Freud's favorite writers, we do not know whether he had read these sketches. That he shared Heine's ambivalent attitude towards Judaism, on the other hand, is easy to demonstrate. If it is the case that Freud was unacquainted with Heine's collection of female portraits, then our admiration for Heine's prescience is all the greater. In the piece entitled "Jessica" Heine says, "When I saw this play performed at the Drury Lane Theater, standing in the box behind me was a fair Briton who at the end of the fourth act was crying bitter tears and cried out several times, 'The poor man is wronged.'"[378]

In the next piece, however, entitled "Portia," Heine himself takes his lead from the fair Briton with the "large black eyes that cried for Shylock"[379]—"I at least, itinerant hunter of dreams that I am, looked everywhere on the Rialto to see if I could find Shylock .... But I could not see him anywhere on the Rialto, so I decided to seek out my old acquaintance in the synagogue. The Jews were celebrating their sacred Day of Atonement and were standing there wrapped in their prayer shawls, making strange movements with their heads, almost looking like an assembly of ghosts."[380]

And, in a remarkable foray into the psychology of religion, which sounds as if it comes from the collective intuition of centuries, Heine goes on "As I, looking round for old Shylock, carefully examined all the pale Jewish faces, I made a discovery which I am afraid I find it impossible to repress. On that same day I had visited the San Carlo lunatic asylum and it struck me now, in the synagogue, that the eyes of the Jews flickered with the same awful, half vacant, half restless, half wily, half imbecile glint I had seen in the eyes of the madmen in San Carlo not long before. This indescribable, mysterious look did not betoken vacuity so much as the domination of an *idée fixe*. Could it be that the belief in that extraterrestrial god of thunder proclaimed by Moses has become the *idée fixe* of a whole people, who refuse to desist, despite the fact that for two thousand years they have been put in a straitjacket and given cold showers?"[381]

The synagogue and the lunatic asylum! Showplaces exhibiting Jewish suffering! Jewishness as pathology of the mind, what a Freudian idea! The *idée fixe* is tied to the belief in the extraterrestrial god of thunder that Moses proclaimed, in Yahweh, whom Freud calls "A coarse, narrow-minded, local god, violent and bloodthirsty; he had promised his followers to give them 'a land flowing with milk and honey' and urged them to exterminate its present inhabitants 'with the edge of the sword.' "[382]

For the young Freud, this God the Father was initially linked in counterpoint to the figure of his own father: parallel to the volcanic eruptiveness of Yahweh was the figure of a father whose sole strength lay in the confession of his own weakness. "I must," Freud says in *The Interpretation of Dreams*, "have been ten or twelve years old, when my father began to take me with him on his walks and reveal to me in his talk his views upon things in the world we live in. Thus it was, on one occasion, that he told a story to show me how much better things were now than they had been in his days. 'When I was a young man,' he said, 'I went for a walk one Saturday in the streets of your birthplace; I was well dressed, and had a new fur cap on my head. A Christian came up to me and with a single blow knocked off my cap into the mud and shouted, 'Jew! get off the pavement!' 'And what did you do?' I asked. 'I went into the roadway and picked up my cap,' was his quiet reply. This struck me as unheroic conduct on the part of the big, strong man who was holding the little boy by the hand."[383] By choosing the word "heroic" in criticizing his father, instead of the more obvious "courageous," the young Freud set up the image of the heroic man as the sign governing his own life. Unlike most other ten- or twelve-year-olds, however, he remained true to this guiding principle, which, from very early on, was intertwined with his other guiding principle—the Oedipus complex.

If one thinks of the role Carl Gustav Jung—his "crown prince" "*in partibus infidelium*"[384]—played in his life, then one can see in the passage from his letter of January 17, 1909, the same interweaving of the Oedipus and Moses themes, though of course, from the perspective of Freud as father, not as son any more. "You," Freud wrote to his "successor,"[385] "are Joshua and will take possession of the promised land of psychiatry, which I shall only be able to glimpse from afar."[386] Moses on Mount Nebo, on the border of the land of Moab, is a Biblical image of Freud, who knew his Bible. "For Freud this image remained a living symbol of the things that were denied him and the things he denied himself."[387] But Freud would not have been "heroic," in the sense of both Oedipus and Moses, if he had not immediately rebelled against self-denial and self-sacrifice.

This rebellion was double-sided. In the name of Oedipus, he demonstrated the existence of infantile sexuality. "Love and hunger ... meet at a woman's breast."[388] In so doing, he released the elemental libidinous forces of society, which initially took its revenge on Freud's for his "heroic deed" through overt or covert hostility, then misinterpreted the release as debauchery and vulgarized his theories to such an extent that all psychological aspects took second place to the technique and gymnastics of coitus. Despite all that, the motto of *The Interpretation of Dreams*—"*Flectere si nequeo superos, Acheronta movebo*"[389]—is not only to be read in a biographical and social sense, that is, directed against "the gods of the academic hierarchy,"[390] but also as a threat of revolution in a religious sense.

Of Michelangelo's "Moses," he wrote in 1914, "How often have I mounted the steep steps from the unlovely Corso Cavour to the lonely piazza where the deserted church stands, and have essayed to support the angry scorn of the hero's [!] glance! Sometimes I have crept cautiously out of the half-gloom of the interior as though I myself belonged to the mob on whom his eye is turned—the mob which can hold fast no conviction, which has neither faith nor patience, and which rejoices when it has regained the illusion of its idols."[391] It was Ernst Simon, who first pointed out that it was here that Freud first used the word "illusion" in the sense in which he was to employ it in *The Future of an Illusion*, to disparage everything religious.[392]

Moses was first published anonymously in *Imago*, with the teasing preface, "Although this paper does not, strictly speaking, conform to the conditions under which contributions are accepted for publication in this Journal, the editors have decided to print it, since the author, who is personally known to them, moves in psycho-analytic circles, and since his mode of thought has in point of fact a certain resemblance to the methodology of psycho-analysis."[393]

Indeed, the interpretation to which Freud subjects the seated figure of Moses is surprisingly analytical. At that time, art history, as far as Freud quotes it, was still completely under the influence of the related humanities. Freud, for his part, uses a process of induction to derive the intention behind the whole from the iconographic detail, relating the structural elements to each other, as if he were an Anglo-Saxon *New Critic* and not a Viennese amateur of 1914.

It is above all the relationship between Moses' beard and his hand which is subjected to the keenest examination. The right index finger and the left-hand strand of the statue's beard become symbols which Freud works to decipher as if they were details from dreams. It is only from them that Freud draws his conclusion as to Michelangelo's state of mind when creating the statue, which was intended to decorate the tomb of Pope Julius II.

Contrary to the assumption, based on the Biblical text, that Moses is about to leap up and shatter the tablets with the Ten Commandments, Freud's detailed analysis leads him to the following conclusion: "What we see before us is not the inception of a violent action but the remains of a movement that has already taken place. In his first transport of fury, Moses desired to act, to spring up and take vengeance and forget the Tables: but he has overcome the temptation, and he will now remain seated and still, in his frozen wrath and in his pain mingled with contempt. Nor will he throw away the Tables so that they will break on the stones, for it is on their especial account that he has controlled his anger.... He remembered his mission and for its sake renounced an indulgence of his feelings."[394]

This corresponds to the Biblical narrative in Exodus 32: 7-35, leaving out verses 19-20, in which Moses, after coming down from the mountain, grinds the golden calf to powder and forces the people to drink it. He remains seated on his rock and, as Freud says, "the giant frame with its tremendous physical power becomes only a concrete expression of the highest mental achievement that is possible in a man, that of struggling successfully against an inward passion for the sake of a cause to which he has devoted himself."[395]

Freud sees Michelangelo's Moses as a figure on his own; the invisible presence of Aaron and the people is omitted, even though it is there in the text. The "highest mental achievement," which is ascribed to Moses, is the heroism Freud desired to share with his model and hero; it is the exultant ideal of German Classicism:

> Freed from the power that every creature binds
> Is he who can his own self overcome.[396]

With no one he can look to for support but himself, Michelangelo's Moses has suppressed his bitterness and wrath, his longing for the

Promised Land. It is the tablets he holds in his hands that are his "destiny"; it is not that they have come to him from above as commandments he has to keep. On the contrary, *he* is keeping *them*, keeping them from his own fury. That is heroic, even if it is not quite tragic: a cathartic victory over the neurotic underground forces through what Freud called the process of sublimation.

It was when Freud discovered in him the founder of a religion who "met with a violent end in a rising of his refractory and stiff-necked people"[397] that the figure of Moses became a tragic one. He owed this discovery to the Old Testament scholar E. Sellin, who found in the prophet Hosea traces of a tradition which, starting out from the idea that Moses was murdered, formed the basis of all later messianic expectations. He could, however, have found the idea in Goethe, in his essay "Israel in the Wilderness." In his *Notes and Essays for a Better Understanding of the West-Eastern Divan*, Goethe, a lover of the Bible, who, however, read it critically, draws a picture of Moses which is anything but monumental: "During these negotiations [between the Israelites and the Midianites, Moabites, and Amorites] Moses disappeared, just as Aaron had; unless we are very much mistaken, Joshua and Caleb had decided to put an end to the matter by terminating the rule of a blinkered man, which they had had to put up with for some years, by dispatching him to join all those unfortunates he had sent on ahead ...."[398]

The place of the murder of Moses in Freud's writings is as follows: while in general Freud insisted on the strictly scientific nature of his works, he marked some as having a dreamlike character. They, too, have a particular logic, but it is not the logic of rational inquiry. His serious writings have their own neat turns of phrase, but here assertions support each other to form sweeping, free-standing arches of rare elegance; it is the truth of dreams, the primal dreams of mankind. And this truth is not interpreted, it is allowed to remain unfathomable. Claude Lévi-Strauss called the truth behind these dreams of mankind "ancient and lasting."[399] Apart from these primal truths, which are transparent and yet axiomatic, these pieces are lyrical constructs because of the character of a personal declaration that lies at their heart. The subject of this personal declaration is the nature of the "great man," which Freud sees as tragic. The tragic features Michelangelo has given his Moses are at the same time features of the father figure: "It is a longing for the father felt by everyone from his childhood onwards, for the same father whom the hero of legend boasts he has overcome.... One must admire him, one may trust him, but one cannot avoid being afraid of him too. We should have been led to realize this from the word itself: who but the father can have been the 'great man,' in childhood?"[400]

The identification of Moses with the "great man" leads to the further identification of this "great man" with the "mighty prototype of a father which, in the person of Moses, stooped to the poor Jewish bondsmen to assure them that they were his dear children."[401] But if the Jews were Moses' "dear children," then after he had freed them from the Egyptian yoke, when they were half grown up, half fledged, so to speak, the Oedipus factor took over and they slew the "great man," their father.

As early as *Totem and Taboo* Freud had boldly gone beneath the surface of the Oedipus dream and linked it to the Darwinian concept of the primal father and the primal horde. A further arch in the bold construct was the concept of the totem meal developed by the anthropologist Robertson Smith and others: "One day the brothers who had been driven out came together, killed and devoured their father and so made an end of the patriarchal horde.... Cannibal savages that they were, it goes without saying that they devoured their victim.... The totem meal, which is perhaps mankind's earliest festival, would thus be a repetition and a commemoration of this memorable and criminal deed, which was the beginning of so many things—of social organization, of moral restrictions and of religion."[402] The murder of the primal father creates primal collective guilt, which is still present in classic Judaism, where the scapegoat as a totemic animal is driven out into the wilderness to expiate his guilt.

All this may be fantasy as Lévi-Strauss understands it, but it was a fantasy embracing mankind. Indirectly, Thomas Mann recognized the flight of fancy (which at the same time means it does not go trawling the depths) which is *Totem and Taboo* when, in 1929, he called the book, "without doubt Freud's outstanding work in a purely artistic sense, a masterpiece which, in construction and literary form, takes its place among all the great examples of the essay in German."[403]

But Freud did not stop at the Jews' feelings of guilt; he traced their continuing presence in Christianity, thus emphasizing the legacy of the Old Testament in the New: "Paul, a Roman Jew from Tarsus, seized upon this sense of guilt and traced it back correctly to its original source. He called this the 'original sin;' it was a crime against God and could only be atoned for by death. With the original sin death came into the world. In fact this crime deserving death had been the murder of the primal father who was later deified."[404] There is a reductionist element underlying Freud's interpretation. Original sin no longer encompasses both the fact and the totality of existence; instead it derives from the primal guilt, the primal murder of the primal father. Since, however, this primal father is ultimately a manifestation of God (the primal father was "deified,") the parricide became a deicide. But along with God, the unambiguous meaning of the world is also slaughtered. Ambivalence is simply another word for the twilight of the God. The intercession of Christ created a scapegoat for Christian original sin: "A son of God had allowed himself to be killed without guilt and had thus taken on himself the guilt of all men. It had to be a son, since it had been the murder of a father."[405] "The poor Jewish people," on the other hand, "who with their habitual stubbornness continued to disavow the father's murder, atoned heavily for it in the course of time. They were constantly met with the reproach 'You killed our God!' And this reproach is true, if it is correctly translated. If it is brought into relation with the history of religions, it runs: 'You will not *admit* that you murdered God (the primal image of God, the primal father, and his later reincarnations).' There should be an addition declaring: 'We did the same thing, to be sure, but we have *admitted* it and since then we have been absolved.' "[406]

The question as to whether, in theological terms, the mere profession of the Christian faith can be seen as atonement is better left open. If, however, in killing Moses the Jews also killed their founding father, then—to use Freud's imagery—at the same time they killed in him the son who has to substitute for God. According to Freud, Moses is actually the son, not of the provincial thunder god Yahweh but, in a figurative sense, the son (disciple and subject) of Pharaoh Amenhotep IV, who, around 1375 B.C., introduced a radical form of monotheism.

Amenhotep, under the name of Akhenaton, was the first ruler in the history of the world to impose the belief in one God on his unwilling subjects. It was the sun, which he praised by the name of the sun god *Aton*, and Freud goes so far as to suggest that this *Aton* reappeared in the Jewish name for God, *Adonai*.[407] "In the two hymns to the Aton which have survived in the rock tombs and which were probably composed by Akhenaton himself, he praises the sun as the creator and preserver of all living things both inside and outside Egypt with an ardor which is not repeated till many centuries later in the Psalms in honor of the Jewish god Yahweh."[408]

It was for the sake of this monotheism that Michelangelo's Moses overcame his fury and spared the tablets on which the prohibitions of the Decalogue were inscribed—and it was for the sake of this monotheism that the great man of the Jews was slain.

When the threat of Nazism was drawing nearer to the Austrian border, Franz Werfel wrote a poem, *Akhenaton's Hymn to the Sun*, the last verse of which runs:

> A million million lives stream out
> From Thee, now I perceive Thee;
> For Thine and my love's sake didst Thou
> Create creation, Aton-Re.
> I gird myself to journey forth,
> Astride my golden chariot throne,
> And with this hymn show to the world
> The Father's love plain in His son.[409]

In contrast to the neopaganism that had arisen in Catholic Austria, Werfel had adapted the *Hymn to the Sun*, transfiguring the golden chariot throne from Verdi's *Aida* with Christian promise. For the publicly professed Catholic Werfel, the "hymn" presumably takes the role of the Holy Ghost.

Against this trinity Freud sets the unconditional monotheism Moses had learned from Akhenaton. He not only opposed the neopaganism of the Nazis, he also opposed the Catholic Church, by whom he felt persecuted, along with his anthropology, to the brink of paranoia. On September 30, 1934 he wrote to Arnold Zweig, "Faced with the new persecutions, one asks oneself again how the Jews have come to be what they are and why they have attracted this undying hatred. I soon discovered the formula: Moses created the Jews."[410] But in *Moses and Monotheism*, Freud takes this idea further: "The great religious idea for which the man Moses stood was, in our view, not his own property: he had taken it over from his King [!] Akhenaton. And he … may perhaps have been following hints which had reached him—from near or distant parts of Asia—through the medium of his mother or by other paths."[411]

But if Moses was an Egyptian, what was his mother's situation? It is astonishing how little attention Freud pays to the princess who, according to Exodus 2: 5-10, took the child out of the Nile. Did he neglect her because she was the precise opposite of the Oedipus model? Like Oedipus, the Moses of the Bible was abandoned; Moses the Egyptian, however, was taken in with compassion. Freud surely knew the old Jewish joke in which the boy in the back row of the class glosses the princess's "This is one of the Hebrews' children" with a whispered, "That's what *she* says." However that may be, Freud contents himself with a variant of Otto Rank's *Der Mythos von der Geburt des Helden,* according to which Moses' abandonment on the river indicates his—probably noble—Egyptian origin, "but, in order to fit in with the fresh purpose, its aim had to be somewhat violently twisted. From being a way of sacrificing a child, it was turned into a means of rescuing him."[412]

The story of the monotheist Moses is the story of the great man who brought the Jews their deity and was killed by them for his pains. It is not, as the Zionist and humanist Ernst Simon maintained, the expression of an "ardent Jewish patriotism," especially as far as the Palestine of the time was concerned. In this Freud was plagued by terrible feelings of ambivalence. On the one hand, during the cold Viennese spring of 1935 he dreamt of visiting Arnold Zweig in his house on Mount Carmel: "If I come to Haifa I will certainly bring Moses for you";[413] on the other, he was annoyed on a matter of principle with the Hebrew University in Jerusalem, whose faculty were clearly of the view that "it is premature to create a chair for psychoanalysis as long as none for psychology exists."[414] Freud, identified as he was with his teaching, had little cause for Mosaic patriotism as long as its object was Palestine. What, moreover, he could not know was that militant Jews inside and outside Palestine, such as Arthur Koestler, identified themselves as "Hebrew" instead of as "Mosaic"[415] because they too rejected the Ten Commandments in order to survive the great assault on the Jews.

The great man concealed a great mystery. In 1936, one year before the publication of his first lecture on Moses, he wrote of his friend, the analyst Eder, "We were both Jews and knew of each other that we carried that miraculous thing in common, which—*inaccessible to any analysis* so far—makes the Jew."[416]

What Jews had in common with other Jews was, in psychoanalytical terms, the guilt for the murder of Moses. That is not sufficient to bind Jews to Jews with the tie of reciprocal recognition; it is "evidence of the presence of a peculiar psychical aptitude in the masses who had become the Jewish people," which "is revealed by the fact that they were able to produce so many individuals prepared to take on the burdens of the religion of Moses in return for the reward of being the chosen people and perhaps for some other prizes of a similar degree."[417] "Prizes" are what you get in the lottery or beauty contests; equating the "reward of being the chosen people" with them makes the "burdens" of Judaism stand out all the more sharply.

Although the structure of Freud's psyche was healthy enough to exclude any Jewish self-hatred, he was above all the great man who became impatient when the riffraff, whether Jewish or non-Jewish, got in his way. On August 18, 1933, six months after Hitler came to power, he wrote to Arnold Zweig, "Our great master Moses was, after all, a strong anti-Semite. ... *Perhaps he really was an Egyptian.*"[418] The revulsion he felt at the Jews dancing round the golden calf was even more compelling than the immediate threat of danger.

And in a letter of June 22, 1937, to Arnold Zweig, when the first two pieces on *Moses and Monotheism* had already appeared, he commented as follows on the sudden death of Alfred Adler: "For a Jew boy out of a Viennese suburb, a death in Aberdeen is an unheard-of career in itself and proof of how far he had got on. The world really rewarded him richly for his service in having opposed psycho-analysis."[419] Apart from the protectiveness he maintained towards his theories right to the end, this was the resident of the city of Vienna dissociating himself from the Jew from the outer working-class districts. (Although Freud was in every respect a well-assimilated Viennese, he was not born there and his establishment at 19 Berggasse was on the extreme edge of the patrician and aristocratic central district).

As Moses, if not as the Egyptian variant, Freud defended monotheism, though with the exclusion of God, by equating it with psychoanalysis. Moses was an anti-Semite (and was killed in tragic circumstances) because the masses succumbed to the demons instead of obeying the laws which drove out the demons. Alfred Adler was a "Jew boy" because, as a socially conscious petty bourgeois, he gave precedence to the practical solution of the problem of power over the mythic solution of the cultural problem of the father-son tragedy. In one bold leap, Freud put his own teaching on a level with Moses' monotheism: "Thereupon there arose from the midst of the people an unending succession of men who were not linked to Moses in their origin but were enthralled by the great and mighty tradition which had grown up little by little in obscurity: and it was these men, the Prophets, who tirelessly preached the old Mosaic doctrine—that the deity disdained sacrifice and ceremonial and asked only for faith and a life in truth and justice (Ma'at). The efforts of the prophets had a lasting success; the doctrines with which they re-established the old faith became the permanent content of the Jewish religion. It is honor enough to the Jewish people that they could preserve such a tradition and produce men who gave it a voice—even though the initiative to it came from outside, from a great foreigner."[420]

Freud presents the tragic image of a secular prophet. His last book is full of "mythic confusion"[421] between the salvation proclaimed by the prophets in messianic mode and the healing he himself ascribed to psychoanalysis.[422] That Napoleon, another of Freud's models, "at least confused himself mythically with Alexander during his oriental adventure"[423] was pointed out by Thomas Mann in his speech on the occasion of Freud's eightieth birthday (and three years later Hitler was to confuse himself with Napoleon when he invaded Poland). In a similar manner, Freud at the end of his life felt himself to be a prophet, and since he felt himself to be one, then he was one.

For Moses to have been Egyptian means he was even more specially chosen. Through Akhenaton's monotheism, he was chosen *before* the Chosen People, who were following the provincial deity Yahweh. If, however, the teachings of Moses were equivalent to psychoanalysis, the *Jewish Science*, then Freud was its prophet, in anger and in love he proclaimed *ma'at* (truth and justice), which are in fact the extreme limits and consequences of a successful analysis. Ultimately, it did not matter whether Moses was an Egyptian, whether monotheism was Mosaic; Freud remained the great man who came to a tragic end in that the "riffraff" slew him before he set foot in the Promised Land. *Nemo propheta in patria.* His book on Moses appeared posthumously, after he had been driven out of Vienna, a city that, in lifestyle and after ten decades of habit, was something like the Promised Land for him, despite all the academic antagonism. His destiny was exile, a destiny even more tragic than that which kept Moses away from his homeland.

For all the literalness he insisted on when it came to his theories, Freud was generous and relaxed compared with the rigidity of Mosaic orthodoxy. (The gentle influence of his liberal teacher of religion, Samuel Hammerschlag, must have had greater effect than it seemed to the student of "the dear old Jewish teacher.")[424]

This is presumably the reason why he placed a taboo on Shakespeare's tragic figure of Shylock. The Jew's insistence on having his bond was anathema to Freud. Basically, psychoanalysis is a method of advocacy to which formal law is foreign, human justice everything. "We do pray for mercy,/ And that same prayer doth teach us all to render/ The deeds of mercy."[425] Those are the words of the Christian Portia, and indeed, at the end Freud's attitude to Christianity is unexpectedly ambivalent: "Christianity, having arisen out of a father-religion, became a son-religion. It has not escaped the fate of having to get rid of the father. Only a portion of the Jewish people accepted the new doctrine. Those who refused to are still called Jews today. Owing to this cleavage they have become even more sharply divided from other peoples than before. They were obliged to hear the new religious community... reproach them with having murdered God. In full, this reproach would run as follows: 'They will not accept it as true that they murdered God, whereas we admit it and have been cleansed of that guilt.' It is easy therefore to see how much truth lies behind this reproach. A special enquiry would have to be called for to discover why it has been impossible for the Jews to join in this forward step which was implied, in spite of all its distortions, by the admission of having murdered God. *In a certain sense* they have in that way taken *a tragic load of guilt* on themselves...."[426] More than that, in a certain sense: *a triple load of tragic guilt*: the murder of Moses, the great man, the persecution of the prophets who proclaimed the Mosaic Law, and the repression of the primal murder.

Shylock adds a fourth: the murder of the son. The pound of Christian flesh, to which he has a justified legal claim, is, in mythic terms, a Laius complex. (Erik H. Erikson has maintained that such "Laius feelings" toward his followers, especially C. G. Jung, were not unknown to Freud.)[427] The Oedipus myth is, so to speak, stood on its head. It is not the father of the primal horde who is murdered but the son. But that cancels out the totem meal, the scapegoat returns from the wilderness having achieved nothing, the Savior descends from the cross to journey into hell, social and moral restraints and religion come to an end.

While Shakespeare does everything to give Shylock's hatred of Christians as human a motivation as he does his daughter Jessica's love of Christians, Freud ventures further, to the tragic substrate where it is no longer a matter of motivations, but of the mythic murder of the son by the father. Freud's unconscious presumably also housed the historical associations of the tragic reversal of morality in the world. Where the father of the primeval horde slays his son, everything is possible, even ritual murder in which the fatherly religion of the Jews desecrates the body of Christ in the host, even if it did not physically violate Christian girls and children. Freud was probably acquainted both with Heine's *Rabbi von Bacherach* and with *Ritualmord in Ungarn* (Ritual Murder in Hungary, 1914), a "Jewish Tragedy in 5 Acts" by his later friend Arnold Zweig, in which the leading role, a Talmud scholar, had been played by the young Elisabeth Bergner. (When he read the play, Franz Kafka was forced "to stop reading, sit down on the sofa and weep. It's years since I wept."[428])

Freud could not but abhor Shylock, who, through the murder of the son, reversed the tragic human linkage between father and son. The demon of lucre, the golden calf Shylock pursues, is not an anticipation of the economy of the modern world but a regression to the time when the primal father could drive out and murder his son if he so desired. Because Freud was too deeply involved in the destiny of the Jews and its paradoxes, he repressed Shylock, replacing him in *The Theme of the Three Caskets* with King Lear.

***

The Italian writer and critic, Giovanni Papini, claims Freud said to him when he visited him on May 8, 1934, "Everybody thinks ... that I stand by the scientific character of my work and that my principal scope lies in curing mental maladies. This is a terrible error that has prevailed for years and that I have been unable to set right. I am a scientist by necessity, and not by vocation. Ever since childhood, my secret hero has been Goethe. I would have liked to have become a poet, and my whole life long I've wanted to write novels. All my gifts—my schoolteachers, too, admitted it—were of a kind to lead me towards literature."[429] Doubts have been cast on the authenticity of this; too many of Freud's remarks about himself speak against it.

When Havelock Ellis, for example, in a 1919 essay entitled "Psycho-Analysis in Relation to Sex," sought to show that Freud's writings should be judged not as scientific publications but as art, Freud replied to the man who was "seriously admired for his researches into sexual science and an eminent critic of psycho-analysis" that "We cannot but regard this view as a fresh turn taken by resistance and as a repudiation of analysis, even though it is disguised in a friendly, indeed in too flattering a manner. We are inclined to meet it with a most decided contradiction."[430] Ellis refused to be put off. He regarded Freud's rejection of the idea that he was an artist as "suspicious." As late as 1936, he could still write to Joseph Wortis, an American psychiatrist, "F. was rather indignant (perhaps a suspicious circumstance!) when I once told him he was an artist. But he is an artist!"[431]

In *The Interpretation of Dreams* Freud had already told how hearing Georg Christoph Tobler's little essay on *Nature* read out at the time he was taking his school-leaving examinations had encouraged him to study science at university.[432] But Tobler's essay (at the time, Freud ascribed it to Goethe) did not describe nature in a scientific style but in a paean of praise, as was the fashion in the *Sturm und Drang* of 1782. No dry pedant, only a man with an artistic bent could be inspired to study nature by poetic prose such as:

> "She [Nature] is acting out a play; whether she sees it herself or not, we do not know, yet she is acting it out for us who are standing in the corner.... Her play is always new, because she is always creating new onlookers. Life is her finest invention and death is the device she employs to allow her an abundance of life."[433]

That Freud, a Viennese schooled in the Paris Opera and the art of Sarah Bernhardt, knew and loved the theater can be seen from the fact that he took the name of his most lasting achievement from Sophocles' tragedy. Of course, we, the onlookers, are put in the corner, like children who have committed the sin of watching where they are not supposed to watch, which, when you come to think of it, is what the sacrilege and prerogative of the play of atonement and consecration in the theater consists of.

Of course, it cannot have been death as a device of nature to make room for an abundance of new life, that is, basically, to avoid a population explosion, that drew Freud, the man of healing, to the study of the natural sciences. Rather, he studied the natural sciences in order to prevent the individual, the tragic death by attempting to heal the onlooker. But even for that he needed drama: "It is an inevitable result of all this," he says in *Thoughts for the Times on War and Death* (1915), "that we should seek in the world of fiction, in literature and in the theatre compensation for what has been lost in life. There we still find people who know how to die—who, indeed even manage to kill someone else.... We die with the hero with whom we have identified ourselves; yet we survive him, and are ready to die just as safely with another hero."[434]

As is clear from these reflections, Freud *was* a very gifted writer, and his gift expressed itself all the more clearly the more personally involved he felt in the subject he had chosen to treat. (That distinguishes him from the scientists of the time who aimed at objectivity.) He loved literature, he loved writers; his writings, like those of Goethe are "fragments of a great confession."[435]

Freud's "personal physician," Max Schur, observed that *The Theme of the Three Caskets* was perhaps the first time Freud approached the principle of the death instinct "head-on."[436] And what can be more poetically conceived and expressed than the end of that little essay? "The dramatist brings us nearer to the ancient theme by representing the man [King Lear] who makes the choice between the three sisters as aged and dying .... We might argue that what is represented here are the three inevitable relations that a man has with a woman—the woman who bears him, the woman who is his mate and the woman who destroys him; or that they are the three forms taken by the figure of the mother in the course of a man's life—the mother herself, the beloved one who is chosen after her pattern, and lastly the Mother Earth who receives him once more. But it is in vain that an old man yearns for the love of woman as he had it first from his mother; the third of the Fates alone, the silent Goddess of Death, will take him into her arms."[437] For all its breadth and wealth of insight, the *Three Caskets* consists of philosophical poetry, of cultural experiences woven round a primal event that becomes clearer and clearer the older, the more mature, the more weary Freud became. This primal event was death.

It is true that Jones maintained death was a subject that was never far from Freud's mind,[438] and certain dreams in *The Interpretation of Dreams*, such as the "*non-vixit* dream" or the "breakfast-ship dream," do spring from a deep level of the death instinct which remained inaccessible to the Freud of the turn of the century. It was only in the years 1912/1913, during which one after the other *Totem and Taboo*, *The Theme of the Three Caskets*, and *The Moses of Michelangelo* were written or appeared, that the "archaeological" or "prehistoric" level was reached. It is the beginning of Freud's study of themes from drama. While before this, the writer inside him had an obligation to prose fiction—see, for example, the beginning of the case study of Katharina...,[439] which reads like a novella—it is now themes from drama which are the subjects of analysis. Whereas he could write, in the final summing-up of the case study on *Fräulein Elisabeth von R.*, "it still strikes me as strange that the case histories I write should read like short stories and that, as one might say, they lack the serious stamp of science,"[440] for an analogy to the totem meal that he postulates, he looks to drama: "I have in mind the situation of the most ancient Greek tragedy. A company of individuals, named and dressed alike, surround a single figure, on whose words and deeds they are all dependent: it is the chorus and the actor playing the Hero. He was originally the only actor. Later a second and third were added, to play as counterpart to the Hero and as characters split off from him; but the character of the Hero himself and his relation to the chorus remained unaltered. The Hero of tragedy must suffer; to this day that remains the essence of a tragedy."[441] As early as the *Studies on Hysteria,* Freud had shown, though in the manner of prose fiction, "an intimate connection between the story of the patient's sufferings and the symptoms of his illness,"[442] thus laying bare the psychoanalytical roots of tragedy.

And Freud goes on to ask, "But why had the Hero of tragedy to suffer? And what was the meaning of his 'tragic guilt'? ... He had to suffer because he was the primal father, the Hero of the great primeval tragedy ... and the tragic guilt was the guilt which he had to take on himself to relieve the Chorus from theirs. ... The crime which was thrown onto his shoulders, presumptuousness and rebelliousness against a great authority, was precisely the crime for which the members of the Chorus, the company of brothers were responsible. Thus the tragic hero became, though it might be against his will, the redeemer of the Chorus."[443]

The possibility of this kind of interpretation was demonstrated by the Swiss literary historian Peter von Matt, using one of Schiller's plays; not surprisingly the play is *William Tell.* [444] In this interpretation, Geßler is the primal father whom the Swiss archer slays. But Tell does not take part in the founding of the Swiss state, the oath on the Rütli, in order not to burden his brothers, the Swiss chorus, with guilt. Acting for the others, he murders the primal father, to be feted at the end as a liberator on the festival meadow as if he were a mastersinger. Moreover, Schiller introduces a dramatic superfluity,[445] giving a double motivation for the redemption of the chorus by introducing Johannes Parricida, the Duke of Swabia who killed his uncle. He does, though, give the Duke lines which boldly stand out from the compendium of familiar quotations contained in the rest of the text:

> I'll bend my steps unto the wilderness,
> The rock-strewn waste, a horror to myself,
> With loathing turn away from my own face
> When mirrored in a stream my form appears.[446]

The wilderness clearly points to the scapegoat, which was sent there in order to bring about the reconciliation with the people. The reflection in the stream, however, merges with the image of the double, which became for Freud "the uncanny harbinger of death."[447] If this scene were not dominated by Tell's unbearable self-righteousness, its disturbing nature would compel us to declare it great tragic literature.

In *Totem and Taboo*, Freud describes the *Darwinian primal horde*: "All that we find there is a violent and jealous father who keeps all the females for himself and drives away his sons as they grow up, nothing more."[448] This "nothing more" also applies to William Tell: Berta von Bruneck, the love interest, is abducted by Geßler without coming to any further harm; both Stauffacher's and Tell's wives fear the same harm might befall themselves and their families; and Baumgarten's slaying of Wolfenschießen, the Emperor's bailiff, in the bath into which the primal father tried to lure his wife,[449] is an overreaction. Wolfenschießen neither forces the woman, nor does he pursue her, but simply awaits his fate all unsuspecting. His crime is stupidity.

Clearly, it was the description of the totem meal, "perhaps mankind's earliest festival,"[450] that made the difference. Freud experienced the murder of the primal father from both sides, so to speak: as Laius he wrote to Ludwig Binswanger on December 12, 1912, the year following the publication of the first *Taboo* article, after he had fainted at the totem meal of the Munich conference and been picked up by Jung: "I am resigned to being declared a candidate for eternity on the basis of my attack in Munich. Recently Stekel wrote that my behavior was already showing the 'hypocritical feature.' All of them can hardly wait for it, but I can answer them as Mark Twain did under similar circumstances: 'Reports of my death grossly exaggerated.'"[451]

As Oedipus, in the following year, when he was plagued by doubts which he had not had with *The Interpretation of Dreams,* he said, "Then I described the wish to kill one's father, and now I have been describing the actual killing; after all, it is a big step from a wish to a deed,"[452] as big a step as that between reporting and carrying out, between prose fiction and drama, and it is perhaps no coincidence that the book ends with Faust's "In the beginning was the deed."[453]

Freud was a "Goethe-Jew," something he shared with many of his disciples and opponents, for example, Martin Buber. He knew the text of *Faust* by *heart*. Despite (or because of) that, he laid the stress on the wrong word. He emphasizes "beginning" when he says, "Primitive men, on the other hand, are *uninhibited*: thought passes directly into action. With them it is rather the deed that is substitute for the thought."[454] That explains the irruption of the primitive when Freud describes the murder of the primal father "in the beginning." It is the deed that is in the beginning, while the hesitation and irresolution of the inhibited neurotic knows neither beginning nor end: "with them [neurotics] the thought is a complete substitute for the deed."[455] That Freud's relationship with the "old man," with his father, was neurotic can be seen, if nowhere else, in the fact that he was a grown man of forty when his father died in 1896, and in 1920 he still expressed his condolences to Jones, whose father had just died, by saying that the death of Jakob Freud all those years ago had "revolutionized"[456] him. The "revolution" consisted of the completion of *The Interpretation of Dreams*: "It was, I found, a portion of my own self-analysis,"[457] which he could only complete after his father's death. The neurotic basis of this he described in one of his letters to Wilhelm Fließ as if it were simply repression: "By one of those dark pathways behind the official consciousness the old man's death has affected me deeply."[458]

The shock Freud suffered when writing *Totem and Taboo* was more that of the primitive man of action than the inhibited neurotic. On the other hand, in *The Interpretation of Dreams*, Freud quoted Goethe when he interpreted Hamlet as the neurotic type "whose power of direct action is paralyzed by an excessive development of his intellect."[459] Freud himself describes Hamlet as perfectly capable of acting, once when he stabs Ophelia's father behind the arras and again when he sacrifices Rosencrantz and Guildenstern without a qualm. "Hamlet," Freud says, "is able to do anything—except take vengeance on the man who did away with his father and took that father's place with his mother, the man who shows him the repressed wishes of his own childhood realized."[460] That is the symptomatology of the neurasthenic and hysteric; tragic it is not.

It was only when Freud, in *Totem and Taboo*, broke through the layers of civilized behavior, of the novelistic interpretation of neurosis, of the inhibition to action, that he, who certainly cannot be accused of being primitive, found himself in the middle of ritual. Carrying out the wish to slay the father is an act of ritual, eminently primitive and therefore in the archaic sense tragic "in the beginning."

This secondary primitiveness, this modern tragic nature was something Freud shared with his age: 1912 saw the premiere of Stravinsky's *Rite of Spring* and Kafka's breakthrough from weary impressionism to the dizzying pace, both primitive and tragic, of "The Judgment" with the transformation of old Bendemann from a retired businessman into a primal father, stamping his feet and jabbing his finger.

The First World War was in the air. Once it had broken out and the streets of Vienna were filled with the wounded and the maimed, Freud dropped the cultured tragedy of classical drama; his new primitivism brought an "altered attitude towards death"[461] since "death is no longer a chance event"—"people really die."[462] It is the tragically primitive layer of the murder of the primal father, which, long repressed, reappears on the surface again. The centuries of Christianity had attempted to dismiss this primal layer as the Devil's work and eradicate it. "In reality there is no such thing as 'eradicating' evil. Psychological—or, more strictly speaking, psychoanalytic—investigation shows instead that the deepest essence of human nature consists of instinctual impulses which are of an elementary nature, which are similar in all men and which aim at the satisfaction of certain primal needs."[463] The First World War itself is an example of the impossibility of ever ridding the world of the elemental tragedy of the primal horde. (In cultural terms, the postwar period was the time of Ernst Toller's Hinkemann, castrated by the war; of Brecht's cannibalistic god Baal and the beginnings of the discovery of the art of the mentally ill.)

During these years there appeared on the horizon, at first unclear and sensed rather than seen, even by Freud, a shadow with a mustache: "The uncanny and coercive characteristics of group formation, which are shown in the phenomena of suggestion ... may therefore with justice be traced back to the fact of their origin from the primal horde. The leader of the group is still the dreaded primal father; the group still wishes to be governed by unrestricted force; it has an extreme passion for authority.... The primal father is the group ideal, which governs the ego in the place of the ego ideal."[464]

It was in 1921 that Freud drew this silhouette. When the shadow appeared more clearly, sweeping the German masses along with it, later even striking out across the Austrian border, Thomas Mann wrote, "I have a private suspicion that the fury he put into carrying out the march on a certain capital was basically directed at the old analyst who had his seat there, his real and actual enemy, the philosopher and revealer of neurosis, the great disillusioner, the one who knew about, and told the world about, 'genius.' "[465] Mann's title for his little essay was "Brother Hitler." As far as Freud was concerned, he could just as well have called it "Son Hitler." There is no doubt that Hitler was out to get Freud and was only prevented from committing this "murder of the primal father" by the combined efforts of his international and—to their great credit—Austrian friends. (One can think what one likes of Hitler, but one thing is certain: he gave the primal tragedy of primitive cannibalism back to the world.)

When the situation was at its worst and there was no hope of escape, Anna Freud asked her father, "Wouldn't it be better if we all killed ourselves?" Freud replied, "Why? Because that's what they want us to do?" It is not only the Jewish fellow-sufferer speaking here, it is also the primal father refusing to commit the murder that would have proved his bastard right: a primal father who commits suicide is not a great man.

With this act of self-assertion, the eighty-two-year-old cancer sufferer demonstrated his greatness, through which he " influence[d] his fellow-men in two ways: by his personality and by the idea which he put forward."466

His personality has long since dissolved into "a whole climate of opinion."467 As far as his ideas are concerned, he seems to have repressed the concept—the tragic concept among his ideas—of the murder of the primal father until his later works. Walter Muschg, who has the credit of having published an essay on Freud as a writer as early as 1930, says of these works, which spread out before us "already imbued with the monumental calm of the approach of death." "When we look on them we are deeply moved because we can discern behind them the whole sweep of his life. In them Freud transmutes the sense of a 'journey' through life into the crystalline transparency of the structure of his writings, looking deep into his own past and that of humanity, mocking himself and us from his birds-eye view and admitting without prevarication the limits of his knowledge."468

Muschg could not have known *Moses and Monotheism* when he wrote his article. That book is far removed from the calm of the late works, which one might call (after Robert Musil) *Posthumous Papers of a Living Author*.469 Even in its external form it is split, the first two of the three essays appearing in Vienna in 1937, the third being brought out in Holland in August 1938. This book, torn apart by exile, is full of cracks, joins, and repetitions; repetitions and digressions make it difficult to read, an outward indication of the tragedy in which the work has its origin. The author, usually so sure of himself, was haunted by doubts to the very end. Jones and at least one of the editors of *Imago*, the art historian Ernst Kris, tried to persuade him to abandon the hypothesis of a repressed "memory-trace" going back to the murder of the primal father. He, however, stuck by it: "The murder of Moses was a repetition of this kind and, later, the supposed judicial murder of Christ, so that these events come into the foreground as causes. It seems as though the genesis of monotheism could not do without these occurrences."[470] The old gentleman refused to give up the assumption of a "memory-trace," even though it was superfluous to the argumentation of his main theme. He clearly needed the murder of the primal father in order to underpin and demonstrate the tragic nature of his own feelings of guilt. Not for nothing did he call the first draft of his book, in a letter of September 30, 1934, to Arnold Zweig, "The Man Moses, a Historical Novel"[471]—in the end such primal fantasies no longer bothered him.

If, elsewhere, he was prepared to abandon the "supposed judicial murder of Christ,"[472] he still considered that it "would obviously be unjust to break off the chain of causes at Moses and to neglect what was effected by those who succeeded him and carried on his ideas, the Jewish Prophets."[473]

As with the "Great Man," an autobiographical confusion of Freud with the tragic situation of the prophets is self-evident. But the tragedy of the zealots, who kept appearing, corresponds to the tragic readiness of the Jews "to take on the burdens of the religion of Moses in return for the reward of being the chosen people and perhaps for some other prizes of a similar degree."[474]

But in Austria, *Prämien*, as well as meaning "prizes," is the word for the money paid out in the lottery or, at best, paid into insurance. Here Freud has unconsciously given expression to his ambivalent feelings toward the "burdens of the religion of Moses," toward the pronouncements of the prophets and the greatness of the great man, his doubts regarding the murder of the primal father—here they appear as ambivalence.

By comparing the Jews' status as the Chosen People, which in the first instance is a religious concept, to a sum of money, he fell victim to a linguistic discrepancy which is not lessened by the fact that he considered religion to consist of the feelings of awe and terror inspired by an "enormously exalted father"[475] and that for him, who started out from such modest beginnings, money certainly did not stink.

What he meant when he spoke of being the Chosen People was, rather, "The pre-eminence given to intellectual labors throughout some two thousand years in the life of the Jewish people.... It has helped to check the brutality and the tendency to violence which are apt to appear where the development of muscular strength is the popular ideal."[476] This was directed more against *Strength through Joy*, the Nazis' physical fitness program, than against the *mens sana in corpore sano* of classical antiquity, for, Freud goes on, "Harmony in the cultivation of intellectual and physical activity, such as was achieved by the Greek people, was denied to the Jews. In this dichotomy their decision was at least in favor of the worthier alternative."[477]

This last sentence sums up Freud's conception of tragedy. As a modest assertion pregnant with meaning, it is, moreover, most appropriate to the modern world. Torn this way and that between pleasure and violence, by disposition both incurable and indestructible, we humans are trapped in our contradictory nature. The primal guilt, which Freud revealed to us in what some may insist on calling his primal fantasy of the murder of the primal father, is unfathomable; bound to the past, our only possible decision is to accept the future. Psychoanalysis can encourage us to make this decision; it cannot make it for us. "The whole trick is to abandon our existence in order to exist."[478] The decision is made, *if* it is made at all, in favor of "the worthier alternative." But this "worthier alternative" is tragic. The road Freud took was strewn with decisions; as far as people were concerned, he was no great judge of character and made mistakes and atoned for them like King Lear; his ideas, on the other hand, were successful, like a zigzag road that eventually does reach the summit of the mountain of taboos and commandments, but the satisfaction of knowing that he was a good doctor was denied Freud. The "worthier alternative" of his research came between him and the ordinary world. The greatness of this great man, the prophetic quality of this prophet, resided in his relentless pursuit of what was "worthier." That he was right can be seen in the amount of tragic experience he accumulated, and not only later when he was old and ill. The opposite of tragedy, such as he experienced and expounded, is the banal.

Appendix

Freud, Oedipus—and Then?

In the first chapter of his book *Angel in Armor*, the American anthropologist, sociologist, and political scientist, Ernest Becker, who died young, writes, "Remarkable things can be surely done with Freud's theory of the Oedipus complex.... Scientists of man of the future will marvel at the perversity of his own ingenuity, even while they give him credit for his true greatness. The judgment on him may well be similar to that on Charles Fourier: a powerful genius, sound in his basic ideas and intuitions, unbelievably liberating to the human spirit, and yet incredibly inverted upon the formulations of his own closed theory. The problem of Freud, as of all science, is to keep what is basic, while breaking out of the confines of a too narrow and constricting general theory."[479] The subtitle of Becker's book is *A Post-Freudian Perspective on the Nature of Man*.

From the very beginning, it was in the nature of the psychoanalytic movement to see its own progress in the reduction or elimination of the father figure of Freud—which in itself is an Oedipal attitude. The main current split up into smaller "away-from-Vienna" movements, which were all the more radical the greater the geographical distance between the original center and the new doctrine. Most of all they would have liked to retain the apostolic succession but without the pope. The elemental power of its founder can be seen in the contradictory multiplicity of sects and conclaves. Psychoanalysis has its gnostics and Manichaeans, its phenomenologists and Existentialists, its Old Analysts and its Reformed Church, the latter not least in America. And again and again, it is over the tragic figure of Oedipus that the paths followed by the schools and movements diverge and turn into crossroads.

There is also social reality. Alexander Mitscherlich has spoken of the overorganized society of the present as a "society without the father," citing Karl Bednarik's 1952 study according to which the young worker in industrial society has "turned into a son who is perpetually only demanding and taking. The only reason why he is not totally indifferent to his father, who has receded very far into the distance, is that he has to listen to his injunctions and decrees in order to be able to evade them."[480]

One could take this further and say that in the affluent society the role of the father has largely fallen to the state. In his *Moles*, Günter Eich has resolutely articulated his Oedipal feelings toward this father image: "Nothing is more repugnant to me than my parents. Wherever I go they pursue me. No removal, no foreign travel helps. As soon as I've found a chair the door opens and one of the two stares in, Father State or Mother Nature."[481] The role of the Great Mother will be discussed in due course; as far as Father State is concerned, it is the target of its subjects' dissatisfaction and resistance—they want to cease being subjects—which, however, apart from criminal borderline cases, find no direct release. We are dealing with a metaphor, if a rather lame one. The result is confusion, diffusion, well-aimed random blows.

Without Laius, no Oedipus; without the tensions between father and son, no Oedipus complex. That is why the periodical *Psyche*, whose editor is Alexander Mitscherlich, redefined Freud's Oedipus complex: "The Oedipus complex is not a 'central concern of orthodox psychoanalysis,' rather the 'Oedipus complex' is the core of what is nowadays understood in the social sciences as the 'process of socialization': the critical moment in the individual's transition from animal to cultural existence which reproduces the history of the development of the human species."[482]

With that, however, psychoanalysis has unquestionably been transformed from an individual to a collective psychological method. Its purpose is no longer to fathom the secret of human beings and their dreams but to explore the structures of society at that, admittedly "critical," moment when the socially definable group emerges from the amorphous horde. The aim of psychoanalysi—to cure individuals—is now understood to be the awakening or strengthening of their ability to adapt to the all but fatherless society.

What is to be understood by the "process of socialization" is clearly shown in the American folk song telling the story of the black laborer John Henry, the central verses of which run as follows:

> Cap'n says to John Henry,
> "Gonna bring me a steam drill 'round,
> Gonna take that steam drill out on the job,
> Gonna whop that steel on down,
> Lawd, Lawd, gonna whop that steel on down."

> John Henry told his cap'n,
> Said, "A man ain't nothin' but a man,

And befo' I let that steam drill beat me down
I'd die with this hammer in my hand,
Lawd, Lawd, I'd die with my hammer in my hand."[483]

Set to an originally Scottish folk tune, the ballad is in the language of the Negro spirituals, but as a whole it touches on the spirit of the American pioneer days, of what, with a complete lack of understanding of the nature of myth, is called the *American myth*. As the hero of this *myth*, the African American John Henry has come to stand for the population of the USA as a whole; the editors simply call the ballad "the greatest."[484] For all their differences in social structure, both black and white can see themselves in this piece of folklore, namely in the confrontation between individual and social power, in the "process of socialization." The foreman tells John Henry, whose job it is to bore holes for dynamite in the Big Bend Tunnel, to use the steam drill. John Henry's reply—he did actually die in the Big Bend Tunnel—represents the heroic revolt of the laborer which encapsulates that "critical moment in the individual's transition from animal to cultural existence," from the horde to the group, into which the editors of *Psyche* had transformed the Oedipus complex. This is quite apart from the fact that the opposition of hammer and steam drill reflects the resistance of man using his natural strength to the advance of industrialization.

Erik H. Erikson, the grand old man of American psychoanalysis, who has never denied his direct descent from Freud's school, sees in John Henry "one of the occupational models of the stray men on the expanding frontier who face new geographic and technological worlds as men without a past .... These workmen," Erikson goes on, "developed to its very emotional and societal limits the image of the man without roots, the motherless man, the womanless man." This image, a primal image, was, says Erikson, to be found in many variations all over the world, but "their common denominator is the freeborn child who becomes an emancipated adolescent and a man who refutes his father's conscience and his nostalgia for a mother, bowing only to cruel facts and fraternal discipline."[485] So the "fatherless society" had already broken out in the murk of the *American myth*.

But what of the foreman, whom the singer calls captain as if he were master of a corps of soldiers and who is the leader of a group who submit to him in "fraternal discipline?" It is he who wants to bring in the steam drill, thus making the white man representative of the industrial society against which the rugged individualist John

Henry defends himself. Can we not discern here yet another Oedipal conflict, the "freeborn" son against the servant of the machine who is both the free man's captain and his father? Of course in this interpretation, the "child of nature" ("A man ain't nothin' but a man") would embody a culturally and biologically earlier stage of human history than his "father," the captain of the gang; in terms of human development, the roles of "father" and "son" are reversed.

Moreover, the editors point out that black laborers such as John Henry saw their hammers as phallic symbols which they were unwilling to allow to be taken away from them.[486] This does not fit in very well with their position as "womanless men" and turns the "fatherly" words of the foremen into a threat against the very center of their existence. Both the "Cap'n" and John Henry call on the "Lawd"—four times in the ten lines of the two verses—a cliché, to be sure, and yet, placed at the beginning of the final lines of the verses, it stands out too much to be a mere filler. Both the plate layer and the foreman swear by the Lord God and, in swearing, they call on him. Heaven—where, according to another spiritual, "the saints go marchin' in"—opens up above the railroads and steam drills. The free society of brothers on the border of the brutal reality of America seems not to have been able to manage entirely without the Heavenly Father.

Erikson himself has pointed out that every trait in the national character of America, as in the national identity of other peoples, has a corresponding opposite which is equally characteristic.[487] The "freeborn child," the man without roots, without parents, has its correlative in the extreme significance the figure of the mother has assumed at the center of the American family, the phenomenon called "momism." Since the days of the frontier, when women possessed rarity value, the mother has developed into a central figure, becoming the conduit for cultural values and the object of a secularized cult of the Virgin Mary.

Repressions on the predominantly Protestant continent may have been sublimated in this cult of the mother. But "momism" was not a phenomenon restricted to a particular confession, it was a product of the cultural climate prevailing on that continent. The mothers of the "Brahmins" from Boston were just as much exposed to it as the black mothers of the slums. Irish and Italian Catholics were caught up in it with extreme intensity, and the most devastating parody of this modern matriarchy was written by a Jew, Philip Roth, in his satire, *Portnoy's Complaint.* In it the hero says of Sophie Portnoy, the mother who has condemned him to a life sentence of submission, "It was my mother who could do anything, who herself had to admit that it might even be that she was actually too good. And could a small child with my intelligence, with my powers of observation, doubt that this was so? ... What a radar on that woman! And this is before radar! The energy on her! The thoroughness! For mistakes she checked my sums; for holes my socks; for dirt my nails, my neck, every seam and crease of my body.... Devotion is just in her blood."[488]

Naturally Sophie Portnoy's husband, a little insurance agent with abundant stomach trouble, is nothing more than the moon which takes its pale light from the central sun of this mother. The matriarchy, too, is a "fatherless society." It is not only through her boundless, and therefore devastating, self-sacrifice, which comes very close to emotional blackmail, that the mother rules and ties her children to her, her sons above all, but also through the principle of permissiveness, of "if you feel like it, do it." The only limits to her lenience are economic ones, often not even those. In one thing, though, she is inflexible: Erikson talks of her "determined hostility to any free expression of the most naive forms of sensual and sexual pleasure on the part of her children, and she makes it clear enough that the father, when sexually demanding, is a bore."[489] The natural consequence of this is that the children, daughters as well as sons, indulge in sexually explicit language, larding their speech with four-letter words. Philip Roth's *Portnoy* is pornography, a parody the purpose of which is to put an end to all pornography. The hero starts and finishes on his psychoanalyst's couch. The taboo on all sexual matters, that his mother has wished on him, has a neurotic character and, like all neuroses, undertones of tragedy. Oedipus is crippled by Jocasta.

***

Erikson's book appeared in 1950. A new generation has made its entrance since then, and almost made its exit, too, a generation which has radically broken the models of American identity developed by Erikson. It is the youth of the *generation gap*, which has consciously and deliberately cut the link between the generations, which even before had not been very reliable in a country so hooked on innovation and youth. During the Vietnam War, the universities were transformed into battle sites. A Pandora's box was opened and America's unsolved problems poured out; partly they were seized on by young people, partly they seized the new generation, taking possession of them to the point of obsession: the question of African Americans and the problem of other minorities, the position of women, the demand for social reform, now on the Russian, now on the Chinese model. Mixed forms presented themselves; the spirit of the rugged individualist John Henry is still alive in the communes, which appear like pre-industrial islands in the highly technological environment. The collision between the two worlds creates the contradiction of which the inhabitants of the communes remain consciously unconscious. Irony is far from them; the *generation gap* is no abyss, let alone a tragic one.

I found the motto of this generation gap inscribed in bold white strokes on the wall of a house between Berkeley and Oakland:

> Love without reserve!
> Enjoy without restraint!
> Live without dead time!

It sounds innocent enough, especially in a society whose members' right to pursue happiness is enshrined in the preamble to the Declaration of Independence, almost making it a duty. However, what this Declaration, a product of the Enlightenment, understood by happiness is anything but a lack of reserve or restraint; nor can one maintain that the young generation has particularly distinguished itself by respect for the Constitution of the United States of America. Yet even this moral about-face is a result of the utopian optimism which is a determining factor in the American temperament. They kick over the traces with self-assurance, provide a model of excess, and pay homage to violence. Even the commune of Charles Manson, who murdered the actress Sharon Tate and a number of her friends in Hollywood, was not free from the pathology of apocalyptic messianism. Optimism alone does not make people happy. As long as this generation can chase after happiness (and, as Brecht said, "Happiness follows on behind") and devote itself to ever more bizarre activities, everything is all right. Otherwise, they will get bored. Boredom is seen as unhappiness and is thus the opposite of happiness. That the constitution—of human beings, not of the United States—can have an unhappy, sometimes even tragic quality is something these young people are totally unaware of. They are not on that wavelength. Boredom, on the other hand, arouses feelings of guilt, which they shift onto the institutions they believe they have sinned against—the prevailing social order, the state. Boredom as the psychological motivation for murder, bombs, homicide.

What is striking about the inscription on the wall of the house between Berkeley and Oakland is that its commandments are basically negative—no line without "without." This is something it largely shares with the Ten Commandments. But there is one more "without" that distinguishes this generation: it is a generation without tragedy. An interpretation of the three lines of which the inscription consists will serve as proof that, the post-oedipal generation has abolished tragedy, along with Oedipus.

"Love without reserve." That sounds like romantic and unconditional devotion, but this generation has taken over their mothers' permissiveness and expanded it into programmatic promiscuity. Not that this did not exist before, only now it has taken on the character of an ideology; it is the done thing, lack of restraint with regard to morality is considered good form, a radical approach to personal relationships has become part of the demands of progress and freedom. And, as Erich Heller has demonstrated,[490] it is our sense of shame that has paid the price. The way that sexual freedom has become programmatic is highlighted by the fact that liberalism, the Civil Rights Movement, has pledged itself to a liberalized relationship between the sexes. The pill does its bit as well. What was once seen as scandalous has now become a plain matter of course, not requiring justification.

Romeo and Juliet no longer have to die. The plague of enmity infecting both their houses does not concern them any more. Their fathers no longer have any say. And even if, by some miracle, they did have some say, an accommodation could always be reached. The bottle Gretchen begs from the woman beside her in church now does not contain smelling salts but the pill she has long since become accustomed to. Even Blanche DuBois in Tennessee Williams' *A Streetcar Named Desire*[491] would probably not have to end up in the lunatic asylum now—the psychiatrist's couch would do just as well. Disaster is avoidable, at least potentially; fate no longer has an individual but a collective face; and desire no longer seeks eternity but insists on immediate satisfaction.

Now it is of course not the case that with this generation the earth has become a paradise where the lion is on peaceable terms with the lamb. There are still ups and downs, as in the case of Patty Hearst, the daughter of an upper-class family who was kidnapped by a radical group, the Symbionese Liberation Army, and thereupon declared her solidarity with the radical aims and methods of her kidnappers. But only the sentimental parents of the girl in their distress could label the incident a tragedy. A tragic situation arises when an individual has to choose between two impossibilities. The fact that, in the same breath as they called the occurrence a tragedy, the upper-class parents tried to lure the girl back with a "Come home, all is forgiven" shows—how could it be otherwise?—that the fateful, compulsive nature of tragedy was a closed book to them. And the girl herself? She stayed missing, in the underground with which she had made common cause. For all the horror of the episode—the discovery, surrounding, and annihilation of the gang of murderers, followed by a nation glued to their television screens—the whole was impelled not by the implacable logic of tragedy but by the arbitrariness of the absurd.

In fact, the absurd is one of the masks in which American life sees itself—and by no means on the stage alone. Things collide, but there is no tragic spark to set off a catastrophe from these things, merely the amazement of the absurd at its own caprices and the laughter of the void at itself. From the very beginning, the fall of President Nixon belonged to the theater of the absurd, not tragedy. Even the White House was subject to the law of the absurd, which states that at any time and in any place both everything and its opposite is possible.

One thing that distinguishes the older from the younger generation is that the latter is only very rarely aware of its own absurdity. From the "Flower People" to the "Jesus Freaks," everything is in deadly earnest. The former went for a combination of European *art nouveau* and oriental elements, which was not difficult since *art nouveau* in its origins was profoundly influenced by motifs from the Far East. The latter, the "Jesus Freaks," have rediscovered the spirit of the original Christian communities; in the oratorio *Jesus Christ Superstar* the guitars twang as if they were the harp on which King David once played. Music is the means of communication of this generation; children's crusades are undertaken to jazz festivals, and the jazz sometimes ends, as does Beethoven's Ninth, with a general gesture in the direction of the brotherhood of man. Some pieces, for example, the songs of Bob Dylan—he took his surname from the poet Dylan Thomas—capture the wistfulness of this muddled generation, the melancholy of a world void of meaning, and the exhaustion after a night of love without reserve.

"Enjoy without restraint" is the anything-goes *carpe diem et noctem* particular to this generation. The limits of consciousness are consciously pushed back with drugs until everything is an inebriated swirl of color and smoke. Self-contradictory as this generation is by its very nature, they reject the oldest and most natural stimulant in intercourse between the sexes—clothing. The dominant style is androgynous. Boyish girls and young men with ponytails reveal an extraordinary assimilation of the sexes to each other. The difference between the sexes disappearing? That is contradicted by the beards of all kinds with which young—and not so young—men screen their faces. And, indeed, any reduction of differences between the sexes is called into question by a "feminine mystique," which has even less to do with mysticism than the "American Myth" has with myth. What it refers to, rather, is one of the phenomena accompanying the radical wing of the American women's movement, the women's liberation movement. Often, though not always, Marx goes hand in hand with Mother Earth; when he does, the double commitment results in twice the aggression: the barriers convention has placed around intercourse between the sexes become barricades to be taken by storm. By storm? Surely not in a storm of passion? Phyllis Chesler, a psychologist and feminist, writes about her—admittedly still utopian—societies of Amazons: "If women take their bodies seriously—and ideally we should," where the question is what this might be, beyond the normal extent of taking anything seriously, "then its *full* expression, in terms of pleasure, maternity and physical strength, seems to fare better when *women* control the means of production and reproduction." (The argument is weakened by the blurring of the boundary between the "means of production," an economic concept, and the "means of reproduction," basically the biological equipment.) "From this point of view," the psychologist goes on, "it is simply not in women's interest to support patriarchy or even a fabled 'equality' with men. That women do so is more a sign of powerlessness than of any biologically based 'superior' wisdom."[492] It is the claim to power heralding a modern race of would-be Amazons and Maenads.

So the great Earth Mother is called upon when it is a matter of achieving equality of opportunity for women in employment. The maenadic frenzy of the matriarchy forms a suitable background: Mother Nature no longer lames her sons, she consumes them. It is striking that a feminist like Phyllis Chesler talks about equality between the sexes as if it were a fable. It is either seen as a political demand which can never be set too high, or it represents revenge and punishment for the thousands of years of patriarchal rule. Both the substance and the tone of such threats have seriously undermined the trust between the sexes. Where the aim is to prove something—in this case the superiority of women—even the most unrestrained enjoyment comes up against its natural restraint. Whereas it used to be the woman who said no to the man, now it is the man who says sorry to the woman.

The Dionysiac, an experience which is on offer on every street corner in the form of pornography, counts for little with the new matriarchy. Bacchus is overshadowed by Demeter, the great Earth Mother, all-comprehending, all-forgiving, all-dominating, all-fertilizing, and fertilized by all. The servants she sends out are women of power, smart and adroit, energetic and pugnacious, and completely uncompromising—a new race.

Bachofen said of the original state of matriarchy, "As many myths demonstrate, for this stage of the force of nature the mother is also seen as the spouse, even the daughter, of the man who comes to fertilize her: all the generations of men in turn visit and fertilize the maternal earth-substance."[493] And Jocasta in *Oedipus* said,

> "Many a man ere now in dreams hath lain
> With her who bare him,"[494]

though it was the censorship of Athens' patriarchal constitution that confined the incest to a dream. But this does not mean that the enjoyment without restraint, which the post-Oedipal generation enjoins on itself, would necessarily include incest, nor that dreams such as Jocasta describes are no longer dreamt. What we are concerned with, however, is Oedipus and the tragedy he embodies. His search for identity takes place within himself. As soon as he has tracked himself down, he performs his self-sacrifice and puts out his eyes. The tragedy in this is lost to the post-Oedipal generation. The search for one's own self—a classic example is Freud's search, in the course of which he discovered the Oedipus complex—has given way to the discovery of new social systems. Sociology, too, begins in dreams, and it is precisely those dreams that drive the new generation. They are dreams that are collective and utopian, not individual and tragic. And it is precisely these dreams that promise enjoyment without restraint; indeed, they are based on it. Barriers fall most quickly when "I" becomes "We."

"Live without dead time." "Dead" is an in-word among the younger generation at the moment. It means something like "empty" or "boring." Death itself is dead and buried. The emptiness and boredom of death has become an embarrassment which is pushed out of the way. The ceremonies for the dead are held in chapels, especially hired for the occasion, which look like airport lounges and, just like them, have sweet music washing through them. Death is probably the only event from which the older and the younger generation turn their eyes away together.

There is, however, *one* kind of death which has made a deep impression on the unconscious of all living people. If the pill has made an immense contribution to the change in the way the sexes see themselves and each other, then the shadow that fell on Hiroshima has changed the way human beings see themselves and their end, a change that comes close to a mutation. This shadow even falls on the dreams which the post-Oedipal generation dreams of a new society and its forms. It has abolished Ernst Bloch's principle of hope.

Sigmund Freud was aware of this fifteen years earlier. "Men," he wrote at the end of *Civilization and Its Discontents*, "have gained control over the forces of nature to such an extent that with their help they would have no difficulty in exterminating one another to the last man. They know this, and hence comes a large part of their current unrest, their unhappiness and their mood of anxiety. And now it is to be expected that the other of the two 'Heavenly Powers,' eternal Eros, will make an effort to assert himself in the struggle with his equally immortal adversary. But who can foresee with what success and with what result?"[495]

The only possible answer to Freud's anything-but-rhetorical question is that less than half a century later both the pleasure principle and the death principle have been subjected to such erosion as to come dangerously close to abolishing the old image of mankind. Lust is naked and filmable, the possibility of mass annihilation is consigned to the unconscious, but it is a permanent fixture there. The mystery of love and death, and the veil of modesty which both spread over themselves, has gone; "a day without illusion has dawned."[496] Death has lost its sting, the grave its victory; all that is left is the doom of a collective end to humanity that is beyond the wit of the boldest fantasies to portray and therefore powerless as an individual threat.

People's disturbed relationship to their existence and their end, their sense of being entirely superfluous, necessarily leads to acts of violence, as happens above all in the big cities and there in particular in the racial conflict between black and white. What is remarkable is that these acts of violence are often committed without respect to the person attacked, that the aggression surfaces at random, unless it is the color of the victim that provoked it. What is also remarkable is the complete indifference of passers-by, who do not even stop to help the victim. Perhaps this conceals a tiny remnant of all-too-well-concealed shame.

A complement and consequence of this, at least among young

people, is a feeling one could describe as a kind of secularized
stoicism. A sixteen-year-old boy, faced with a life-and-death operation
on the brain, can write:

> Life goes on without you,
> a small minority know you.
> But when you die,
> your ideas,
> thoughts,
> feelings,
> loves and happiness
> linger on within many.
>
> Many people whom I don't know
> pray for me.
> That touches me deeply.
> to love a man,
> to pray for a man,
> to feel for a man,
> whom they don't know,
> is more than I can express in words.

What is seeking expression here is a kind of substitute immortality
in the spirit of a group, which becomes a mystical, self-transcending
concept. (The group does not know the dead man who lives on in its
memory.) This fearlessness in the face of death, which is interwoven
with a good deal of the general devaluation of individual death, is
presented as a model to the community, whose love, prayers, and
feelings support the sixteen-year-old "man" they do not know, enfold
him, one might say, in his hour of need. The "man" remains
anonymous, his feelings hidden. What is impressive about these lines
is their matter-of-fact tone, which is impersonal and therefore
exemplary. He accepts his fate in as untragic manner as possible,
without any talk of guilt and retribution; he regards his affliction as a
vicissitude which could befall any other member of the community
praying for him. Because life is absurd and therefore unpredictable, it
sent Stephen to the operating table—from which, moreover, he got up
fit and well.

In *The Interpretation of Dreams* Freud said, "King Oedipus, who slew
his father Laius and married his mother Jocasta, merely shows us the
fulfillment of our childhood desire."[497] Bound up with this wish

fulfillment are powerful feelings of guilt, feelings of guilt which in the past contributed a good deal to mankind's fear of death. Having freed themselves from the basic Oedipal conflict, the post-Oedipal generation is also spared the fear of death. In return, they have laid themselves open to the "soup-everlasting"[498] of boredom. They are not even aware of being sent out into a world without meaning or purpose; they have become accustomed to it; it has sunk to the depths of their consciousness, where, at most, it fools around making absurd jokes. They can even, as the example of the *Jesus Freaks* shows, go to church and pay effusive homage to a heavenly father—or is Jesus their brother? But just as they like to prescribe their own marriage rites, they also refuse to celebrate death as a tragic ritual. America is a young country; its inhabitants are *novarum rerum cupidi* as a matter of principle. Every generation starts afresh; history has never been a force to shape consciousness, apart from the old families in the South and on the East Coast. Everything is geared to a future which has no place for the death of the individual. Thus, the cult of the dead is seen as a relic from the past, like the belief in ghosts, and, like the latter, produces a mild frisson in semi-pornographic films such as *The Exorcist*. Those left behind do not need comforting; their eyes are fixed on the future, on the community, however vague and mystical that term might be. In brief, even death has been socialized; at best, it is a social affair that one gets out of in as dignified a manner as possible.

Now one might object that the preceding generations did not exactly celebrate their death. Arthur Miller's *Death of a Salesman* portrays the tawdriness of death among the middle classes, just as, on the other side of the Atlantic and twenty years earlier, Franz Werfel's *Death of a Poor Man* had done. And yet Arthur Miller has endowed Willy Loman's deathbed with all the arcana of a paranormal experience, orchestrating it as a mystery:

> "Willy (*uttering a gasp of fear, whirling about as if to quiet her*): Sh! (*He turns around as if to find his way; sounds, faces, voices, seem to be swarming in upon him and he flicks at them, crying, 'Sh! Sh!' Suddenly music, faint and high, stops him. It rises in intensity, almost to an unbearable scream. He goes up and down on his toes, and rushes off around the house.*) Shhh!
> Linda: Willy?
> (*There is no answer.*)"[499]

That is still a tragedy, if one set in the petty bourgeoisie. (Accordingly, the relationship of the sons, Biff and Happy, to Willy Loman is still charged with all the tensions of the Oedipus complex.) Even the modest funeral rites Arthur Miller accords his dubious hero are fundamentally alien to the new generation. For them, individual heroism, however dubious it might be, is no longer *relevant*, to use one of the shibboleths with which they distance themselves from the older generation. The mass destruction which looms over their horizon like a black cloud demands collective solutions, not a dwelling on individual fates. They have made themselves at home in the atomic apocalypse; what they have left in the way of dreams and wishes is a life without boredom, without emptiness, a life without dead time.

***

In the second of his *Three Essays on the Theory of Sexuality*, Freud talks of infantile sexual impulses, which during periods of sexual latency are diverted from their sexual use, continuing, "Historians of civilization appear to be at one in assuming that powerful components are acquired for every kind of cultural achievement by this diversion of sexual instinctual forces from sexual aims and their direction to new ones—a process which deserves the name of 'sublimation.'"[500] The post-Oedipal generation has extended Freud's pleasure principle so far beyond its limits that one can no longer talk of either pleasure or principle. Pleasure which has been excreted cannot be sublimated. Something similar could be said of Freud's death principle. Otto Rank[501] and, following him, Norman O. Brown[502] were of the opinion that it was not the pleasure principle but the death principle which, repressed, was the basis of all cultural achievements. But it is not the repressed, it is the sublimated death instinct on which culture is founded. Even the sublimated death instinct is not strong enough in itself to bear the edifice whose arches and vaults are due to the tension between Eros and Thanatos. It is the tension of tragedy (non-dialectical, since the emotions and nerves are involved as well as thought) which produced *Hamlet*, *Don Giovanni*, and the late self-portraits of Rembrandt. Hamlet's "Ripeness is all" expresses a sublime sublimation; even as a linguistic image, the phrase is a strange weave of growing and dying (as of a fruit, for example). The end of *Don Giovanni*, of which Eduard Mörike said, "As if coming from distant galaxies, the notes swoop down through the blue night from silver trombones, ice-cold, cutting to the very marrow, to the core of being,"[503] certainly did not derive from repression; it is the old tension between the Don's lust and his descent into death and hell which, in Mörike's words, is resolved in the silver tones of the trombones. Body and mind, "the very marrow, the core of being," created this tension and are part of it. It is the same tension as that between passion and its withering which breathes into the paintings of Rembrandt's old age a life defiantly accepting the inevitable. It was also this tension in which both the myth of Oedipus and Freud's interpretation of it presented themselves, in which the scientist's intuition and his scientific approach held each other in a precarious balance.

When the death instinct alone is active, repressed and not sublimated, it tends to lead to neuroses, to what Ernest Becker in his "post-Freudian perspective on the nature of man" called "paranoia." Becker says, "The more we study man the more the striking realization dawns that what we call perversity is really an impoverished poetry, a creative ingenuity from a desperate position. And this is, after all, a definition of even the best poetry: a cry, a reaching out, an attempt to make sense, with patterns of words, of the confines of the human condition. Nowhere is this more clear than in the behavior we call paranoia." [504]

Now the connection between genius and madness is not a discovery of Becker's. But the anthropologist, who sees paranoia as the "most intense and focused functioning of the mind," also observes "that everyone is paranoid at some time or other—if he has any sensitivity at all. And in our modern world one mild paranoid fantasy per week would be about par for the average person; and to have no paranoid fantasies at al, should certainly mark one off as an uninteresting clod."[505]

Ernest Becker knew what he was talking about. As a university professor in America and Canada, he had enough contact with students. His observations assume the egalitarian democracy of abnormal behavior. The generation of love without reserve and enjoyment without restraint can easily lose control, especially when they gather together for communal events such as mass jazz concerts. The alienation which is rife in middle-class American society, as it is elsewhere, is not quite sufficient to explain this abnormal behavior. Immense repressions are at work, without the outlet of sublimation in cultural creativity. It is as if the fatherless generation were looking for the image of the father at least, like the European Expressionists, in order to send him out into the desert as a scapegoat. They find him in the person of Indian sages, gurus who teach transcendental meditation and other things; they go in for yoga. All this is seen primarily as technique, but it has the aura of a doctrine that brings healing, if not salvation.[506] They pick up the crumbs from the tables of exotic countries, though nothing could be farther from their thoughts than to sacrifice to their gods. Exposed to a world which revolves eccentrically, without a past and averse to any historical consciousness, even alienated from the history of their own childhood, matter-of-fact to the point of simple-mindedness, craving highs, this generation is heading for a future, for new forms of communal living, in which they cannot quite believe, under the shadow cast by the great bomb.

The paranoia to which this generation has an academic right at least once a week expresses itself in an all-too-obvious lack of precisely that ability to *relax* that earlier generations regarded as the ideal and keyword of their existence. On this continent, relaxation was seen as a guarantee, so to speak, that the world was in order, that the happiness they were officially enjoined to pursue was attainable. The post-Oedipal generation has completely lost this ability to relax. And who can blame them? Already separated from the blessings of catharsis by worlds of tradition, the *ennui* the young fear more than death is the precise opposite of any kind of purgation of the emotions. (That this *ennui* drove Baudelaire and Edgar Alan Poe to drink, drugs, and death is something they are largely unaware of, given their rejection of all historical consciousness.) Catharsis occurs when the spark of tragedy ignites (even if, as in the theater, only vicariously), passions discharge, and the atmosphere is cleared. An echo of this can be found in the psychiatric practices which try to get patients to release their suffering in a primal scream. But that too is technique rather than tragedy; all that "clearing the atmosphere" means to the younger generation is ridding the air of the exhaust fumes from the cars they are driving. They are a technological generation, even where they despise technology, conceived and born without tragedy. What does it matter that today many of them have come to terms with an American society which has been completely disillusioned by the Watergate scandal and identify with it, for worse rather than for better? That the libraries are crowded, the ringleaders of yesterday's revolt have become today's model students and yuppies? What has happened goes too deep and is of too great consequence to be reversed from one decade to the next. And perhaps, if the generation gap, which still operates, really does have the nature of a mutation, it is the lack of any relationship to the tragic which distinguishes the younger generation. The shadow of Oedipus no longer falls across their road through life, and it is not a crossroads.

Notes

[1] Ernst Kris, "Zur Psychologie älterer Biographik" in *Imago*, XXI (1935), pp. 320-344; p. 323. Translation by M. M.

[2] Ibid., p. 341.

[3] Ibid., p.342. Italics in original.

[4] See Ernst Robert Curtius, *European Literature and the Latin Middle Ages*, tr. Willard R. Trask, London: Routledge & Kegan Paul, 1953.

[5] Kris, op. cit., p. 343.

[6] Thomas Mann, "Freud und die Zukunft" in T. M., *Gesammelte Werke*, vol. IX, Frankfurt/M.: Fischer, 1960, p. 492. Translation by M. M.

[7] Ibid., p. 496.

[8] The title of Hanns Sachs, *Gemeinsame Tagträume*, Leipzig etc.: Internationaler psychoanalytischer Verlag, 1924 (= Imago-Bücher V).

[9] See, for example, Heinz Politzer, *Hatte Ödipus einen Ödipus-Komplex?*, Munich: Piper, 1974, p. 43-44.

[10] Sophocles, *King Oedipus* (line 1525), in Sophocles, *The Seven Plays in English Verse*, tr. Lewis Campbell, London: Oxford University Press (*The World's Classics*), 1911, p. 128.

[11] Ernest Jones, *Sigmund Freud. Life and Work* (3 vols.), London: Hogarth Press, 1953-1957, vol. 2, p. 15.

[12] Cf. Ernest Becker, *The Denial of Death*, New York: Free Press, 1973, p. 112.

[13] Virgil, *Aeneis*, Book VII, line 312.

[14] Sigmund Freud, *The Interpretation of Dreams*, tr. and ed. by James Tyson; in *The Standard Edition of the Complete Psychological Works of Sigmund Freud*, vol. 5, London: Hogarth Press, 1953, p. 608. Further references to Freud's works will give the title, sometimes in shortened form, followed by SF/CPW plus the volume and page number.

[15] *Letters of Sigmund Freud 1873-1939*, ed Ernst L. Freud, tr. Tania and James Stern, London: Hogarth Press, 1963, p. 255 f. Translation adapted by M. M.

[16] *Dreams,* SF/CPW vol. 5, p. 608.

[17] *Dreams*, SF/CPW, vol. 4, p. 262

[18] *The Complete Letters of Sigmund Freud to Wilhelm Fließ 1887-1904*, tr. and ed. Jeffrey Moussaieff Masson, Cambridge, Mass: Harvard University Press, 1985, p. 268.

[19] Jones, vol. 1, p. 14.

[20] *Dreams*, SF/CPW, vol. 5, p. 459.

[21] Ibid., vol. 4, p. 247.

[22] Ibid., vol. 4, pp. 262-263

[23] *New Introductory Lectures on Psycho-analysis,* SF/CPW vol. 22, p. 80.

[24] *Dreams,* SF/CPW, vol. 5, p. 615 .

[25] *Dreams,* SF/CPW vol. 4, pp. 261-262. Politzer's italics.

[26] Sophocles, *King Oedipus* (l. 980 ff.), op. cit., p. 112.

[27] *Dreams,* SF/CPW vol. 4, p 264.

[28] Sophocles, *King Oedipus* (l. 1490 ff.), op. cit., p. 127.

[29] *Dreams,* SF/CPW, vol. 4, p. 264.

[30] *Dreams,* SF/CPW, vol. 4, p. 264-265.

[31] Shakespeare, *Hamlet,* Act III, i, 60-68.

[32] *Hamlet,* Act III, i, 70-74.

[33] Shakespeare, *Sonnet LXVI.*

[34] *Hamlet,* Act III, i, 83.

[35] Shakespeare, *Julius Caesar,* Act I, ii, 193.

[36] Erich Heller, *The Artist's Journey into the Interior and Other Essays,* New York: Random House, [1959, 62, 64] 1965, p. 142.

[37] *Hamlet,* Act III, i, 84-88.

[38] *Dreams,* SF/CPW, vol. 4, p. 265.

[39] *Dreams,* SF/CPW, vol. 4, p. 265.

[40] *Hamlet,* Act V, i, 279 -280.

[41] *Hamlet,* Act III, i, 79-80.

[42] *Dreams,* SF/CPW, vol. 4, p. 265.

[43] *Hamlet,* Act V, ii, 301.

[44] Thomas Mann, "Tonio Kröger" in T. M., *Death in Venice, Tonio Kröger and Other Writings,* tr. David Luke, Ed. Frederick A. Lubich, *The German Library,* vol. 63, New York: Continuum, 1999, p. 25.

[45] Ibid., p. 22.

[46] *Hamlet,* Act III, i, 144.

[47] Heller, *The Artist's Journey,* p.145.

[48] Thomas Mann, *Tonio Kröger,* p. 4.

[49] Ibid., p. 29. Italics in original.

[50] Ibid., p. 30.

[51] *Civilization and Its Discontents,* SF/CPW, vol. 21, p. 122.

[52] Thomas Mann, *Tonio Kröger,* p. 55.

[53] Ibid., p. 54.

[54] Ibid., p. 55.

[55] Thomas Mann, "Freud und die Zukunft," in T. M., *Gesammelte Werke,* Bd. VII, pp. 478-501. Translation here by M. M.

[56] Ibid., p. 501. Italics in original.

[57] Erich Heller, *The Ironic German: A Study of Thomas Mann,* Boston, Toronto: Little, Brown and Company, 1958.

[58] Thomas Mann, "Bruder Hitler," in *Gesammelte Werke,* Bd. XII, Frank-

furt/M.: Fischer, 1960, p. 845; translated by M. M. (There is a not very satisfactory translation in Thomas Mann, *Order of the Day: Political Essays and Speeches of Two Decades*, tr. H. T. Lowe-Porter and others, New York: Alfred A Knopf, 1942, p. 153.) Later in Mann's essay on "this rather unpleasant and mortifying brother" (p. 849) he says, "How a person like that must have hated analysis! I have a private suspicion that the fury he put into carrying out the march on a certain capital was basically directed at the old analyst who had his seat there, his real and actual enemy, the philosopher and revealer of neurosis, the great disillusioner, the one who knew about, and told the world about, 'genius.'" (p. 850) The idea that Freud was "unmistakably one of those very Jews whose extermination became [Hitler's] dedicated purpose" is also expressed by Vincent Brome, *Freud and his Early Circle: The Struggles of Psycho-Analysis*, London: Heinemann, 1967, p xi.

[59] *New Introductory Lectures on Psycho-analysis*, SF/CPW, vol. 22, pp. 79-80.

[60] Stanley Edgar Hyman, "Psychoanalysis and the Climate of Tragedy" in: *Freud and the 20th Century*, ed. Benjamin Nelson, London: Allen & Unwin, 1958, p 167. Italics added by H. P. The essay first appeared in the spring of 1956 in the *Partisan Review*.

[61] *New Introductory Lectures on Psycho-analysis*, SF/CPW, vol. 21, p. 64.

[62] *Civilization*, SF/CPW, vol. 21, pp. 64-65. The "somewhat eccentric dramatist" Freud refers to here is Christian Dietrich Grabbe (1801-1836) and his hero Hannibal.

[63] *The Future of an Illusion*, SF/CPW, vol. 21, p. 50.

[64] *Civilization*, SF/CPW, vol. 21, p.74.

[65] Quoted from Becker, *The Denial of Death*, p.105.

[66] *The Future of an Illusion*, SF/CPW, vol. 21, pp. 26-27. Translation modified by M. M.

[67] *Civilization*, SF/CPW, vol. 21, p. 122.

[68] A letter from Emma Jung to Freud in *The Freud/Jung Letters*, ed. William McGuire, tr. Ralph Mannheim and R. F. C. Hull, London: Hogarth Press/ Routledge & Kegan Paul, 1974, p. 456.

[69] For an opposite view, see: David Balkan, *Sigmund Freud and the Jewish Mystical Tradition*, New York: Schocken Books, 1965.

[70] *Letters of Sigmund Freud*, ed. Ernst L. Freud, tr. Tania and James Stern, London: Hogarth Press, 1963, p. 345. Translation adapted by M. M.

[71] Ibid., p. 403. Translation modified by M. M.

[72] See for example Tilman Moser, *Years of Apprenticeship: Fragments of My Psychoanalysis*, intro. Heinz Kohut, tr. Anselm Hollo, New York: Urizen, 1977. Although the author talks of a successful analysis, he is aware that he can never say his neurosis has been completely cured. Both the content and the style of the book confirm this.

[73] Rainer Maria Rilke, *Duino Elegies*, in *The Selected Poetry of Rainer Maria Rilke*,

tr. Stephen Mitchell, London: Pan, 1987, p 151.

[74] See, for example, his letters to Lou Andreas-Salomé (of January 20, 1920) and to Emil, Freiherr von Gebsattel (of January 24, 1920) in *Selected Letters of Rainer Maria Rilke 1902-1926*, tr. R. F. C. Hull, London: Macmillan, 1946, p. 198 ff. and pp. 204-205.

[75] *Analysis Terminable and Interminable*, SF/CPW, vol. 22, p. 243.

[76] See, for example, Bernd Urban, "Die Wunscherfüllung unserer Kindheit. Psychoanalytische-archivalische Notizen zu Hugo von Hofmannsthal's Tragödie *Ödipus und die Sphinx*" in *Psychoanalytische Textinterpretationen*, ed. Johannes Cremerius, Hamburg: Hoffmann und Campe, 1974, pp. 284-302.

[77] See, for example, the letter about his play *Elektra*, written about the same time, to Ernst Hladny; the letter is contained in Hugo von Hofmannsthal, *Briefe 1900-1909*, Vienna: Bermann-Fischer, 1937, pp. 393-394.

[78] Letter of January 1908 to O. A. H. Schmitz, quoted from Rudolf Hirsch, "Zwei Briefe über den *Schwierigen*" in *Hofmannsthal Blätter*, Heft 7 (1971), pp. 70-75; p. 74, footnote 1. Translation by M. M.

[79] Hugo von Hofmannsthal, *Ödipus und der Sphinx. Tragödie in drei Aufzügen* in H. v. H., *Gesammelte Werke, Dramen II*, ed. Herbert Steiner, Frankfurt/M.: Fischer, 1954, pp. 313-314. Translation by M. M.

[80] It has long been the author's desire to write a fictitious reply of Hermann Kafka to his son Franz's letter of indictment of November 1919. This would have shown that the family likeness between father and son was greater than either, father or son, would have liked. In his imaginings, the author never got beyond the first line of the letter. It ran, "Dear Franz, You will tell me your story."

[81] Hugo von Hofmannsthal, *Ödipus und die Sphinx*, p. 296.

[82] Ibid., p. 315.

[83] Gerald S. Stein, "Can the Freudians and the Jungians Close their Ranks" in *San Francisco Chronicle*, 17 November 1974 (This World), p. 26.

[84] *Freud/Jung Letters*, p. 456.

[85] Ibid.

[86] C. G. Jung, "The Psychology of Dementia Praecox," in C. G. Jung: *The Psychogenesis of Mental Disease*, tr. R. F. C. Hull, London: Routledge & Kegan Paul, 1960, p. 4. Translation modified by M. M.

[87] C. G. Jung, *Memories, Dreams, Reflections*, recorded and ed. by Aniela Jaffé, tr. Richard and Clara Winston, London: Collins and Routledge & Kegan Paul, 1963, pp. 147-148. Translation modified by M. M.

[88] Ibid., p. 147.

[89] Ibid., p. 11.

[90] Friedrich Nietzsche, *On the Genealogy of Morality*, ed. Keith Ansell-Pearson, tr. Carol Diethe, Cambridge: CUP, 1994, p. 107 .

[91] Note the repetition of the words in Jung, *Memories*, p. 149, p. 151.

[92] *New Introductory Lectures on Psycho-analysis*, SF/CPW, vol. 22, pp. 79-80. H. P.'s italics. See also the chapter "Sigmund Freud and the Tragedy of Interpretation," footnote 59.

[93] Jung, *Memories,* pp. 148-149.

[94] *Freud/Jung Letters*, p. 95. Italics in original; translation modified by M. M.

[95] Ibid., pp.110-111.

[96] Ibid., p. 121.

[97] See the *Freud/Flieβ Letters.*

[98] *Freud/Jung Letters*, p. 122.

[99] Ibid., pp. 211-212.

[100] Jones, vol. 2 p. 37.

[101] Ibid.

[102] *Freud/Jung Letters*, p. xvi.

[103] Jones, vol. 2, pp. 30-31.

[104] *Freud/Jung Letters*, p. 120.

[105] Jones, vol. 2, p. 38.

[106] *Freud/Jung Letters*, p. 135. Letter to Freud of March 11, 1908.

[107] Ibid., pp. 196-197.

[108] Jones, vol. 2, p. 37.

[109] Jung, *Memories*, p. 146.

[110] *Freud/Jung Letters*, p. 300.

[111] Ibid.

[112] Ibid., pp. 218-219.

[113] Goethe, *Faust,* Part II, Act 2, Scene 2. Translation by M. M.

[114] Paul Roazen, *Freud: Political and Social Thought*, London: Hogarth Press, pp. 177-178.

[115] Becker, *The Denial of Death*, pp. 109-110.

[116] See, for example, the anecdote about their meeting in 1909 when there was a loud report in Freud's bookcase. "I said to Freud: 'There, that is an example of a so-called catalytic exteriorisation phenomenon.' 'Oh come,' he exclaimed. 'That is sheer bosh.' 'It is not,' I replied. 'You are mistaken, Herr Professor. And to prove my point, I now predict that in a moment there will be another loud report!' Sure enough, no sooner had I said the words than the same detonation went off in the bookcase." Jung, *Memories*, p.152.

[117] Jones, vol. 2, p. 67.

[118] Jung, *Memories*, pp. 152-153.

[119] Ibid.

[120] See, for example, Lionel Trilling, "The Freud/Jung Letters," *The New York Times Book Review*, April 21 1974, pp. 32-33.

[121] Jung, *Memories*, p. 153.

[122] Jones, vol. 2, p. 61.

[123] Jones, vol. 1, p. 348.

[124] Jung, *Memories*, p. 153. [Amenophis IV is now generally known as Akhenaton, Amon-hotep as Amenhotep — MM.]

[125] *On the History of Psycho-analysis*, SF/CPW, vol. 14, p. 58. The letter is not contained in Freud's *Correspondence* so must presumably be considered lost.

[126] Jones, vol. 2, p. 165.

[127] *Totem and Taboo*, SF/CPW vol. 13, p. 141.

[128] *Freud/Jung Letters*, p. 517; letter of November 14, 1912.

[129] Freud must have been deeply wounded by the term "modifications." In the passage in *On the History of Psycho-analysis* where he sums up his relationship with Jung, he uses it twice, the second time with the following remark: "It may be said lastly that by his 'modification' of psycho-analysis Jung had given us a counterpart to the famous Lichtenberg knife. He has changed the hilt, and he has put a new blade into it; yet because the same name is engraved on it we are expected to regard the instrument as the original one." SF/CPW, vol. 14, p. 66.

[130] *Freud/Jung Letters*, p. 517.

[131] Trilling, op cit., p. 32.

[132] Jung, *Memories*, p. 153.

[133] Once before Jung had laid Freud on the couch, if only in a metaphorical sense. During their trip to America, Freud had got Jung to analyze one of his dreams. When, for clarification, Jung asked about details of Freud's private life, the latter refused, saying, "But I cannot risk my authority!" Jung recounts this episode in his *Memories*, adding, "The sentence burned itself into my memory; and in it the end of our relationship was already foreshadowed. Freud was placing personal authority above truth." (p. 154) Even before *Memories*, Jung mentioned this traumatic experience in a seminar given in English in Zurich and went on to say, "This experience with Freud ... is the most important factor in my relation to him." *Freud/Jung Letters*, p. 526, fount 3.

[134] *Freud/Jung Letters*, p. 522.

[135] Ibid.

[136] Ibid.

[137] Ibid., p. 457.

[138] Jung, *Memories*, p. 154.

[139] *Freud/Jung Letters*, p. 456. (See also note 9).

[140] For the problem of identification associated with such last words, see the arguments in Ernst Kris' *Zur Psychologie älterer Biographik* as well as footnote 1 in the chapter "Sigmund Freud and the Tragedy of Interpretation."

[141] Horace, *Carminum Liber tertius*, II, 13. (It is sweet and honorable to die for one's country).

[142] Jones, vol. 2, p. 192.

[143] Ibid., p. 66.

[144] Ibid., p. 67.

[145] Ibid.

[146] Ibid.

[147] Ibid. p. 63.

[148] *An Autobiographical Study,* SF/CPW vol. 20, p. 52.

[149] Jones, vol. 2, p. 67

[150] *History of Psychoanalysis,* SF/CPW, vol. 14, p. 58..

[151] *Freud/Jung Letters,* p. 523. Translation amended by MM.

[152] Ibid., p. 529. Letter of December 5, 1912.

[153] Ibid., p. 524.

[154] Jung's suggestion and Freud's rebuke are in the letters of December 3 and 5, which will be dealt with elsewhere. See *Freud/Jung Letters,* pp. 525-527 and pp. 529-530.

[155] *The Complete Correspondence of Sigmund Freud and Ernest Jones 1908-1939* ed. R. Andrew Paskauskas, Cambridge, Mass: Harvard U. P., 1993, p 182.

[156] See Jones, vol. 2, p. 467.

[157] *Three Essays on the Theory of Sexuality,* SF/CPW, vol. 7, p. 143.

[158] Jones, vol. 1, pp. 346-347. Jones also shows that Freud should have named Fließ in third place among the "discoverers" of bisexuality, instead of in sixth.

[159] See also Freud's letter of October 6, 1910, to Ferenczi , quoted in Vincent Brome, *Freud and his Early Circle,* p. 127; also in *The Correspondence of Sigmund Freud and Sándor Ferenczi,* vol. 1: 1908-1914, ed. Eva Brabant and others, transcribed Ingeborg Meyer-Palmedo, tr. Peter T. Hoffer, Cambridge, Mass: The Bellknap Press of Harvard U. P., 1993, p. 221.

[160] Jones, vol. 2, p. 467.

[161] Goethe, *Faust* Part 2, Act 5, Scene 7.

[162] Jones, vol. 2, p. 165.

[163] See Karl Kraus's pun: "In Austria the word for sending a letter is *aufgeben* [= 'to post' and 'to abandon']." Karl Kraus, "Nachts," in K. K., *Die Fackel,* Vienna, 1899-1936, nos. 381-383 (1913), p. 71.

[164] *Freud/Jung Letters,* p. 509. Jung himself was not above postal misunderstandings. The invitation to the Munich meeting which he sent to Jones not only had a misleading address but also gave the wrong date for the meeting. When Jones told Freud about this slip, the latter merely remarked, "A gentleman should not do such things even unconsciously." (Jones, vol. 2, p. 164)

[165] See Jones, vol. 2, pp. 164-165.

[166] *Freud/Jung Letters,* p. 523. Letter of November 29, 1912.

[167] Marthe Robert, *The Psychoanalytic Revolution; Sigmund Freud's Life and Achievement* tr. Kenneth Morgan, London: George Allen & Unwin, 1966, p. 173.

[168] Jones, vol. 2, p. 165.

[169] *Some Character-types met with in Psycho-analyic Work,* SF/CPW, vol. 14, p. 316.

[170] *A Disturbance of Memory on the Acropolis,* SF/CPW, vol. 22, pp. 247-248. Italics in original.

[171] Becker, *The Denial of Death,* p. 101.

[172] Ibid., p. 115.

[173] See Paul Roazen, *Brother Animal. The Story of Freud and Tausk,* New York: Knopf, 1969, and the response of K. H. Eissler, *Talent and Genius. The Fictitious Case of Tausk contra Freud,* New York: Quadrangle, 1971.

[174] Trilling, "The Freud/Jung Letters," p. 32.

[175] *Freud/Jung Letters,* p. 526.

[176] In 1910, Jung had published and article entitled "On the Criticism of Psychoanalysis" in the *Jahrbuch für psychoanalytische und psychopathologische Forschungen* II (pp. 743-746). In it he reproduced verbatim a report by Kurt Mendel of an account of Freud's views; in this report, which had appeared in the *Neurologisches Centralblatt* (Leipzig 1910), he says, "For you are corrupt from birth. Your father had the reputation of being unusually tidy and economical, and the Freudians say he is stubborn because he won't give full acceptance to their teachings. Unusually tidy, economical and stubborn! A hopeless anal-erotic, therefore!... As for your mother, she cleans out the house every four weeks 'Cleaning, and particularly spring-cleaning, is the specific female reaction to suppressed anal eroticism'.... You are a congenital anal-erotic from your father's and your mother's side!" Jung described this as "a valuable contribution to the knowledge of personal undercurrents beneath so-called scientific criticism" and as a "*document humain.*" In C. G. Jung, *Freud and Psychoanalysis, Collected Works* vol. 4, tr. R. F. C. Hull, London: Routledge & Kegan Paul, 1961, p. 76, p. 75.

[177] *Freud/Jung Letters,* pp. 526-527. Translation adjusted by M. M.

[178] Ibid., p. 583.

[179] Ibid., p. 524.

[180] Ibid., p. 526.

[181] Jones, vol. 2, p. 162.

[182] *Freud/Jung Letters,* p. 456.

[183] Jung, *Memories,* p. 162.

[184] C. G. Jung, *Symbols of Transformation: An Analysis of the Prelude to a Case of Schizophrenia,* tr. R. F. C. Hull, London: Routledge & Kegan Paul, 1967 (2nd, revised edition), p. 157.

[185] *Civilization,* SF/CPW, vol. 21, p. 74.

[186] Ibid.

[187] Edward Glover, *Freud or Jung?,* London: Allen & Unwin, 1950, p. 57.

[188] *Freud/Jung Letters,* p. 529.

[189] Ibid., p. 533.

[190] Ibid., pp. 534-535.

[191] Matthew, 5: 7 (King James Version).

[192] C. G. Jung, *Collected Works*, vol. 10, tr. R. F. C. Hull, London: Routledge & Kegan Paul, 1964, p. 166.

[193] Jung, *Memories*, p. 150.

[194] *Freud/Fließ Letters*, p.358; also in Schur: *Living and Dying*, op cit., p 353. Translation amended by MM.

[195] *Dreams*, SF/CPW, vol. 4, p. 264.

[196] *The Uncanny*, SF/CPW, vol. 17, p. 249.

[197] Ibid., p. 252.

[198] Schur, p. 353. [*Ablöse* only means redemption in a financial sense. M. M.]

[199] Goethe, *Maximen und Reflexionen über Kunst*, in Goethe, *Werke*, Weimarer Ausgabe, Bd. 48, p. 205. Translation M. M.

[200] Cf. Max Schur, *Living and Dying*, p. 526.

[201] Goethe, *Faust*, Part II, Act 1, Scene 2.

[202] *The Complete Correspondence of Sigmund Freud and Karl Abraham 1907-1925*, transcribed and ed. Ernst Falzeder, tr. Caroline Schwarzacher and others, London: Karnac, 2002, p. 378.

[203] See Schur, *Living and Dying*, p. 353.

[204] Albert Camus, *Le Mythe de Sisyphe*, Paris: Gallimard, 1942, p. 17.

[205] Jones, vol. 3, p. 95.

[206] Freud, *Letters*, p. 349.

[207] Quoted from Schur, p.360.

[208] *Freud/Fließ Letters*, p. 268.

[209] Quoted in Schur, p. 406.

[210] Thomas Mann, *The Story of a Novel. The Genesis of Doctor Faustus*. Tr. Richard and Clara Winston. New York: Alfred A. Knopf, 1961, pp. 217-218.

[211] Thomas Mann, *Doctor Faustus*, tr. H. T. Lowe-Porter, New York: Alfred A. Knopf, 1948, pp. 466-467.

[212] Source not traced. In the margin H. P. noted, "Sterba Beethoven," presumably a reference to Richard F. Sterba's book *Ludwig van Beethoven und sein Neffe*; a passage corresponding to Politzer's text could not be found there.

[213] Quoted from Jones, vol. 3, p. 20.

[214] Schur, p. 360.

[215] *Freud/Abraham Correspondence*, p. 470.

[216] Schur, p. 364.

[217] Ibid., p. 505.

[218] Ibid., p. 505, footnote 3.

[219] Ibid., p. 412.

[220] *Freud/Fließ Letters*, p. 287.

[221] Schur, pp. 410-411. Italics in original.

[222] Ibid., p. 411.

[223] Ibid., p. 412.

[224] Ibid., p. 410.

[225] *Beyond the Pleasure Principle*, SF/CPW, vol. 18, p. 38. Italics in original.

[226] E.g. Robert, p. 331.

[227] Friedrich Nietzsche, *Beyond Good and Evil*, tr. Helen Zimmern, Edinburgh: T. N. Foulis, 1909, p. 98; (*Complete Works*, vol. 12).

[228] *Beyond the Pleasure Principle*, SF/CPW, vol. 18, p. 39.

[229] Nietzsche, *Beyond*, p. 98.

[230] Letter of November 6, 1911, from Emma Jung to Freud; in *Freud/Jung Letters*, p. 456.

[231] Fritz Wittels, *Sigmund Freud: His Personality, His Teaching, His School*, tr. Eden and Cedar Paul, London: George Allen & Unwin, 1924.

[232] Wittels, pp. 251-252; quoted in Robert: pp. 328-329; also quoted in Jones, vol. 3, p. 43, though with a different translation. H. P.'s italics.

[233] Cf. Robert, p. 328.

[234] See footnote 194.

[235] *Dreams*, SF/CPW, vol. 5, p. 421.

[236] Cf. Jones, vol. 2, p. 15.

[237] See Schur, pp. 155-157.

[238] *Dreams*, SF/CPW, vol. 5, p. 422.

[239] Ibid., p. 487. Italics in original.

[240] Ibid., p.485. Italics in original; translation modified by M. M.

[241] *Dreams*, SF/CPW, vol. 5, p. 422. Translation adjusted by MM.

[242] See Schur, p. 157.

[243] *Dreams*, SF/CPW, vol. 5, p. 483.

[244] Ibid., p. 463.

[245] See my interpretation of this dream in H. P., "Hatte Ödipus einen Ödipus-Komplex," op. cit., pp. 119-121. References to further literature can be found there.

[246] *Dreams*, SF/CPW, vol. 5, p. 463.

[247] Ibid., p. 465.

[248] Ibid., p. 149. H. P.'s italics.

[249] See ibid., pp. 195-196.

[250] Ibid., p. 264.

[251] Ibid., p. xxvi. Translation slightly modified by M. M.

[252] *A Disturbance of Memory on the Acropolis*, SF/CPW, vol. 22, p. 248; p. 247.

[253] See chap. 2.

[254] *Dreams*, SF/CPW, vol. 4, p. 255

[255] *On Transience*, SF/CPW, vol. 14, p. 305 ff. In a marginal note to "poet," H. P. wrote, "who?"

[256] Ibid.

[257] Heinrich Heine, "Serafine X" from the collection *Neue Gedichte*. Translation by M. M.

258 *Transience*, SF/CPW. vol. 14, p. 305.

259 Ibid., p. 306.

260 Ibid., p. 307.

261 Ibid.

262 Friedrich Nietzsche, *Untimely Meditations*, tr. R. J. Hollingdale, introduction J. P. Stern, Cambridge: CUP, 1983. p. 132.

263 *Thoughts*, SF/CPW, vol. 14, p. 291.

264 Ibid.

265 Rainer Maria Rilke, *The Book of Hours* in R. M. R., *Selected Works*, Volume II: *Poetry*, tr. J. B. Leishman, London: Hogarth Press, 1960, p. 90.

266 *Thoughts*, SF/CPW, vol. 14, p. 293.

267 Ibid., p. 292.

268 Ibid., p. 293. Translation adjusted by MM.

269 Ibid.

270 Ibid., pp. 293-294.

271 *Why War?*, SF/CPW, vol. 22, p. 213.

272 Ibid., p. 213.

273 *Thoughts*, SF/CPW, vol. 14, p. 299. [*Diebstahlbad* combines *Stahlbad* = bath of steel (cf. Ernst Jünger's First World War diary *In Stahlgewittern*, *Storm of Steel*) with *Diebstahl* = theft.]

274 *Why War?*, SF/CPW, vol. 22, p. 213

275 *Group Psychology and the Analysis of the Ego*, SF/CPW, vol. 18, p. 93.

276 Ibid., p. 94.

277 Ibid., p. 95.

278 Karl Kraus, "Die letzte Nacht. Epilog zu der Tragödie *Die letzten Tage der Menschheit*, in K. K., *Werke*, Bd V, ed. Heinrich Fischer, Munich: Kösel, 1957, p. 731. Translation by M. M.

279 *Group Psychology*, SF/CPW, vol. 18, p. 94.

280 Kraus, *Die letzten Tage*, final line.

281 *Why War*, SF/CPW, vol. 22, p. 215.

282 Ibid., pp. 214-215. Translation slightly modified by M. M.

283 Ibid., p. 215.

284 *Thoughts*, SF/CPW, vol. 14, p. 299.

285 Ibid., p. 299.

286 Hugo von Hofmannsthal, *Der Tor und der Tod* in H. v. H., *Gedichte und kleine Dramen*, ed. Herbert Steiner, Stockholm: Bermann-Fischer, 1946, pp. 279-280. Translation by M. M.

287 *Psycho-Analysis and Faith. The Letters of Sigmund Freud and Oskar Pfister*, ed. Heinrich Meng and Ernst L. Freud, tr. Eric Mosbacher, London: Hogarth Press, 1963, p. 131. Translation modified by M. M.

288 Ibid., p. 133.

289 Becker, *Denial*, p. 100. Italics in original.

[290] *Beyond*, SF/CPW, vol. 18, p. 22.

[291] Ibid., p. 20.

[292] See *Introductory Lectures on Psycho-analysis*, SF/CPW, vol. 16, p. 270.

[293] *Beyond*, SF/CPW, vol. 18, p. 21. Translation slightly amended by M. M.

[294] Ibid., p. 22.

[295] Thomas Mann, *Freud und die Zukunft*, p. 488. Translation by M. M.

[296] Ibid. Italics in original.

[297] Schur, p. 325.

[298] *Beyond*, SF/CPW, vol. 18, p. 22.

[299] *Analysis Terminable*, SF/CPW, vol. 23, p. 243.

[300] Cf. *Ego and Id*, SF/CPW, vol. 19, p. 46.

[301] *Beyond*, SF/CPW, vol. 18, p. 24.

[302] Ibid., p. 59. Italics in original. Translation adjusted by M. M.

[303] *The Ego and the Id*, SF/CPW, vol. 19, pp. 40-41.

[304] Ibid., p. 42.

[305] Ibid., p. 58.

[306] Konrad Lorenz used this expression in the German title (*Das sogenannte Böse. Zur Naturgeschichte der Aggression*) of his book, which appeared in English, as *On Aggression*, tr. Marjorie Latzke, London: Methuen, 1966.

[307] Konrad Lorenz, Introduction to: Friedrich Hacker, *Aggression. Die Brutalisierung der modernen Welt*, Zurich: Molden, 1971, p. 10. Translation M. M.

[308] Ibid.,

[309] *Ego,* SF/CPW, vol.19, p. 47.

[310] Günter Eich, *Pigeons and Moles. Selected Writings of Günter Eich*, tr. with an introduction by Michael Hamburger, Columbia, NC: Camden House, 1991, p. 185.

[311] *The Economic Problem of Masochism*, SF/CPW, vol. 19, p. 164.

[312] Schur, p. 373.

[313] *Masochism,* SF/CPW, vol. 19, pp. 163-164.

[314] Ibid., p. 164. Italics in original.

[315] *Analysis Terminable*, SF/CPW, vol. 23, p. 243. Translation by M. M.

[316] *Totem*, SF/CPW, vol. 13, p. 142.

[317] *Masochism*, SF/CPW, vol. 19, pp. 167-168. Translation adjusted by M. M.

[318] Ibid., p. 168.

[319] *Civilization*, SF/CPW, vol. 21, p. 74.

[320] Franz Kafka, "The Judgment" in Franz Kafk, *Stories 1904-1924*, tr. J. A. Underwood, London: Futura, 1983, p. 56.

[321] Thomas Mann, "Dem Dichter zu Ehren. Franz Kafka und *Das Schloß*" in T. M., *Gesammelte Werke*, Bd. X, Frankfurt/M.: Fischer, 1960, p. 778. Translation by M. M.

[322] *Masochism*, SF/CPW vol. 19, p. 167. H. P.'s italics.

[323] *Address delivered at the Goethe House at Frankfurt*, SF/CPW, vol. 21, p. 210.

324 See Erich Heller, "Goethe and the Avoidance of Tragedy" in *The Disinherited Mind: Essays in Modern German Literature and Thought*, London: Bowes & Bowes, 1952, pp. 37-63.

325 Philip Rieff, *The Mind of the Moralist*, New York: Viking Press, 1959, p. 301.

326 *Civilization*, SF/CPW, vol. 21, p. 84. H. P.'s italics.

327 *Three Essays*, SF/CPW, vol. 7, p. 225, footnote 1. Translation adjusted by M. M.

328 *Sigmund Freud and Lou Andreas-Salomé: Letters*, ed. Ernst Pfeiffer, tr. William and Elaine Robson-Scott, London: Hogarth Press, 1972, p. 181.

329 See Schur, p. 420.

330 *Dreams*, SF/CPW, vol. 4, p. 238. Translation adapted by M. M. David Riesman comments: "Note the carefree manner in which he talks of 'my usual way' instead of 'symptom' when he is talking about himself." D. R., *Freud und die Psychoanalyse*, Frankfurt/M.: Suhrkamp, 1969, p. 20. Translation by M. M.

331 *Freud and Andreas-Salomé: Letters*, p. 181.

332 Letter to Oskar Pfister of October 9, 1918. *Freud/Pfister Letters*, p. 61.

333 W. H. Auden, "In Memory of Sigmund Freud," in W. H. A., *Collected Shorter Poems 1927-1957*, London: Faber and Faber, 1971, p. 170.

334 Quoted from Paul Roazen, *Freud and his Followers*, New York: Knopf, 1975, p. 537. Roazen's information is based on Maryse Choisy's book on Freud, *Sigmund Freud: A New Appraisal*, London: Owen, 1963, pp. 83-84.

335 *Civilization*, SF/CPW, vol. 21, p. 111.

336 *Jokes and their Relation to the Unconscious*, SF/CPW vol. 8, p. 236.

337 Johann Nestroy (1801-1862) an Austrian actor-dramatist with a dark sense of verbal humor.

338 *Civilization*, SF/CPW, vol. 21, p. 111.

339 Ibid., p. 119.

340 Ibid., p. 122.

341 Riesman, *Freud*, p. 104.

342 "This life seems to resemble a race-course." In Andreas Gryphius, "Abend" (Evening) in *The Penguin Book of German Verse*, introduced and edited with plain prose translations by Leonard Forster, 2nd ed., Harmondsworth: Penguin, 1959, p. 133.

343 *Civilization*, SF/CPW, vol. 21, p. 145.

344 Ibid., p. 112-113.

345 W. B. Yeats, "The Second Coming," in *Poems of W. B. Yeats. A New Selection*. Selected with an Introduction and Notes by A. Norman Jeffares, London and Basingstoke: Macmillan, 1984, p. 246.

346 *Civilization*, SF/CPW vol. 21, p. 145.

347 See Vincent Brome, *Freud and his Early Circle: The Struggles of Psycho-Analysis*, p. xi; or Thomas Mann, "A Brother" in *Order of the Day: Political Essays and*

Speeches of Two Decades, tr. H. T. Lowe-Porter, New York: Alfred A. Knopf, 1942, p. 159.

[348] See Schur, p. 499.

[349] *Heil* can mean both "hail" and "heal" in German. Freud was not alone in his view nor in his use of the pun. When the Rector of Vienna University, Julius Wagner von Jauregg, who held the first chair in psychiatry there, entered the great hall, filled with rampaging Nazis, to be greeted with cries of "*Heil Hitler!*" from the students, he is said to have replied, "Even I can't do that."

[350] Roazen, *Freud and his Followers*, p. 536.

[351] *Moses and Monotheism: Three Essays,* SF/CPW, vol. 23, p. 114.

[352] Jones, vol. 3, p. 241.

[353] *New Introductory Lectures,* SF/CPW, vol. 22, p. 80.

[354] Schur, p. 501-502.

[355] Freud, *Letters 1973-1939*, pp. 441-442.

[356] See Schur, p. 498, footnote 3.

[357] Roazen, *Freud and his Followers*, p. 542.

[358] Jones, vol. 3, pp. 245-246.

[359] Psalm 137, v. 5. *The New English Bible*, Oxford/Cambridge: Oxford University Press/Cambridge University Press 1970, p. 735.

[360] Schur, p. 408.

[361] Ibid., p. 529. Translation adjusted by M. M.

[362] *The Theme of the Three Caskets,* SF/CPW, vol. 12, p. 301.

[363] *The Correspondence of Sigmund Freud and Sándor Ferenczi,* vol. 1: 1908-1914, p. 387.

[364] *Caskets,* SF/CPW, vol. 12, p. 291.

[365] See also Schur, p. 274.

[366] Shakespeare, *The Merchant of Venice*, Act III, 2, 16-18.

[367] *The Psychopathology of Everyday Life,* SF/CPW, vol. 6, p. 98.

[368] *New Introductory Lectures,* SF/CPW, vol. 15, p. 38.

[369] *Merchant of Venice*, Act II, 7.

[370] Ibid., Act II, 9.

[371] Ibid., Act III, 2, 63-72.

[372] Ibid., Act III, 2, 11-13.

[373] Ibid., Act V, 1, 83.

[374] *Future,* SF/CPW, vol. 21, p. 50. Freud applied the expression to Heinrich Heine, who used it of Spinoza.

[375] Sophocles, *Oedipus at Colonos* (l. 1226), op. cit., p. 297.

[376] *Those Wrecked by Success,* SF/CPW, vol.14, p. 331.

[377] Arthur Schnitzler, *Tagebuch 1920-1922*, Vienna: Verlag der österreichischen Akademie der Wissenschaften, 1993, p. 319. Translation by M. M.

[378] Heinrich Heine, "Shakespeares Mädchen und Frauen" in H. H., *Sämtliche*

Werke, Bd. VIII, op. cit., p. 252. Translation by M. M.

379 Ibid.

380 Ibid., p. 267-268.

381 Ibid., p. 268-269.

382 *Moses and Monotheism: Three Essays,* SF/CPW, vol. 23, p. 50.

383 *Dreams,* SF/CPW, vol. 4, p. 197.

384 *Freud/Jung Letters,* pp. 218-219.

385 Ibid.

386 Ibid., pp. 196-197.

387 Ernst Simon, "Freuds Moses" in *Sie werden lachen—die Bibel. Erfahrungen mit dem Buch der Bücher,* ed. H. J. Schulz, Munich: Deutscher Taschenbuch Verlag, 1985, pp. 169-180; p. 171. Translated by M. M.

388 *Dreams,* SF/CPW, vol. 4, p. 255.

389 *Dreams,* SF/CPW, vol. 4, p. ix. (If I cannot bend the powers above to my will, I will stir up Hades.)

390 Peter Heller, "Zur Biographie Freuds" in *Merkur* 10 (1956), pp. 1233-1239; p. 1236. See also: Walter Schönau, *Sigmund Freuds Prosa. Literarische Elemente seines Stils,* Stuttgart: Metzler, 1968, p. 67.

391 *The Moses of Michelangelo,* SF/CPW, vol. 13, p. 213. Translation adjusted by M. M.

392 Simon, p. 172.

393 *Moses of Michelangelo,* SF/CPW, vol. 13, p. 211.

394 Ibid., pp. 229-230.

395 Ibid., p. 233.

396 Goethe, "Die Geheimnisse. Ein Fragment," verses 191-192 in J. W. v. G., *Werke,* WA I, Bd. 16, p. 178. Translation by M. M.

397 *Moses and Monotheism,* SF/CPW, vol. 23, p. 36.

398 Goethe, "Israel in der Wüste" in J. W. v. G., *Noten und Abhandlungen zum besseren Verständnis des Westöstlichen Diwans* in J. W. v. G., *Werke,* WA I, Bd. 7, pp. 170-171. Translation by M. M.

399 Claude Lévi-Strauss, *The Elementary Structures of Kinship,* tr. James Harke Bell, John Richard von Sturmer, Rodney Needham (editor), Boston: Beacon Press, p. 491.

400 *Moses and Monotheism,* SF/CPW, vol. 23, pp. 109-110. [The German phrase "der große Mann" can, of course, mean "the big man" as well as "the great man."]

401 Ibid., p. 110.

402 *Totem,* SF/CPW, vol. 13, p. 142.

403 Thomas Mann, "Die Stellung Freuds in der modernen Geistesgeschichte," in *Die psychoanalytische Bewegung* 1 (1929), pp. 3-32, p. 3. Reprinted in T. M.: *Gesammelte Werke,* Bd. X, op. cit., pp. 256-280. Translation by M. M.

404 *Moses and Monotheism,* SF/CPW, vol. 23, p. 86.

405 Ibid.

406 Ibid., p. 90. Italics in original. Translation adjusted by M. M.

407 See ibid., p. 25.

408 Ibid., p. 22. The psychoanalytical discussion on Amenhotep IV goes back to 1912, when a paper on the pharaoh by Karl Abraham was discussed at the fateful Munich conference. Earlier in that year, Freud had warned Abraham not to describe the Pharaoh as a neurotic, "which is in sharp contrast with his exceptional energy and achievements, as we associate neuroticism, a term that has become scientifically inexact, precisely with the idea of being inhibited. After all, we all have these complexes, and we must be careful not to call everybody neurotic." Jones, vol. 2 (appendix), p. 503.

409 Franz Werfel, "Echnatons Sonnengesang," in F. W., *Gesammelte Werke. Das lyrische Werk*, ed. Adolf D. Klarmann, Frankfurt/Main: Fischer, 1967, p. 466. Translation by M. M.

410 *The Letters of Sigmund Freud and Arnold Zweig*, ed. Ernst L. Freud, tr. Professor and Mrs. W. D. Robson-Scott, London: Hogarth Press, 1970, p. 91. The letter also contains symptoms of Freud's paranoia.

411 *Moses and Monotheism*, SF/CPW, vol. 23, p. 110. Minor modification to translation by M. M.

412 Ibid., p. 15.

413 *Freud/Zweig Letters*, p. 104.

414 Letter of December 5, 1933, to Leon Judah Magnes, in *Letters 1873-1939*, p. 414.

415 Arthur Koestler, *Promise and Fulfilment, Palestine 1917-1949*, London: Macmillan, 1949, p. 74. At this point in the margin of his manuscript H. P. quotes from that page of Koestler's book, "Orde Wingate ... a Lawrence of the Hebrews."

416 Letter of April 19, 1936, to Barbara Low in *Letters 1879-1939*, p. 424. Original in English; H. P.'s italics.

417 *Moses and Monotheism*, SF/CPW, vol. 23, p. 111.

418 Quoted in Schur, p. 468. Italics in original.

419 Quoted in Jones, vol. 3, p. 223. Translation modified by M. M.

420 *Moses*, SF/CPW, vol. 23, p. 51.

421 Thomas Mann, "Freud und die Zukunft" op. cit., p. 492. Translation by M. M.

422 Here Politzer is playing on the connection between the German words *Heil* (=salvation) and *Heilung* (=healing).

423 Thomas Mann, "Freud und die Zukunft," op. cit., p. 492.

424 Letter of January 10, 1884, to Martha Bernays in *Letters 1879-1939*, p. 103.

425 Shakespeare, *The Merchant of Venice*, Act IV, 1, 200 ff.

426 *Moses and Monotheism*, SF/CPW, vol. 23, p. 136. Italics added by H. P.

427 Gerald S. Stein, *Can the Freudians and the Jungians Close Their Ranks?*, op. cit.,

p. 26.

428 Franz Kafka, *Letters to Felice*, ed. Erich Heller and Jürgen Born, tr. James Stern and Elisabeth Duckworth, New York: Schocken, 1973, p. 530.

429 Giovanni Papini, "A Visit to Freud (8 May 1934)" in *Freud As We Knew Him*, ed. Hendrik M. Ruitenbeek, Detroit: Wayne State Univ. Press, 1973, pp. 98-102; p. 99.

430 *A Note on the Prehistory of the Technique of Analysis*, SF/CPW, vol. 18, p. 263.

431 Letter of October 2, 1936, quoted from: Joseph D. Wortis, *Fragments of an Analysis with Freud*, New York: Simon and Schuster, 1954, p. 176.

432 See *Dreams*, SF/CPW vol. 5, p. 431.

433 J. W. v. Goethe, "Die Natur. Fragment," in J. W. v. G., *Werke*, WA II, Bd. 11, pp. 6-7. Translation by M. M.

434 *Thoughts*, SF/CPW, vol. 14, p. 291.

435 J. W. v. Goethe, *Aus meinem Leben. Dichtung und Wahrheit*. Zweiter Teil, Buch 7, in J. W. v. G., *Werke*, WA I, Bd. 27, p. 110.

436 Schur, p. 274.

437 *Casket*, SF/CPW, vol. 12, p. 301.

438 See Jones, vol. 2, p. 362.

439 *Studies on Hysteria*, SF/CPW, vol. 2, pp. 125-134.

440 Ibid., p. 160.

441 *Totem*, SF/CPW, vol. 13, pp. 155-156.

442 *Hysteria*, SF/CPW, vol. 2, p. 161.

443 *Totem*, SF/CPW, vol. 13, p. 156.

444 Peter von Matt, *Literaturwissenschaft und Psychoanalyse. Eine Einführung*, Freiburg: Rombach, 1972, pp. 54-65.

445 For the contrary view, see Peter von Matt, op. cit. p. 59.

446 Friedrich Schiller, *Wilhelm Tell*, Act 5, Scene 2. Translation by M. M.

447 *Uncanny*, SF/CPW, vol. 17, p. 235.

448 *Totem*, SF/CPW, vol. 13, p. 141.

449 Schiller, *Wilhelm Tell*, Act 1, Scene 1.

450 *Totem*, SF/CPW, vol. 13, p. 142.

451 Quoted from Roazen, *Freud and his Followers*, p. 249. See also Ludwig Binswanger, *Erinnerungen an Sigmund Freud*, Bern: Francke, 1956, pp. 63-64.

452 Quoted from Jones, vol. 2, p. 397.

453 Goethe, *Faust*, Part 1, l. 1237.

454 *Totem*, SF/CPW, vol. 13, p. 161. Italics in original.

455 Ibid.

456 Jones, vol. 3, p. 21.

457 *Dreams*, SF/CPW, vol. 4, p. xxvi.

458 *Freud/Fließ Letters*, p. 202.

459 *Dreams*, SF/CPW, vol. 4, p. 265.

460 Ibid., p. 265.

[461] *Thoughts*, SF/CPW, vol. 14, p. 275

[462] Ibid., p. 291.

[463] Ibid., p. 281.

[464] *Group Psychology*, SF/CPW, vol. 18, p. 127.

[465] Thomas Mann, "A Brother" in *Order of the Day: Political Essays and Speeches of Two Decades*, New York: Alfred A. Knopf, 1942, p. 159. Translation modified by M. M.

[466] *Moses and Monotheism*, SF/CPW, vol. 23, p. 109.

[467] W. H. Auden, "In Memory of Sigmund Freud," in W. H. A., *Collected Shorter Poems 1927-1957*, London: Faber and Faber, 1971, p. 170.

[468] Walter Muschg, "Freud als Schriftsteller," in W. M., *Die Zerstörung der deutschen Literatur* Bern: Francke, 1956, pp. 153-197; p. 195; first published in *Die psychoanalytische Bewegung* 5 (1930), pp. 467-509. Translation by M. M.

[469] See Robert Musil, *Posthumous Papers of a Living Author*, tr. Peter Worstman, Hygiene, Colorado: Eridanos Press, 1987.

[470] *Moses and Monotheism*, SF/CPW, vol. 23, p. 101.

[471] *Freud/Zweig Letters*, p. 91.

[472] *Moses and Monotheism*, SF/CPW, vol. 23, p. 101.

[473] Ibid., p. 110.

[474] Ibid., p. 111.

[475] *Civilization*, SF/CPW, vol. 21, p.74.

[476] *Moses and Monotheism*, SF/CPW, vol. 23, p. 115

[477] Ibid.

[478] J. W. v. Goethe, *Maximen und Reflexionen* no. 78, in J. W. v. G., *Werke* WA I, Bd. 42/2, p. 150. Translation by M. M.

[479] Ernest Becker, *Angel in Armor. A Post-Freudian Perspective on the Nature of Man*, New York: Braziller, 1969, p. 4.

[480] Alexander Mitscherlich, *Society Without the Father: A Contribution to Social Psychology*, tr. Eric Mosbacher, London: Tavistock Publications, 1969, p. 163.

[481] Günter Eich, *Pigeons and Moles*, p. 185.

[482] *Psyche*, 6/7 (1971), p. 536. Translation by M. M.

[483] *Folksong USA*, ed. John A. Lomax and Alan Lomax, New York: Duell, Sloan and Pearce, 1947, p. 259.

[484] Ibid., p. 246.

[485] Erik H. Erikson, *Childhood and Society*, New York: Norton, p. 299.

[486] *Folksong USA*, p. 247.

[487] Erikson, *Childhood and Society*, p. 285.

[488] Philip Roth, *Portnoy's Complaint*, New York: Bantam, 1969, pp. 10-11.

[489] Erikson, *Childhood and Society*, p. 290

[490] Erich Heller, "Vom Menschen der sich schämt," in *Merkur*, 315 (XXVIII), pp. 727-740.

[491] Tennessee Williams, *A Streetcar Named Desire*, New York: New Directions,

1947.

[492] Phyllis Chesler, *Women and Madness*, Garden City: Doubleday, 1972, p. 237.

[493] *Der Mythus von Orient und Occident. Eine Metaphysik der alten Welt. Aus den Werken von J. J. Bachofen*, ed. Manfred Schroeter, Munich: Beck, 1956, p. 265. Translation by M. M.

[494] Sophocles, *King Oedipus*, l. 980-981.

[495] *Civilization*, SF/CPW, vol. 21, p. 145.

[496] Hugo von Hofmannsthal, *Der Turm. Ein Trauerspiel*, in H. v. H., *Gesammelte Werke, Dramen IV*, ed. Herbert Steiner, Frankfurt/M.: Fischer, 1958, p. 458. Translation by M. M.

[497] *Dreams*, SF/CPW, vol. 4, p. 262.

[498] Thomas Mann, *The Magic Mountain*, tr. H. T. Lowe-Porter, Harmondsworth: Penguin, 1960, p. 183.

[499] Arthur Miller, *Death of a Salesman. Certain Private Conversations in Two Acts and a Requiem*. New York: Viking, 1958, p. 136.

[500] *Three Essays*, SF/CPW, vol. 7, p. 178.

[501] See especially Otto Rank, *Will Therapy. Truth and Reality*, New York: Knopf, 1945.

[502] Norman O. Brown, *Life versus Death. The Psychoanalytical Meaning of History*, New York: Vintage, 1959.

[503] Eduard Mörike, *Mozart auf der Reise nach Prag*, in E. M., *Sämtliche Werke*, Bd. I, ed. Gerhart Baumann, Stuttgart: Cotta, 1954, p. 905. Translation by M. M.

[504] *Angel in Armor*, p. 123, p. 124.

[505] Ibid.

[506] Here Politzer is again playing on the connection between the German words *Heil* (=salvation) and *Heilung* (=healing).

Editor's Afterword

A few years after Heinz Politzer's death, his papers were deposited with the German Literary Archives in Marbach am Neckar. Among them was a substantial bundle of manuscripts on Sigmund Freud, including lectures in English and manuscripts and notes for his projected book *Freud and Tragedy*.

The archivist in charge of Politzer's papers intended to write an article indicating the importance of this material but unfortunately died in a road accident. Thus, it remained hidden in the archives for a further ten years until I came across it when I was working there at the beginning of the 1990s. Given its significance, I saw it as my duty to have the manuscript published.

In order to come as close as possible to the author's intentions, I consulted, among other things, his correspondence with Alexander Mitscherlich, Hans Paeschke, and Friedrich Torberg. Initially Politzer had envisaged "five or six chapters," but he very quickly let Alexander Mitscherlich talk him out of a "chapter on the tragedies Freud caused." Thus in a letter to Mitscherlich of February 1, 1977, he named "three main chapters," adding in the early summer of that year a further "fourth and last chapter." An essay "Freud, Oedipus—and Then?," which Politzer had written in 1975 for publication in *Merkur*, possibly as a fourth chapter or afterword to his book, only to reject it after criticism by Paeschke, has been included in the present publication as an appendix.

The first chapter, "Sigmund Freud and the Tragedy of Interpretation," appeared separately in *Dauer im Wandel. Aspekte österreichischer Kulturentwicklung*, (ed. Walter Strolz and Oscar Schatz, Vienna, Freiburg, Basel: Herder, 1975). Politzer's personal copy has hand-written corrections, which have been incorporated in the present edition.

The second chapter, on Freud and Jung—"Oedipus in practice, so to speak," as Politzer called it—has a pendant in the manuscript of a program broadcast in 1975 by Hessen Radio on the occasion of the hundredth anniversary of Jung's birth. "The chapter itself is three times as long," Politzer told Mitscherlich; the typescript, with its many handwritten corrections, served as the basis for the present edition.

"The first sketch of the third chapter of my Freud book (on death and dying) is finished. It still requires many corrections, much tightening up," Politzer wrote to Hans Paeschke in the summer of 1975, "but at least I can now see my way more clearly." This manuscript, dated June 8, 1975, does indeed have many corrections and is described by Politzer, in a letter to Mitscherlich of February 1, 1977, as "complete in manuscript, but not yet typed." This is the version used in the present edition.

There is also a pendant to the fourth and last chapter, namely the essay "Why Freud Placed a Taboo on Shakespeare's Shylock," which Politzer extracted from the chapter for a festschrift for Mitscherlich's seventieth birthday. The fourth chapter itself uses parts of an afterword Politzer wrote around the same time for a facsimile edition of Freud's *The Theme of the Three Caskets*. He completed the chapter between July 4 and 19, 1977, before undergoing a serious operation. In the winter of the same year, he wrote to Paeschke telling him he intended to look at it again; it needed much revision. And in his last letter to Paeschke, he was still saying how much work needed to be done on that chapter and on the book as a whole. The manuscript of the fourth chapter has a whole host of corrections, and there is no doubt that the argument is less fully developed than in the first two chapters. Stylistically, however, Politzer's unmistakable, darkly glowing tone can be clearly heard.

Wilhelm W. Hemecker